The World's Best

MARCHETTE CHUTE, distinguished writer, scholar and critic, provides new insight and understanding of William Shakespeare's work in these superb retellings of all his great tragedies, comedies and histories from the First Folio.

About her book *Stories from Shakespeare,* Miss Chute writes, "I wrote it to share as far as possible the joy I have had in Shakespeare's plays. . . . I hope I have made a small but clear path of entrance to the most varied and glorious world ever created by one man."

Miss Chute clarifies the plots and characterizations with timely comments and well-chosen quotations. She also includes a brilliant introduction which places the playwright, his theatre and his period in proper perspective.

"The reader is immediately aware of Miss Chute's wit, sense of humor, scholarship, and straightforward interpretation without condescension in this book that so greatly adds to the enjoyment and understanding of Shakespeare by all age groups."
—*Saturday Review*

MARCHETTE CHUTE

Stories from
SHAKESPEARE

A MERIDIAN BOOK

MERIDIAN
Published by Penguin Group
Penguin Group (USA) Inc., 375 Hudson Street, New York, New York 10014, U.S.A.
Penguin Group (Canada), 90 Eglinton Avenue East, Suite 700, Toronto, Ontario,
Canada M4P 2Y3 (a division of Pearson Penguin Canada Inc.)
Penguin Books Ltd., 80 Strand, London WC2R 0RL, England
Penguin Ireland, 25 St. Stephen's Green, Dublin 2, Ireland (a division of Penguin Books Ltd.)
Penguin Group (Australia), 250 Camberwell Road, Camberwell, Victoria 3124, Australia
(a division of Pearson Australia Group Pty. Ltd.)
Penguin Books India Pvt. Ltd., 11 Community Centre, Panchsheel Park,
New Delhi – 110 017, India
Penguin Group (NZ), 67 Apollo Drive, Rosedale, North Shore 0632, New Zealand
(a division of Pearson New Zealand Ltd.)
Penguin Books (South Africa) (Pty.) Ltd., 24 Sturdee Avenue, Rosebank,
Johannesburg 2196, South Africa

Penguin Books Ltd., Registered Offices: 80 Strand, London WC2R 0RL, England

Published by Meridian, a member of Penguin Group (USA) Inc.
This is an authorized reprint of a hardcover edition published by Liveright Publishing Corporation.
For information address Liveright Publishing Corporation, a subsidiary of
W. W. Norton & Co., Inc., 500 5th Avenue, New York, NY 10110.

First Meridian Printing, June 1987
28

 REGISTERED TRADEMARK—MARCA REGISTRADA

LIBRARY OF CONGRESS CATALOGING-IN-PUBLICATION DATA

Chute, Marchette Gaylord, 1909–
Stories from Shakespeare / Marchette Chute.
p.   cm.
First published: 1987.
Includes index.
ISBN 978-0-452-01061-1
1. Shakespeare, William, 1564–1616—Adaptations.   2. English
drama—Early odern, 1500–1700—Adaptations.   I. Title.
[PR2877.C53   1993]
823'.52—dc20   93–33372

Printed in the United States of America

CONTENTS

Introduction **7**

The Comedies

The Tragedies

The Histories

INTRODUCTION

WILLIAM SHAKESPEARE was the most remarkable story-teller that the world has ever known. Homer told of adventure and men at war, Sophocles and Tolstoy told of tragedies and of people in trouble. Terence and Mark Twain told comic stories, Dickens told melodramatic ones, Plutarch told histories and Hans Christian Andersen told fairy tales. But Shakespeare told every kind of story—comedy, tragedy, history, melodrama, adventure, love stories and fairy tales—and each of them so well that they have become immortal. In all the world of storytelling, his is the greatest name.

Nowadays most storytelling is done in prose, whether in books or in the theatre. But in early times stories were told in verse, because they were recited instead of being written down and verse was easier to remember. By Shakespeare's time, stories in books were usually in prose but stories in the theatre were still in verse. Audiences were accustomed to it and enjoyed the musical sound of the words, and the actors found it easier to memorize.

Shakespeare told his stories for the theatre and so he used verse. And the world is fortunate that he did, for he is England's greatest poet. He combines Chaucer's clearness and Milton's magnificence with Keats' magic and the lovely singing line that has been the glory of so many English poets. He could write about battlefields or country flowers, witches or children, dying heroes or young lovers or chatty old men, and could do it in poetry which is not only perfect in itself but which joins hands with the storytelling, so that the two go together like the words and music of a song.

Shakespeare used prose also, especially in his comedies, for there was no rule in those days against mixing poetry and prose and Shakespeare was free to do as he pleased. So he pleased himself, and by doing so he not only pleased the audiences of his own day, but he has given more joy ever since than any other writer in the world's history.

Shakespeare was not only one of the greatest of poets and storytellers, but he was also one of the greatest of playwrights. He understood so well the demands of the theatre that time has not aged or weakened his plays and they still leap into life on any stage. Something of this can be explained by the fact that he was a genius, but part of the explanation lies also in the fact that he was a practical man of the theatre, spending the whole of his adult working life as an actor and producer on the London stage.

Since Shakespeare was a man of the theatre, he did not write his plays to be printed. He wrote them as theatre scripts for the use of his fellow actors, and he expected them to last only so long as his fellow actors wished to show them on the stage. But his audiences enjoyed his plays so much in the theatre that they wanted to experience them again, and during his lifetime about half of them found their way into print. After his death, the actors in his company realized that all his plays ought to be printed or many of them would be lost. They loved him so much, both as a writer and as a human being, that they could not permit this to happen, and two of his oldest friends in the company, John Heminges and Henry Condell, gathered all his plays together in a single book. It was published in 1623, seven years after Shakespeare's death, and is now known as the First Folio. Heminges and Condell wrote at the beginning of the book that they had collected Shakespeare's plays, not for "self-profit or fame, only to keep the memory of so worthy a friend and fellow alive." And they succeeded beyond their dreams, for no one is more alive than William Shakespeare.

Since then his plays have been published and republished in almost every country in the world. Yet the plays are plays, and Shakespeare did not intend them to be read but to be acted. He did not wish the speeches to lie flat on the page but to be spoken by real people, and when he wrote a stage direction he expected it to come to life with gay costumes and banners and the sound of trumpets. His audience was not a single reader sitting quietly in a chair but a large group of people waiting excitedly in a theatre.

Because this was so, Shakespeare never stopped to explain anything. If he had been telling his stories in the form of a novel he would have let his readers know what his characters looked like, what clothes they wore, what kind of houses they lived in and what they were thinking about. But since he was a playwright he put his people onstage without any explanations, and as they move about and start talking they begin to explain themselves. After a time they come so completely to life that they seem to be real people, and it may be that they seem all the more real because the author himself never comes forward to explain them.

All this, however, demands a great deal of the reader. Since Shakespeare will not help him, the reader has to do the extra work for himself. He has to discover the line of the story and the personalities of the characters, and some people find this so confusing that they say Shakespeare is too hard for them. If they see one of his plays on the stage in a really good production they can follow the story easily enough and understand the people, but they find it much more difficult when they are left to themselves with a book.

A further difficulty lies in the fact that so many of Shakespeare's plays are taught in the schools as "required reading." This is an excellent idea in itself, since some people would make his acquaintance in no other way, but it has the disadvantage of anything that is compulsory. The average person does not like to be told what to do, and he might begin to study a play like *Romeo and Juliet* with the conviction already formed in his mind that he is not going to enjoy himself. He starts to read the first act and finds that two characters named Sampson and Gregory are talking about coals and seem to be making very little sense. He begins leafing through the pages, looking for some kind of a story, and finds a great many Italian names that he cannot keep apart and speeches full of long words. So he puts the book down, convinced that Shakespeare is much too difficult to be read for pleasure and that the whole subject is overrated.

It is in the hope of preventing this that *Stories from Shakespeare* was written. Its purpose is to give the reader a preliminary idea of each of the thirty-six plays by telling the stories and explaining in a general way the intentions and points of view of the characters. It will not give much conception of Shakespeare's vastness, his wisdom, or his profound knowledge of people, any more than indicating the theme of the Fifth Symphony will give an adequate conception of Beethoven. But it may open a door that to some people is closed and give a glimpse, however slight, of what lies beyond.

Shakespeare himself considered it of great importance that the stories of his plays should be clearly understood. It was the custom in his own day for an actor called the Prologue to come on-stage before the action started and explain exactly what the play was going to be about. Moreover, Shakespeare chose stories whose plots were already familiar to his audiences. Most of his comedies and tragedies come from tales that had already been shown on the stage or were available in the bookstores, and his history plays are dramatizations of events in the lives of English kings that were already familiar to his audiences. Shakespeare never confused his own public, and he would not wish anyone to be confused today.

There is one disadvantage that faces a modern reader

of Shakespeare which did not exist in his own period, and that is the unfamiliarity of some of the words. The language was still changing in Shakespeare's day; there were no English dictionaries and new words were still being added and discarded. Words like "savage" and "method" that are familiar now were new and strange in Shakespeare's day, while words like "twink" and "reechy," which were familiar enough then, have vanished from the language. Moreover, some words are still in use but have changed their meanings. In *Hamlet,* for instance, the word "rivals" is used in the sense of "partners," and when Hamlet's mother accuses him of "ecstasy" she means temporary insanity. In the latter case, the meaning is clear enough because Hamlet answers with a denial: "It is not madness."

In most cases it is easy enough to guess a word from the context, but the wise reader will get an edition of Shakespeare that has a full glossary in which all the unfamiliar words can be looked up. There will not be many of them, and after a while the meaning of the sentences will not be hard to understand. For as the story moves along and the people come to life, each play will begin to explain itself.

As far as the background of the plays is concerned, the reader's best guide is his own imagination. This was the same guide that was used by Shakespeare's own audiences, and he trusted it completely. His plays were not staged in the box-like area of the present-day theatre, with three walls, a proscenium arch, a curtain and a great deal of scenery. The theatre of his day was shaped more like a modern stadium, a curved shell open to the sky and with the audience grouped around three sides of it. The fourth side held the stage area, with a platform jutting out into the audience and various levels of acting space behind it. There was no curtain and no formal scenery, and each scene followed the last one without pause. Shakespeare was able to plan his plays in a continual flow of action and the result was more like a modern motion picture, which runs for two hours without stopping, than like a modern play with its long pauses between the acts. Shakespeare's plays were divided into scenes and acts when they were printed, but this is only for convenient reference and does not indicate any pause in the action.

Shakespeare faced some disadvantages in not being able to close his stage off with a curtain. When a character was killed in the course of the action, the playwright had to devise a way of getting him off unless the corpse was to remain on-stage for the rest of the play. Nor was it possible to introduce important articles of furniture, like beds and thrones, unless they were pushed out in full view of the audience or were used only on the small inner stage that could be curtained.

But the advantages far outweighed the difficulties, for the action could be kept fluid and always in motion. The actors could stage a battle scene, for instance, on the jutting platform stage, with plenty of room for shouting men and waving banners. Then a different group of actors could appear on one of the side balconies and show a scene taking place within the besieged castle, and the next scene might move to the top level, which would become for the moment a turret, with the defenders' flag flying from the battlements. Once the play started, the audience was given no time to remember that they were in a London theatre on a sunny afternoon. They stayed inside the play, believing in it, until it was finished.

Since Shakespeare had the imagination of the audience on his side, he did not need scenery. If he wanted an orchard by moonlight, he wrote the setting into the lines—

Lady, by yonder blessèd moon I swear
That tips with silver all these fruit-tree tops . . .

and the audience saw the moonlit orchard for themselves.

This atmosphere of willing make-believe, which is the essence of true theatre, made it possible for Shakespeare to conquer time and space in his plays. *Antony and Cleopatra*, for instance, covers about twelve years and ranges over the whole of the ancient world from Egypt to Rome. There are forty-two changes of scene in this particular play, and if the actors had been obliged to stage them literally they would have had to omit most of them or keep the audience waiting until midnight while the scenes were being shifted. But as it was, the imagination of the playgoers and Shakespeare's poetry worked together to build Pompey's ship or Cleopatra's palace, and they did it much better than even the busiest of carpenters.

Shakespeare knew his stage thoroughly, both its limitations and its magnificent possibilities, and handled it with an assurance that came through years of close intimacy. He was an actor before he began his career as a playwright, and he continued to be an actor during the twenty years that followed until he finally retired from the London stage. Shakespeare helped with every detail of the productions, for in those days the actors produced their own plays. They worked on a cooperative basis, with joint ownership of the scripts, the costumes and the properties, and in the case of Shakespeare's company they owned the theatre also. He and his fellow players like Heminges and Condell were responsible for everything—the choosing of the script, the financing, the casting, the costuming, the licensing, the rehearsals and the advertising—and this gave Shakespeare a practical knowledge of his profession that no other playwright ever had to a like degree.

As a result, there was never any writer who knew as much about stagecraft as William Shakespeare. He knew how to keep a story moving, how to build his climaxes and how to give actors the kind of parts that are brilliantly effective, and it is no wonder that every actor longs for a chance to appear in one of his scripts. When his plays fail in the theatre, as they sometimes do, it is usually because they have been produced poorly, either too carelessly or too reverently.

The same thing is true of reading Shakespeare's plays. They should never be read carelessly, with only half the attention, for they demand the full stretch of the reader's mind and all the intelligence and imagination he possesses. On the other hand, they should not be read with misplaced reverence, as though they were stuffed and labeled objects in an old-fashioned museum where it would be disrespectful even to breathe on the glass. This sort of approach leads to reading him through a sense of duty, which is unfair both to Shakespeare and to his plays.

There is, of course, nothing wrong with reverence.

Shakespeare is one of the world's greatest playwrights and he has a right to the most profound respect. But he also has a right to be read with understanding and enjoyment, and if Shakespeare himself had any say in the matter he would undoubtedly settle for the enjoyment and let the respect go. For he wrote to give delight, and the happy reader of Shakespeare is the best one.

NOTE

The plays in this book are the thirty-six plays that are included in the First Folio, and they are arranged in the three divisions that are given in the Folio: comedy, history and tragedy. The comedies and tragedies are arranged in the probable order in which Shakespeare wrote them. The histories are all concerned with kings of England and are therefore arranged in the order in which the kings reigned.

The Comedies

THE COMEDY OF ERRORS

THE COMEDY OF ERRORS takes place in a Greek seaport of Asia Minor, and the joke on which the story is based is one that used to be popular with the playwrights of ancient Greece. Nevertheless, Shakespeare did not take the location of his play seriously. He had not read any Greek stories but he had read a great many Italian ones, and the background of *The Comedy of Errors* reflects the spirit he found in Italian romances. Names like "Angelo" are Italian rather than Greek, the city is ruled over by a duke in the Italian manner, and there is even a lady abbess to help the story along. It would have been quite impossible to find a lady abbess in the real city of Ephesus, but Shakespeare was working in the world of make-believe and had no interest in exact realism.

The plot he used was based on an old and popular joke that had been flourishing for a long time on the Italian stage—the joke of the mixed-up twins. Two brothers who look exactly alike become separated at birth, and when they are grown one of the brothers arrives by accident in the town where the other brother lives. Of course they are mistaken for each other, and everyone in the cast becomes involved in the confusion. This kind of joke is effective on the stage because an audience enjoys the feeling of knowing more than the characters do. It can look down on them and laugh, and the more baffled and distraught the characters become the more the audience laughs.

A story of this kind does not depend on characterization or on skill in language. It depends on speed, on a plot that winds itself as tight as a top, spins hard on its own momentum and then comes to a sudden finish. *The Comedy of Errors* is really a farce rather than a comedy, and an excellent one of its kind.

17

The story opens when an elderly merchant from the city of Syracuse arrives in the great seaport city of Ephesus. The two cities are at war with each other, and when old Aegeon makes his appearance in Ephesus he is condemned to death unless he can pay a large ransom by nightfall. The duke of the city is sorry for Aegeon and, although he cannot change the law, he is willing to listen to the old man's story.

Aegeon was once the father of twin baby boys, and he had selected two other identical twin boys to be brought up as their servants. But the family was separated in a shipwreck, and Aegeon was left without his wife and with only one son. The son was named Antipholus, and when he grew up he went out to look for his brother, taking with him his servant whose name was Dromio. He never returned, and Aegeon has spent five years looking for him. He almost welcomes death in Ephesus, since he has lost both his sons and no longer wishes to go on living.

The scene shifts to the mart, the trading center of Ephesus, where another stranger has arrived in town. This is young Antipholus himself, still looking for his lost brother. Antipholus wishes to do a little sight-seeing in the town before his noon dinner, and he sends his servant Dromio back to the inn to deposit a bag of gold that has been given him.

A moment later, Dromio reappears. At least Antipholus thinks it is Dromio, since he looks exactly like him, but in reality it is Dromio's twin, the servant of his lost brother. His brother has been living in Ephesus for many years, with a wife and a house of his own, and his servant has been sent to the mart to fetch his master home to dinner.

The name of this brother is also Antipholus, and the name of his servant is also Dromio. The fact that the twins have the same name makes it a little difficult to keep them apart when the play is being read, and so Shakespeare calls the husband Antipholus of Ephesus and the brother who has been searching for him Antipholus of Syracuse. (It is a help to remember that "Syracuse" has the same first letter as "stranger," and it is Antipholus of Syracuse who is the stranger in town.)

Dromio of Ephesus of course thinks that he has found

his own master when he finds Antipholus of Syracuse. Dromio wants him to come at once to dinner, because it is noon and the food is burning up. All Antipholus wants to know is what has become of the bag of money he gave his servant, who now seems to have no knowledge of the gold but is full of strange talk about a wife and dinner. Antipholus has heard that the city of Ephesus is full of witches and sorcerers and he decides to leave as soon as possible, once he is sure that his money is safe at the inn.

The next scene takes place in the house of Antipholus of Ephesus, where his wife and his sister-in-law are waiting for him to return home to dinner. He naturally does not return, since Dromio brought the message to the wrong man, and the annoyed servant arrives back at the house with a full report.

> *He asked me for a thousand marks in gold:*
> *' 'Tis dinner time,' quoth I; 'My gold!' quoth he:*
> *'Your meat doth burn,' quoth I; 'My gold!' quoth he:*
> *'Will you come home?' quoth I; 'My gold!' quoth he:*
> *'Where is the thousand marks I gave thee, villain?'*
> *'The pig,' quoth I, 'is burned;' 'My gold!' quoth he:*
> *'My mistress, sir,' quoth I; 'Hang up thy mistress!*
> *I know not thy mistress . . .'*

The mistress of the house, whose name is Adriana, is much shocked by this report. She tells Dromio that he must go back at once and fetch his master, and Dromio says that he feels "like a football," being pushed back and forth between the two of them. After he has gone, Adriana wails to her sister that she has given her husband the best years of her life and now he treats her with cruelty. Luciana, the sister, remains calm, but after all she is not the one who is in trouble.

Meanwhile Antipholus of Syracuse has found that his bag of gold was safely delivered to the inn and that his servant Dromio claims to know nothing about their recent conversation. The two men are talking together and joking with each other when the two sisters, Adriana and Luciana, find them. Adriana attaches herself to the man she believes to be her husband, for the two brothers look so much alike that not even a wife can tell them apart, and she is determined to get him to come home to dinner. Antipholus feels his head swimming with thoughts of goblins and elves, and since this is "fairy land" he decides he might as well go with the two ladies. His servant Dromio accompanies them, to act as porter at the gate and keep out unwelcome visitors, and the four of them go off together to the house of Antipholus of Ephesus.

The unwelcome visitor who naturally arrives for dinner is the real husband, Antipholus of Ephesus. He has brought a business friend with him, and his servant Dromio, and the three of them arrive trustingly at the gate. However, Dromio of Syracuse, who is acting as porter, refuses to let them in and shouts insults while the rightful owners pound indignantly at their own door. The embarrassed business friend tries to persuade Antipholus of Ephesus to go somewhere else for dinner, but Antipholus, quite naturally, is in a bad temper at being locked out of his own house. To revenge himself, he decides to have dinner with a courtesan and to give her the gold chain he has ordered for his wife Adriana.

Meanwhile Antipholus of Syracuse has been having a difficult time also, since during dinner he fell in love with Adriana's sister. Luciana, being a virtuous lady, is unwilling to listen to words of love from the man she believes to be her brother-in-law, and Antipholus is not a success with his love-making. His servant Dromio has the reverse problem. A fat kitchenmaid has wrapped herself affectionately around him, under the impression he is his twin brother, and she is determined to marry him. Antipholus, by now hopelessly confused, resolves to escape from the town before nightfall and sends Dromio to find him a ship. A goldsmith brings him a chain and he accepts it as one more odd aspect of the town of Ephesus; it is actually the chain that Antipholus of Ephesus had ordered for his wife and is now planning to give the courtesan.

The goldsmith is in a hurry to be paid for the chain, since he has a pressing debt of his own, and he tries to collect the money from Antipholus of Ephesus. Antipholus, a much-tried man, becomes highly indignant and points out that he never received the chain. The goldsmith

THE COMEDY OF ERRORS

says that he did and, when Antipholus still refuses to pay for it, the goldsmith has him arrested. When his brother's servant makes an appearance to report he has found a ship, Antipholus sends him to Adriana to get the money for his bail. The money is in a desk at home, and Antipholus of Ephesus goes off to prison to wait for it.

Dromio gets the money without any difficulty but of course brings it to the wrong man, Antipholus of Syracuse. Antipholus is beginning to think that he has encountered a remarkably generous town, in which people press gold chains and money on him, but he is nevertheless determined to catch his boat and leave Ephesus as soon as possible. He becomes even more determined when the courtesan accosts him on the street and demands to know the whereabouts of the chain he has promised her. Antipholus rushes off muttering of witches, and the courtesan, now also beginning to feel annoyed, goes and tells Adriana that her husband has turned into a lunatic.

Antipholus of Ephesus, in the meantime, has been waiting for the money for his bail. Instead all three women descend on him—his wife, her sister and the courtesan— and along with them is a skinny conjurer named Pinch who is supposed to have some skill in calling forth evil spirits out of lunatics. Pinch tries to feel his pulse and Antipholus hits him over the head, confirming everyone's opinion that he is mad indeed. His servant Dromio seems to be touched with lunacy also, and the two of them are taken away by Doctor Pinch.

The other Antipholus has decided to fight his way to the inn, get his luggage and then board the boat at once. His servant, on the other hand, is beginning to enjoy himself, for the citizens of Ephesus are so kind to strangers. "They speak us fair, give us gold; methinks they are such a gentle nation, that, but for that mountain of mad flesh that claims marriage of me, I could find it in my heart to stay here still and turn witch." He has reason to change his mind when the goldsmith demands the money for his chain. Antipholus, pushed too far, draws his rapier, and there is a wild struggle. The three ladies, still convinced they are dealing with a madman, add to the confusion, and the harried strangers from Syracuse finally retreat into the shelter of a neighboring abbey.

The abbess herself comes out to quiet the multitude and tries to find out why Antipholus was driven mad. She is inclined to blame his wife, who probably made him lose his wits by nagging him, and the outraged Adriana decides to appeal to the duke to get her husband back out of the abbey.

The duke happens to be passing by, for it is sundown and he has come to supervise the execution of old Aegeon. Adriana pours out to him the shocking details of her husband's wild behavior and her report is confirmed by a servant. He enters to say that Antipholus has broken from his bonds and is busy singeing Doctor Pinch's beard, but Adriana knows that this is quite impossible since her husband is in the abbey.

At this point Antipholus of Ephesus enters, fresh from his triumph over Pinch, and demands justice from the duke. He wants his wife punished for having locked him out of his own house. Moreover, he has had a hard day and he wishes the duke to know all about it.

The duke, a conscientious man, tries to get at the truth through questioning everyone and becomes more confused than ever. The problem is not solved until the abbess enters, and then she brings the second Antipholus and the second Dromio with her.

Once the two brothers stand face to face, everything straightens itself out. Aegeon joyfully discovers that he has two living sons, and he further discovers that the abbess is his lost wife. Antipholus of Syracuse is now free to court the fair Luciana, and Dromio of Syracuse is delighted to learn that he will not be expected to marry his "fat friend" the kitchenmaid. The abbess invites the duke and all her new-found family to a joyful celebration, and the two Dromios go off contentedly, hand in hand, as the story ends.

LOVE'S LABOUR'S LOST

THE STORY *of Love's Labour's Lost* is laid in Navarre, an ancient kingdom in Spain, but there is nothing in the least Spanish about the play. If it has any reality at all, it is an English reality. The young lords and ladies are storybook versions of some of the men and women who could be seen around the English court, and the country people are cheerful parodies of types Shakespeare could have met in his native Warwickshire.

The play is less a story than a game. The plot is as light as a soap bubble, and its charm lies in the kind of dancing light that it throws on some of the subjects which fascinated young men and women in Shakespeare's day. It is almost a Valentine of a play, half a love-Valentine and half a comic-Valentine, and has to be read in the spirit in which it was written.

The story opens in the park of the king of Navarre, where he and his lords are discussing a highly idealistic project. They wish to retire from the world for three years and dedicate themselves to contemplation and the pursuit of knowledge instead of worldly enjoyment and the pursuit of young ladies. The king and two of his lords are quite content with the idea, but the liveliest of them all, Berowne, has strenuous objections.

He finally agrees to sign a pledge along with the rest and then begins to study some of the special statutes that are designed to keep the court of Navarre pure, virtuous and womanless. He is especially interested in the law that forbids anyone to talk to a woman, since, as he points out helpfully, the princess of France is arriving in Navarre on a diplomatic mission and it will be rather difficult to avoid talking to her. The king hastily withdraws this particular statute, and Berowne signs with pleasure.

23

The rule against women is intended to apply to everyone in the court, but word comes that the new law has already been broken. A country boy named Costard has been seen walking out in the park with a maid named Jaquenetta, and he is brought before the king by the local constable. The constable also brings a letter from a Spanish knight named Armado, who saw the whole thing and was deeply shocked.

Armado's letter is a parody on a certain kind of ornamental and highly decorated writing that was popular in the days when *Love's Labour's Lost* was written. Instead of saying that he went for a walk because he felt sad, Armado writes: "Besieged with sable-coloured melancholy, I did commend the black-oppressing humour to the most wholesome physic of thy health-giving air." It takes a long time for Armado to explain in his elegant letter that he has merely been in the park at suppertime and seen Costard and Jaquenetta together. What he does not explain is the real reason for his indignation: he is in love with Jaquenetta himself.

Armado is convinced that he is too mighty a soldier to fall in love with a mere country girl, and he has a long chat with his page on the subject. He finally decides that if Hercules and other men of valor could be overcome by Cupid, the god of love, then it is no disgrace for the great Armado to be overcome also. "Adieu, valor, rust, rapier, be still, drum; for your manager is in love. Yea, he loveth. Assist me, some extemporal god of rhyme, for I am sure I shall turn sonnet."

The conquest of Armado by the god of love is followed by the even more sudden defeat of the king of Navarre and his three lords, for they succumb to the power of Cupid as soon as they meet the princess of France and her three ladies. The princess has been obliged to pitch her tent in the king's park, since his oath does not permit him to lodge her in the palace, but he cannot avoid going to pay her a formal diplomatic call. At least, he does his best to keep it formal, but it is only too clear that the king has fallen in love. Berowne attaches himself to a lovely dark-eyed lady of France named Rosaline, who teases him while he is there and calls him a "merry madcap lord" after he departs. The two other ladies of France look with equal favor on the two remaining lords of Navarre, and it is evident that Armado is not the only one who will be writing love sonnets.

Berowne has never been in love before and he is extremely indignant at his unexpected plight. He has always mocked at lovers, and in his opinion wives are like German clocks, never behaving properly. Moreover, Rosaline is dark and, if she were an ideal beauty, she would be fair. The whole thing is extremely unjust in Berowne's eyes, and evidently a penance that Cupid has imposed

for my neglect
Of his almighty dreadful little might.

The whole austere and womanless community of Navarre is now in love, in spite of all the laws and statutes that have been made on the subject, and the only person who gets any real advantage from the situation is Costard. He is given three farthings by Armado to carry a love letter and a poem to Jaquenetta, and a shilling by Berowne to carry a similar one to Rosaline. Costard does his best to be helpful but he is a minnow in intelligence, and when he finds the princess out hunting deer in the park he gives her the letter that was meant for the country maid.

The local schoolmaster also tries his hand at writing poetry and composes a poem on the death of a deer killed by the princess, while the curate and the constable listen in reverence. The schoolmaster, whose name is Holofernes, is extremely proud of his writing ability but tries to be outwardly casual about it. "This is a gift that I have, simple, simple; a foolish extravagant spirit, full of forms, figures, shapes, objects, ideas, apprehensions, motions, revolutions . . . The gift is good in those in whom it is acute, and I am thankful for it." Their discussion on the art of writing is interrupted by Jaquenetta, who has received the letter that Berowne meant for Rosaline and asks the curate to read it to her. Berowne has written a sonnet and Holofernes is quite severe about it, since in his opinion it lacks the "elegance, facility and golden cadence" of the best poetry. In any case, the sonnet was clearly not intended for Jaquenetta and he sends her off to give it to the king, then settles down to tell the curate exactly what is wrong with the poem he so mistakenly admires.

Berowne is now incurably addicted to writing sonnets, and he is carrying a piece of paper around with him in the park when he sees the king approaching. Berowne hastily conceals himself, and the love-stricken king betrays his emotions immediately with a melancholy "Ah, me!" The king, like everyone else, has just composed a sonnet and plans to leave it where the princess will be sure to pick it up.

One of his lords approaches, and with a tact to equal Berowne's the king steps aside and hides himself in a bush. Again a sonnet has been composed to the fair eyes of a lady, and then the fourth lord turns up with an ode. The king rises up out of his bush and informs the two false lords that they have broken their oath, and then Berowne comes out of hiding to reveal that the king has been writing sonnets too.

Berowne is deeply disappointed in his three friends for falling from grace. "Are you not ashamed?" He is just remarking that no one would ever get him to "write a thing in rhyme" when Jaquenetta appears, bearing in her hand the sonnet he wrote to Rosaline. Berowne tries to tear up the paper but one of the lords alertly finds his name on it, and Berowne has to confess that he is a fellow sinner. He endures a good deal of teasing on the subject but takes the position that in reality they are all still faithful to their vow. They made an oath to spend three years in study, and the best thing for any young man to study is a woman. So the four of them decide that they will openly woo the young ladies of France and plan to present revels and entertainments for their delight.

Armado, the Spanish knight, is assigned to work out the show, which, as Armado puts it, is to be presented to the princess in her pavilion "in the posteriors of this day, which the rude multitude call the afternoon." He asks Holofernes to help him and they decide to do the Nine Worthies. They are rather short of actors, since they have no one but the curate and the page to help them, but Holofernes feels capable of playing three of the Nine

Worthies all by himself, and the constable, who is baffled by everything else in the arrangements, feels that he can at least supply a little music.

The lovesick lords have been sending gifts to their ladies —gloves and pearls and poetry—and the ladies have decided to tease their ardent hosts. They learn that the young gentlemen intend to call on them disguised as Russians, and they decide to put on masks and change their gifts about so that each young man will woo the wrong young lady. The disguised lords have brought the page along with them to deliver a preliminary speech, but he has a difficult time with it because the ladies will not cooperate. The baffled Russians discover that the ladies will not cooperate with them either, and they are finally forced to retire.

The king and his three lords reappear without their disguises, and the king tries to persuade his royal guest to enter the palace. The princess says demurely that she could not possibly agree, since she would be assisting him to break his solemn oath. The king suggests that she may be lonely where she is, and the ladies explain that, on the contrary, they have just been visited by some very foolish Russians. Finally they admit that they know who the Russians were. The lords turn pale, and Rosaline inquires sweetly if they feel seasick, coming so far from Russia. The lords then make the further discovery that each of them has been wooing the wrong lady. They can see now that they are completely forsworn, since all day they have been making promises and none of them has been kept.

They also discover, Berowne in particular, that it is better to court a lady in prose and do it honestly than to "woo in rhyme" in the high-flown way they have all been doing. Berowne resolves to forsake from that time forward all "taffeta phrases, silken terms precise" and he promises Rosaline that he will use only plain, homespun words in making love to her.

> *Henceforth my wooing mind shall be expressed*
> *In russet yeas and honest kersey noes:*
> *And to begin, wench,—so God help me, la!—*
> *My love to thee is sound, sans crack or flaw.*

Rosaline points out that "sans" is not a word he should be using under the circumstances, and Berowne can see that the love of fantastical phrases is a sickness from which a man can recover only by degrees.

Meanwhile the amateur actors have been anxiously waiting to put on their show, and they finally send Costard to see if the lords and ladies are ready for them. The king does not want them to perform, since he feels that Navarre has already disgraced itself sufficiently without offering the ladies some bad amateur theatricals. Berowne, however, thinks he would enjoy seeing "one show worse" than the one he and his three friends have already supplied.

Costard is convinced that it will be an excellent show, since he has all the witless enthusiasm of a really bad amateur actor. He starts the proceedings off by playing Pompey, an achievement of considerable difficulty because the audience keeps interrupting him. When he announces with pride that he is Pompey the Big, they inform him that he is supposed to be Pompey the Great, but he acknowledges the correction graciously and manages to get through his lines with great aplomb. The princess, who is a courteous lady, is very kind to him: "Great thanks, great Pompey," and he receives her gratitude with a judicious mixture of modesty and pride. " 'Tis not so much worth; but I hope I was perfect. I made a little fault in 'Great.' "

The next Worthy is Alexander, who turns out to be the curate. He starts his speech in a mad rush and is interrupted by his unhelpful audience. He starts over again, forgets his lines and stands paralyzed until Costard has to push him off the stage. Costard, secure in the magnificence of his own performance, is inclined to be forgiving. "He is a marvelous good neighbour, faith, and a very good bowler; but, for Alexander—alas, you see how 'tis."

The next Worthies are Judas Maccabeus and Hercules, played by the schoolmaster and the page. The page is rather small for Hercules, but the amateur actors have solved that problem by presenting Hercules when he was "a babe, a child, a shrimp." Judas Maccabeus manages to finish only one line of his speech because he descends into an argument with the audience, and when Armado comes on as Hector he has no better luck. Armado argues that the audience should be more gentle with Hector. "The sweet war-man is dead and rotten; sweet chucks, beat not the bones of the buried; when he breathed, he was a man."

The amateur theatricals break up when Costard and Armado forget the Worthies and get into a fight over Jaquenetta, and the audience is hoping for a duel between them when a messenger arrives from the French court. The news he brings sobers them all abruptly, for the king of France is dead.

The princess is so heavy-hearted that she cannot imagine why she ever spent her time in laughter and teasing, and she prepares to go home to France. The four men who will be left behind are really in love, and they make one final promise. During the year in which the princess is in mourning for her father they too will retire from the world, and Berowne, the lively mocker, has an extra penance laid upon him. For a year the man who has laughed at so many people will go around to the hospitals and see if he can persuade laughter there, and Berowne is sobered enough to accept the challenge.

It is winter now in their spirits, after a short, gay spring, and the amateur actors have a final offering in the shape of a dialogue between the cuckoo and the owl. They present two of the loveliest songs in Shakespeare, the ones he used to describe a country winter and a country spring.

> *When daisies pied, and violets blue,*
> *And lady-smocks all silver-white*
> *And cuckoo-buds of yellow hue*
> *Do paint the meadows with delight . . .*

But winter has the final word, with the owl in the snow, and so the little story ends.

THE TAMING OF THE SHREW

THE TAMING OF THE SHREW tells a story within a story, a device that Shakespeare tried only once and then discarded as of no use to him.

The first story, which is called the Induction, opens with a drunken tinker who is pushed out of an alehouse and falls asleep on the ground. A great lord who has been out hunting finds him there and decides to play a joke on him. He will house him in his castle and surround him with respectful servants, and when the tinker wakens they will pretend he is their noble master who has temporarily gone mad. A page dressed in the clothes of a great lady is assigned to act the part of his wife, and when the tinker first wakes he is hopelessly befuddled. Then he begins to develop a real enthusiasm for his new life, and the joke lies in the contrast between the earth-like realism of the tinker and the elegance of his silken background.

A play has been arranged for his amusement, presented by a group of traveling actors, and as the play starts the second story begins. This is the tale of the taming of the shrew, the hot-tempered woman who is finally conquered by her husband, and it takes up the rest of the action. There is no real connection between the two stories, except for a kind of cheerful heartlessness in the tone of both.

The story of the shrew opens in the busy Italian city of Padua, a center of the arts. A rich young tourist named Lucentio arrives there with his servant to round out his education, and almost at once he finds himself a spectator to a vigorous family argument. A rich merchant of the town has two daughters, Katharina and Bianca. Katharina, the elder, has such a violent temper that no one will marry her, but her sister Bianca is so gentle and soft-spoken that she has two ardent suitors, one young and one old. The merchant announces that he will not let Bianca marry until he first finds a husband for Katharina and thus leaves the two suitors with the problem of finding someone who is willing to marry a shrew. Meanwhile young Lucentio, who has been listening to the whole discussion, falls in love with Bianca himself. He decides to let his servant take his place in Padua society while he disguises himself and tries to get a position as schoolmaster to so pretty and gentle a lady.

A vigorous young man named Petruchio arrives in town with only one thought in his head: to marry a rich wife.

I come to wive it wealthily in Padua;
If wealthily, then happily in Padua.

He is a friend of the younger of the two suitors, who is delighted to present him to Katharina's father as a potential son-in-law. In return, Petruchio agrees to present his friend, in disguise, as a music master who has come to teach Bianca.

Still another suitor for Bianca's hand turns up in the person of Lucentio's servant, dressed as a fine gentleman to help his master in his wooing; and the whole troop of men, half of them disguised and all of them anxious to see Katharina married, go in a body to the house of the merchant.

Katharina is furious at her father, jealous of her sister, and in general in a bad temper with the whole world. Petruchio is told what a violent woman she is, and he can judge for himself when his unhappy friend comes back into the room. He has tried to teach Katharina to play the lute and has foolishly found fault with her fingering; and she, being a woman of direct action, has broken the lute over his head. But Petruchio refuses to worry. She is rich, and he is sure he can tame her.

Katharina enters, and there is the first of a series of lively scenes between herself and Petruchio. Audiences have always enjoyed these scenes, for the fun of seeing two strong wills pushing against each other, both of them quite without scruple or any sense of fair play and both of them determined to win. Petruchio has hit upon a technique that maddens Katharina all the more because she cannot find a way to turn it back on him. When she shouts, he tells her he loves her sweet and gentle voice, and when she rages about the room, he admires her charming way of walking. The rest of the company returns, and Petruchio reports blandly that Katharina loves him devotedly. He will be back on Sunday to marry her, although Katharina assures him she will see him hanged first.

Now that the older sister is safely betrothed, Bianca is free to marry, and at once the suitors fall to arguing among themselves. The elderly suitor and the servant who is disguised as Lucentio vie with each other in offering huge sums of money to her father, while the other two, disguised as schoolmasters, try to give Bianca lessons in music and Latin while they make love to her. Neither of them is wholly successful, and the scene ends when Bianca is called away to help with the preparations for her sister's wedding.

The wedding is a peculiar one. Petruchio arrives late, dressed like a lunatic, on a horse that is almost falling apart and with his servant Grumio as untidy as he is. He behaves like a madman throughout the wedding ceremony, upsetting the priest, throwing wine in the sexton's face and kissing the new-made bride with "such a clamorous smack" that the whole church rings with it. When Katharina tries to make him stay for the bridal dinner, he seizes her bodily and carries her away, shouting energetically that he is rescuing her from thieves. "Fear not, sweet wench; they shall not touch thee, Kate."

All through the long, cold journey to his country house Petruchio keeps up his performance. Grumio, his servant, is finally sent on ahead and staggers into the front hall completely worn out and feeling like "a piece of ice." He has a wonderful tale to tell about the outrageous behavior of his master, and the servants are waiting with fascinated interest to see the new bride. "Is she so hot a shrew as she's reported?"

They are all well trained in the parts they are to play when Katharina and Petruchio enter, Katharina bewildered and half frozen and Petruchio in full swing. He knocks the servants about when they try to serve supper, calling

them names like "beetle-headed, flap-eared knave," and
in the end Katharina gets no food at all. Then he makes
such a commotion about the way the bed is arranged that she
gets no sleep either. Petruchio does all this with an air of
the warmest regard for his wife's comfort, singing snatches
of song with unsinkable good cheer and bidding his
"sweet Kate" welcome to his house. He is behaving more
violently than Katharina herself at her worst, but with such
a sunny air of doing it all for her comfort that she has no
weapons against him.

Meanwhile, back in Padua, Bianca has fallen in love
with Lucentio, the rich young tourist who disguised himself as her teacher. The younger suitor, much upset by her
inconstancy, goes off to marry a wealthy widow, and this
leaves only the elderly suitor to be disposed of. He is
outbid by Lucentio's disguised servant, who agrees that
Lucentio's father will put in an appearance to guarantee
the promised dowry and then picks up a stray old man
who is willing to act the father's part.

The action turns back to the country house of Petruchio, where a half-starved Katharina is trying to bribe
Grumio to get her a piece of meat.

> *I, who never knew how to entreat*
> *Nor never needed that I should entreat,*
> *Am starved for meat, giddy for lack of sleep,*
> *With oaths kept waking, and with brawling fed,*
> *And that which spites me more than all these wants,*
> *He does it under name of perfect love.*

Grumio is extremely helpful and sympathetic, and he ends
by offering her mustard without any beef in the very image
of his equally helpful master.

Petruchio has decided it is time to pay a visit back to
Padua and has ordered a special outfit for Katharina to
wear. The haberdasher enters with a little cap he has made
for her, and Katharina's heart goes out to it. Petruchio
says in contempt that it is no better than a walnut shell,
and his wife is roused to fury in her desire for the cap.
Petruchio says she is indeed right. It is "a paltry cap, a

custard-coffin," and he loves her for disliking it. Katharina fights back:

> Love me or love me not, I like the cap,
> And I will have it, or I will have none.

So she gets none.

Then the tailor comes in with the gown and again Petruchio finds fault with everything. The sleeve is carved like an apple tart and nothing is the way he ordered it. The tailor tries to defend himself, and Petruchio turns on him with some of his most talented insults.

> Thou flea, thou nit, thou winter-cricket thou!
> Braved in mine own house with a skein of thread!
> Away, thou rag, thou quantity, thou remnant!

The tailor is actually safe enough and will be paid; but as long as he is in front of Katharina Petruchio never forgets the part he is playing. It ends with their setting out for Padua with no new clothes at all, but with Katharina beginning to realize that this is a warfare she can never win.

In Padua itself, young Lucentio's plan for a secret marriage to Bianca progresses. The pretended father is introduced to Bianca's father and the pretended son is given leave to marry her, but the real arrangement is for Lucentio to slip away with the bride and marry her in St. Luke's Church. The chief difficulty, which no one knows about, is that Lucentio's real father is journeying to Padua to see his son.

On the road to town he meets Katharina and Petruchio. Petruchio has been chatting about the moonlight, and when Katharina points out, quite reasonably, that it is the sun, he says he will turn around and go home if she persists in arguing with him. Katharina says hastily that of course it is the moon, and when Petruchio reverses himself and says it is the sun she agrees with that also. When they meet Lucentio's father she addresses him as though he were a young girl, because Petruchio has told her to, and then apologizes charmingly when Petruchio reverses himself. Her manners are so excellent, in fact, that she gives the impression of enjoying the role of a meek wife as much as she enjoyed being a shrew. Katharina can do nothing by halves and Petruchio's worries are over.

The same cannot be said for Lucentio's father when he arrives at his son's lodgings to find an elderly stranger and a counterfeit son in possession. They accuse him of being a madman, but as soon as Lucentio himself arrives, newly married to Bianca, he kneels at his father's feet and asks for pardon. He is given it freely, and so all the couples are satisfactorily mated. Lucentio has Bianca, Petruchio has Katharina, the young suitor has his widow, and the old suitor, although he remarks frankly, "My cake is dough," is at least invited to the wedding feast.

The banquet is a lively one, with Katharina's wit as sharp as ever, and after the ladies have left the table the gentlemen sympathize with Petruchio for having married a shrew. Petruchio offers to wager that he possesses the most obedient wife of the three, and the other two husbands, convinced they will win, agree. Lucentio sends word to his wife, who is sitting by the parlor fire, that he wishes to see her, and Bianca sends back word she is too busy. The husband of the widow sends an entreaty to his wife to come, and she sends back a flat refusal. Then Petruchio commands his wife to come, and she comes instantly.

Katharina does more than that. She explains to the two erring wives the kind of obedience they owe their husbands, and the delighted Petruchio applauds her:

> *Why, there's a wench.*
> *Come on, and kiss me, Kate.*

So the shrew is at last tamed, and the farce has a happy ending.

THE TWO GENTLEMEN OF VERONA

THE TWO GENTLEMEN OF VERONA is Shakespeare's first attempt at a romantic comedy, and like most first attempts it is not altogether successful. It includes a great many situations and scenes that were popular in his day and that Shakespeare used again later—the rope ladder, the helpful friar, the forest of outlaws, the girl in love who dresses as a boy, and so on—but none of them seems very interesting and it is chiefly because the people are not very real. They move about in obedience to the plot instead of to themselves and the men in particular are cut out of lace paper.

The chief justification for the plot is that it takes place in a kind of never-never land of lovers where nothing is expected to be consistent.

> *O, how this spring of love resembleth*
> *The uncertain glory of an April day,*
> *Which now shows all the beauty of the sun,*
> *And by and by a cloud takes all away.*

Everything is done in the name of love, and love is expected to be unreasonable.

The young men who give the play its title are two close friends named Valentine and Proteus, who are saying good-bye to each other as the story opens. Valentine is going to the great city of Milan to finish his education, while Proteus is staying at home to woo a lady named Julia. He has hopefully sent her a love letter by Valentine's servant, a country boy named Speed who is much annoyed because he failed to get a tip for delivering it.

The letter has actually been delivered to Julia's maid, who cannot resist teasing her mistress a little about Proteus. For Julia is in love with him but unwilling to admit it. She makes a great show of tearing up his letter and then goes down on the floor to try to piece together the fragments. Finally she brings herself to write him in return, and Proteus is reading her letter when he encounters his father. The old gentleman has just decided to send his son to Milan, to finish his education and to be near Valentine, and when Proteus hastily pretends that the letter he is reading has been sent from Valentine, his father is sure he has made a wise decision.

Valentine, meanwhile, has been spending his time educationally in Milan by falling in love. The object of his affections is the daughter of the duke of Milan, a gray-eyed, auburn-haired lady named Silvia. Speed feels no sympathy for his lovesick master, and since most of Shakespeare's servants have a cheerful disregard for their masters' dignity, Speed is quite willing to lecture him on the subject. Valentine has also been writing love letters, since Silvia has asked him to. She pretends she is using him as a kind of secretary to write love letters for her to a "secret nameless friend" and then delivers the letters back to him again, since he of course is the friend.

Proteus is ready to set sail and bids Julia an emotional farewell. His servant Launce has undergone an equally emotional scene of parting with his family—"my mother weeping, my father wailing, my sister crying, our maid howling, our cat wringing her hands." Fortunately he can take his dog Crab with him, although Crab is a hard-hearted animal who was not in the least impressed by all the family emotion.

It becomes evident in Milan that Silvia has another suitor, a knight named Thurio who has the warm approval of her father the duke. She acquires a third when Proteus arrives at court, for he falls immediately in love with her and forgets all his promises to Julia. Proteus knows very well he is betraying his friend, for Valentine has already told him how much he loves the daughter of the duke.

Why, man, she is mine own,
And I as rich in having such a jewel
As twenty seas, if all their sand were pearl,
The water nectar, and the rocks pure gold.

But Proteus has a name that means "changeable" and he ~annot help himself.

Julia finds that she cannot bear to live in Verona any longer since Proteus is not there and she decides to follow him to Milan. She will disguise herself as a page, since a lady cannot travel alone, and her maid is extremely helpful. "What fashion, madam, shall I make your breeches?"

Proteus continues to disgrace himself in Milan. He finds out that Silvia and Valentine are planning to run away together and that Valentine is bringing a ladder of rope to Silvia's room in the upper tower. Proteus betrays his friend to Silvia's father, and the duke finds the ladder of cords hidden under Valentine's cloak. The young man is banished from the kingdom and Proteus, pretending to sympathize, escorts him as far as the city gate. Speed, Valentine's servant, goes with him, after listening to all the troubles his friend Launce has been having with a milkmaid.

Proteus offers to help Thurio in his wooing of Silvia, but with no intention of having him succeed. He advises Thurio to court her with "wailful sonnets" and they arrange to stage a concert under Silvia's window.

Valentine makes his way through the woods outside the city and is set upon by a band of outlaws. They are storybook outlaws who swear "by the bare scalp of Robin Hood's fat friar," and they promptly ask Valentine to be their captain. He is a noble youth and agrees only on condition that they will never prey on women or on the poor.

The concert is performed under Silvia's window and the musicians sing that lovely song,

> *Who is Silvia? what is she?*
> *That all our swains commend her?* . . .

Among the listeners is Julia, who learns from the host at the inn that the faithless Proteus has been courting Silvia, and her heart is nearly broken by the news. Proteus has promised Thurio to woo Silvia on his behalf, but as soon as the knight has departed he attempts to make love to her himself, and he continues to be hopeful in spite of the open contempt that Silvia shows for him.

Next morning, to speed his wooing, Proteus sends his servant Launce to the lady with a little dog as a present. Launce loses the small object, which he considers no better than a squirrel in any case, and substitutes his own ungainly cur, who is ten times bigger and therefore ten times better. Silvia is not pleased with the gift and Launce is bringing it back again when he encounters his master and a young page who has just been engaged by him. The page is Julia, still disguiesd as a boy, and since Launce is such an unsatisfactory messenger, Proteus sends Julia instead with a ring to his beloved.

There is a charming little scene between Julia and Silvia, a kind of dress rehearsal on Shakespeare's part for a much better use of the same situation later in *Twelfth Night*. Julia tells Silvia of the sad lady that Proteus left behind him, and Silvia is deeply sympathetic. She has already decided to run away and look for Valentine, and at sunset she leaves the city.

Proteus discovers that she has run away to the forest and goes to look for her, with Julia following. As soon as he discovers Silvia, he tries to make violent love to her and is stopped by Valentine, now the leader of the outlaws. Proteus is instantly repentant of his bad behavior, and Valentine, his affection for his friend running away with him, makes a magnificent offer. "All that was mine in Silvia I give thee." At this Julia faints, and when she recovers she admits her identity. Proteus promptly reverses himself and decides he loves Julia after all, Valentine is at last free to marry Silvia, and the duke of Milan suddenly appears and forgives everyone, even the outlaws.

So the story ends, a little abruptly but in "mutual happiness," as any comedy should.

A MIDSUMMER NIGHT'S DREAM

A MIDSUMMER NIGHT'S DREAM is one of the most magical plays ever written. It is a story of flowers and young lovers and dreams, and of the fairies who lived in an enchanted wood near Athens in the days when Theseus came back a conqueror. Most of it is played by moonlight, and anyone who has been outdoors on a moonlit night knows how changed and how lovely the world can be.

Everyone is a little moonstruck in the play, a little touched by magic. But it is not the fairies' magic, potent as that might be. It is Shakespeare's magic and the power he had over words, a power stronger than that of Theseus the conqueror or Oberon the fairy king.

The story opens in the palace of Theseus, who is looking forward with longing to his wedding with the queen of the Amazons. It is to be held on the first night of the new moon, and Theseus finds the waiting difficult.

One of his subjects comes to him with a formal complaint that his daughter is disobeying him. Her name is Hermia, and her father wishes her to marry an Athenian youth named Demetrius. But Hermia will do almost anything to avoid marrying the man of her father's choice, for she herself is in love with Lysander. Finally the two lovers decide to run away together and they arrange to meet the following night in a wood near Athens.

Hermia discloses the plan to the dearest of her friends, whose name is Helena. She had supposed her friend would be pleased, for Helena is in love with Demetrius and he may turn to her if Hermia is no longer in the city. But Helena is so much in love she is willing to hurt herself for his sake. She tells Demetrius of the plan, knowing that he will pursue the escaping lovers but that she at least can accompany him.

Meanwhile a group of Athenian workmen have heard that the duke Theseus intends to have mirth and revelry on his wedding night, and they decide to put on a play for him. They meet at the house of a carpenter named Peter Quince, who is acting as director and who is harried by a self-appointed assistant director named Nick Bottom.

The play has an excellent title, "The most lamentable comedy and most cruel death of Pyramus and Thisby," and everyone is prepared to work hard to make it a great success. It is the workmen's intense earnestness that makes them so funny, for they are convinced that they are men of great wit, talent and competence, while they are actually the worst group of amateur actors who ever choked an audience with laughter.

Quince has a great many troubles as director, even apart from the fact that Bottom is determined to run the whole show for him. No one is really prepared to do what Quince wants. He tries to cast Bottom as Pyramus the hero, but Bottom pictures himself in a more grandiloquent role and cannot be prevented from declaiming lines from quite a different play. Quince then attempts to cast Flute, the bellows-mender, as Thisbe the heroine. Flute does not want to take the part of a lady because he has a beard coming, and this gives Bottom a chance to demonstrate how charmingly he could play Thisbe if anyone would let him.

Quince then casts Snug, the joiner, in the part of the lion, and Snug is a little reluctant because he is slow at memorizing his lines. He is assured he will have nothing to do but roar, and this too strikes Bottom's wandering fancy. He is eager to play the lion because he could roar so excellently, in two different keys. Quince, asserting himself, says that Bottom must play Pyramus and no other, for Pyramus was, after all, "a most lovely, gentleman-like man"; and Bottom, versatile to the end, has a whole series of different beards with which he is prepared to decorate himself for the part.

Quince informs them they must all know their lines by the following night. And since too many people will watch them if they rehearse in town, they will meet "in the palace wood, a mile without the town, by moonlight." So there will be two groups of people in the wood that night, the lovers and the workmen.

The fairies will be there also. It is a wood of cowslips and primroses, and both the king and queen of the fairies plan to hold their revels there. But they will not hold them together, for the king and queen have been quarreling, so stormily that the elves have hidden in acorn cups and rains have drenched the land. Titania, queen of the fairies, is bringing up a changeling whom Oberon, the king, wants as his page, and he is angry because she will not give the boy up to him.

Among Oberon's servants is Puck, a teasing mischief-maker who spends most of his time playing jokes, and the king sends him on a wicked little errand. There is a flower called love-in-idleness, and Oberon plans to use it to play a trick on the queen. If the juice is squeezed on her eyelids while she is sleeping she will fall in love with the next thing she sees, and Puck speeds around the globe to get the flower.

I'll put a girdle round about the earth
In forty minutes.

Into the moonlit wood comes Demetrius, searching for the escaping lovers and followed by the faithful Helena. The watching king of the fairies is regretful that the young Athenian obviously does not return her love, and he sends Puck to put some of the flower juice on his eyes while he goes to do the same with Titania.

Oberon finds Titania upon a bank of flowers. Her fairies sing a lullaby to protect her from the wild things of the wood, beetles and hedgehogs that might do her harm. Then they leave her sleeping among the violets and the wild thyme, and Oberon puts the magic juice upon her eyelids.

The two escaping lovers enter, weary and confused and having lost their way. They decide to lie down in the moonlit wood until daybreak, and Puck, searching for an Athenian, decides that the sleeping Lysander must be the man that Oberon meant. But Puck has chosen the wrong man, and Lysander, when he wakens, sees the wrong woman. For Helena has been wandering in the wood since

Demetrius cast her off, and Lysander, misled by the magic, falls instantly in love with her. Hermia wakens and finds herself alone, and she sets out grieving to look for her lover.

Bottom and his friends arrive in the wood for their rehearsal, and Peter Quince is ready to start immediately. But Bottom has been brooding over the script and has decided that it needs some changes. It is possible that the ladies in the audience may become upset by the bloody death of Pyramus, and therefore the play needs a prologue to assure everyone that Pyramus is not really dead at all. Bottom then manages to solve all the other production problems that have come up, and the rehearsal is ready to begin.

The play is full of large words which no one can pronounce, and Flute, as the lovely Thisbe, has a tendency to run all his lines together. Still, all is progressing satisfactorily until Bottom enters on cue. He has been waiting in a hawthorn thicket for his time to enter, and Puck has slipped the head of an ass on his shoulders. Bottom cannot understand why his fellow actors run away from him in terror. He is even more astonished when Titania wakens and falls in love with him, although, as he remarks philosophically, "Reason and love keep little company together nowadays."

Titania, under the spell of the flower's enchantment, is enthralled by Bottom and calls on all her fairies to do him service.

> *Be kind and courteous to this gentleman,*
> *Hop in his walks, and gambol in his eyes,*
> *Feed him with apricocks and dewberries,*
> *With purple grapes, green figs and mulberries,*
> *The honey-bags steal from the humble-bees,*
> *And for night-tapers crop their waxen thighs,*
> *And light them at the fiery glow-worm's eyes,*
> *To have my love to bed and to arise,*
> *And pluck the wings from sleeping butterflies,*
> *To fan the moonbeams from his sleeping eyes,*
> *Nod to him, elves, and do him courtesies.*

The elves and the ass bow graciously to one another, and Bottom, always the master of any situation he finds himself in, conducts a polite conversation with them until Titania leads him away.

Hermia enters, followed by the devoted Demetrius and still looking for her lost Lysander. She is sure that Demetrius in his jealousy has killed him, although Demetrius indignantly protests his innocence. He dares not follow her while she is angry with him, and he in his turn lies down to sleep.

Oberon points out to Puck that he has put the wrong Athenian under the spell. Demetrius is supposed to fall in love with Helena, and Puck is sent to find her while his master anoints the second Athenian with the flower juice. Now both the young men are in love with Helena, after both have scorned her, and the situation delights Puck since it confirms his opinion of the whole human race. "Lord, what fools these mortals be!"

Demetrius and Lysander attempt to woo Helena, who is naturally convinced that they are making fun of her, while Hermia is appalled to find that both suitors have forsaken her and is sure the whole thing is Helena's fault. Hermia is small and spirited while Helena is tall and rather timid, and she appeals to the men to protect her.

She was a vixen when she went to school;
And though she be but little, she is fierce.

The men, however, are occupied with their own quarrel, and they go off to fight a duel with each other.

Oberon is inclined to suspect that Puck arranged the whole mix-up deliberately, but Puck assures him that he meant no harm. "Believe me, king of shadows, I mistook." He is sent to straighten everything out and manages to collect all the confused and sleepy lovers in the same place. Then, through his magic power, he makes sure that each man will choose the right maid when he wakens.

Meanwhile Titania's obedient little fairies have been encountering a certain amount of difficulty in trying to serve anyone as large and hairy as Bottom. Titania wishes to wreathe musk-roses around his large ears, while her elves bring him nuts, but what Bottom wants is a peck of oats and some sleep. When Oberon asks for the little changeling boy Titania is willing to give him up, and Oberon lifts the enchantment from her eyes. By this time it is daybreak, and the king and queen do a dance to music. Then, with the lark's song, all the fairies fly away.

Duke Theseus is out hunting that morning in the forest with his pack of hounds. He comes upon the four sleeping lovers and has his huntsmen wake them with their horns. Demetrius explains to the duke that he followed his rival into the wood the night before; but now he is a rival no longer, for Demetrius is in love with Helena and quite content to let Hermia marry Lysander. The duke is delighted that everything has turned out so well and graciously arranges to have the two young couples married on his own wedding day. This leaves only Bottom in the empty wood; and when Bottom awakens, with the ass's head no longer upon him, he is so charmed with the strange dream he has had that he decides to have it turned into a ballad and sung at the play.

Bottom's fellow actors meet at the house of Peter Quince to mourn the loss of their leading man. With three weddings in the same day, they could have made their fortunes presenting the tragedy before the duke. Then Bottom enters full of enthusiasm and a list of final instructions, and the cast goes off rejoicing to collect their costumes.

The duke's bride and his master of the revels try to persuade Theseus not to waste his time with a ridiculous group of amateur actors. But the duke is a gentleman and mindful of their good intentions, and moreover he is willing to bring his own imagination to a play. "The best in this kind are but shadows; and the worst are no worse, if imagination amend them." And so the story of Pyramus and Thisbe begins, a tragedy presented with lunatic solemnity by Bottom and his woolly-headed friends.

Peter Quince has unwisely decided to present the prologue himself and, since he pays no attention to the punctuation marks, it comes out just the reverse of what he intended. Then he goes on to present the characters in verse of determined elegance which rises to a height of alliterative awfulness when he reaches the suicide of Pyramus.

> *Whereat, with blade, with bloody blameful blade,*
> *He bravely broached his boiling bloody breast . . .*

Snout, who is acting the wall, earnestly explains himself to the audience and then Pyramus enters on a wave of woe and rhetoric.

> *O grim-looked night! O night with hue so black!*
> *O night, which ever art when day is not!*
> *O night! O night! alack, alack, alack!*
> *I fear my Thisby's promise is forgot.*

The wall that has been separating the lovers kindly opens its fingers so that Pyramus can peer through; but there is no Thisbe on the other side and Pyramus curses the wall for deceiving him. This rouses Theseus to the suggestion that the wall ought to curse him back and Bottom emerges from his role long enough to assure the duke earnestly that he is mistaken. "No, in truth, sir, he should not. 'Deceiving me' is Thisby's cue; she is to enter now, and I am to spy her through the wall. You shall see, it will fall pat as I told you. Yonder she comes."

So she does; and the play lurches on its well-intentioned way in spite of the candid comments made by the members of the audience. Finally it arrives at Ninus' tomb, which the whole cast is determined to pronounce Ninny's. Pyramus and Thisbe have arranged to meet there, but Thisbe runs away because the lion, roaring most dreadfully, has frightened her. Pyramus finds her mantle and promptly concludes that she has been eaten. So he stabs himself, taking rather a long time to die after he has pronounced himself dead because he has a speech to deliver.

Thisbe, who has not been eaten after all, returns to mourn Pyramus in a final, idiotic effusion that lists all his lovelier aspects.

> *These lily lips,*
> *This cherry nose,*

These yellow cowslip cheeks
Are gone, are gone;
Lovers make moan.
His eyes were green as leeks.

Then Thisbe kills herself which, as the duke says, makes
an excellent ending. "For when the players are all dead,
there need none to be blamed." And thus the silliest and
most engaging of tragedies is ended.

By this time it is midnight, which is "almost fairy time."
The whole household goes to bed, leaving Puck and the
fairies to place a blessing on the three bridal couples and
to encircle the play with a final garland of poetry as the
Dream ends.

THE MERCHANT OF VENICE

THE MERCHANT OF VENICE is a romantic comedy, but of a most unusual kind. For the theme is money, and the climax tells of an attempted murder.

No one but Shakespeare would have tried to place material like this in such a romantic framework, and perhaps no one but Shakespeare could have succeeded. He succeeded partly because his control over his material was so complete that he could do almost anything he pleased with it, and partly because the fascination of his two chief characters is so strong that no audience can resist them. They are Portia the heiress and Shylock the moneylender, and between them they create an extraordinary play.

The story opens in the busy commercial city of Venice, and the talk is mostly of money. A merchant of Venice named Antonio is in a melancholy mood and his friends are sure he is worrying about his business ventures. He says he is not, but his closest friend, a young man named Bassanio, has good cause to be worrying about money. He has been spending lavishly and is deeply in debt just at a time when he has an opportunity to court an heiress. Bassanio needs enough money to go to Belmont and make a good showing against the other suitors, and since Antonio's ships are all at sea he has no ready money to give his friend. But he loves him so much that he is willing to borrow the money somewhere in Venice so that he can speed Bassanio on his wooing.

Then the scene shifts to Belmont and to the house of that lovely lady with the "sunny locks," Portia the heiress. Portia, like Antonio, is in a melancholy mood. "My little body is aweary of this great world." Her chief difficulty is boredom and the fact that she does not like any of her suitors. The Neapolitan prince understands nothing but horses, the Frenchman is quite unsatisfactory ("God made him, and therefore let him pass for a man"), the Englishman refuses to learn Italian, the Scot is quarrelsome and the German drinks too much. Portia has no wish to "be married to a sponge" and in fact has no wish to be married to any of her current crop of suitors. In the days when her father was alive she once met a young Venetian gentleman named Bassanio, and she still remembers him with favor.

Back in Venice, Bassanio is trying to raise enough money to go to Belmont. He needs three thousand ducats and arranges with a moneylender named Shylock to let him have the money for three months. If the money is not paid back in the specified time, Shylock can demand it from Antonio, who is acting as his friend's bondsman. Shylock wishes to see Antonio, to talk over the final arrangements, and Bassanio suggests he come to dinner with them.

Shylock refuses, and for a very old and sad reason. Shylock is a Jew, and in Venice the Jews were treated as though they belonged to an outcast race. They were obliged to live in a special part of town and wear special garments to keep them separate from the Christians, and almost the only trade they were permitted to practice was that of lending money.

Shakespeare had almost certainly never met a Jew, since all the Jews in England had been exiled long ago. But Shakespeare knew enough about human nature to realize how angry such treatment would make the members of a proud and ancient people. Shylock hates all Christians, especially Antonio, and while he is forced to do business with him, he will go no farther. "I will not eat with you."

Shylock has always been treated with the most savage contempt by Antonio, and now he finds that the man wants to ask a favor of him.

> You call me misbeliever, cut-throat dog,
> And spit upon my Jewish gaberdine . . .
> Well then, it now appears you need my help . . .
> Shall I bend low, and in a bondman's key,
> With bated breath and whispering humbleness,

Say this,—
'Fair sir, you spit on me on Wednesday last;
You spurned me such a day, another time
You called me dog; and for these courtesies
I'll lend you thus much moneys'?

It is only for a moment that Shylock indulges the deep anger which burns so constantly in him. Then he assumes the mask he wears whenever Christians are about and is almost cringing in his politeness, for he has thought of a way to destroy his enemy. Pretending that the whole thing is in jest, he gets Antonio to sign an agreement that, if the money is not repaid in time, Shylock may cut a pound of flesh from his body. Antonio is sure it is safe to sign the bond, for he is expecting all his ships to return to Venice within a month or so and will be able to repay the money easily.

Shylock has a servant named Launcelot Gobbo, who leaves him to go into service with Bassanio. Shylock also has a daughter, a pretty girl named Jessica who falls in love with a friend of Bassanio. She runs away with him one night, taking with her some of her father's gold and jewels, and Shylock's hatred of the Christians becomes a settled and almost uncontrollable mania.

Meanwhile, back in Belmont, Portia has been receiving a new series of suitors, and the first of them is the stately, dark-skinned prince of Morocco. Portia's father had realized it would be hard for her to choose a husband and when he died he left a test for her suitors. Each man was to be presented with three caskets, of gold, silver and lead. Inside one of them was Portia's picture, and whoever chose the right casket would become her husband.

The prince of Morocco chooses the gold casket, since gold is the most valuable of all metals; but inside it he finds a skull and a warning against putting any faith in outward appearances. The next suitor, the prince of Arragon, chooses the silver casket, and inside it he finds the portrait of an idiot and another warning. Then Portia hears that a third suitor is approaching, a young Venetian, and her maid cannot help hoping that the new suitor is Bassanio, with whom Portia is already in love.

Back in Venice Shylock is roaming the streets, followed by jeering small boys and half-crazed with anger and grief. He has lost his daughter, his money and his jewels, even the turquoise his wife gave him when they married. He has nothing left except his revenge, the terrible joy of returning evil for evil.

I am a Jew. Hath not a Jew eyes? hath not a Jew hands, organs, dimensions, senses, affections, passions? fed with the same food, hurt with the same weapons, subject to the same diseases, healed by the same means, warmed and cooled by the same summer and winter, as a Christian is? If you prick us, do we not bleed? if you tickle us, do we not laugh? if you poison us, do we not die? and if you wrong us, shall we not revenge? If we are like you in the rest, we will resemble you in that.

At first Shylock has nothing but the loneliness of his own hatred—"no satisfaction, no revenge . . . no sighs but o' my breathing; no tears but o' my shedding." Then he learns the great news that Antonio's ships have all been wrecked and knows that at last he will have a Christian for company in his despair, someone whom he can harm even more than he himself has been harmed.

Meanwhile Portia has tried to delay the casket test in case Bassanio should fail, but he is determined to test his fortune immediately. She gives him a hint that he should choose the third casket by having a song sung to him in which the words rhyme with "lead."

Tell me, where is fancy bred,
Or in the heart or in the head? . . .

Bassanio is not misled by the glitter of silver and gold. He chooses the plain casket, the one with Portia's picture inside it, and she gives her love to him in lines of nobility and loveliness.

You see me, Lord Bassanio, where I stand,
Such as I am . . .

It is a household full of matchmaking, for one of Bassanio's friends announces that he would like to marry Portia's maid, and Shylock's runaway daughter Jessica also makes her appearance in Belmont with her Venetian husband.

With them comes a letter from Antonio that throws a sudden shadow over all the happiness; for the pound of flesh is forfeit to Shylock and Antonio knows he must die. Portia is willing to offer any amount of money to save him, and she sends Bassanio back to Venice to see if he can bribe Shylock away from his revenge. But Shylock does not want money. He wants what in his own mind he calls justice against Antonio and for himself.

> Thou call'dst me dog before thou hadst a cause,
> But, since I am a dog, beware my fangs . . .

Portia has given out that she and her maid have planned to retire from the world and live in prayer and contemplation until their husbands return. But such a plan is quite alien to Portia's lively spirit. She not only intends to go to Venice herself, but to go disguised as a lawyer and attend Antonio's trial. She has a cousin from whom she can get the necessary robes and the proper legal advice, and she will dress herself as a young doctor of laws with her maid as the lawyer's clerk. She leaves Jessica and her husband to manage the house in her absence and sets off in high spirits for Venice and the duke's court of justice.

The duke and all the great men of Venice have been trying to persuade Shylock to forego his revenge, and when the court is gathered together the duke makes one last appeal. Shylock is quite unmoved by all the arguments. For once, the laws of Venice that have pressed so heavily upon his people are on his side and he sees no need to justify his course of action. He feels that he is doing no more than ridding his house of a rat, and let no one talk to him of mercy. The great men of Venice, for all their fine talk, hold slaves, and where the slaves are concerned they do not deal in compassion or brotherhood. The slaves are their property, and in the same way the pound of flesh is Shylock's property and no man can take it from him.

"I stand here for the law." It gives him great pleasure when Antonio's friends rage at him, for he knows they are helpless. Antonio knows it too and has lapsed into a mood of doomed resignation.

It is a court of confused and angry men, locked in a dilemma and with Shylock whetting his knife in the midst of them. Into it comes the young lawyer's clerk who is really Portia's maid. She brings a letter from Portia's cousin, introducing the brilliant young lawyer he has sent in his stead, and all the company turns to greet the new arrival.

Portia makes her entrance, a small figure in flowing dark robes among the glittering throng of Venetian grandees. Facing her is that other robed figure in his gaberdine, Shylock with his knife, and the play rises to its climax as a duel of the mind is fought between the two antagonists.

Portia begins by putting the problem on a higher level than the duke has been able to. She speaks not of justice but of mercy, which is a free gift and cannot be forced or constrained, and she does it in words so beautiful that they have become some of the most familiar in the English language.

> The quality of mercy is not strained.
> It droppeth as the gentle rain from heaven
> Upon the place beneath; it is twice blest,
> It blesseth him that gives and him that takes;
> 'Tis mightiest in the mightiest; it becomes
> The thronèd monarch better than his crown . . .

All religions pray to God, and it is not justice they pray for.

> In the course of justice, none of us
> Should see salvation: we do pray for mercy,
> And that same prayer doth teach us all to render
> The deeds of mercy . . .

But Shylock is unmoved and continues to rest his case on the Venetian law.

Then Portia shifts ground and moves in her turn to the

strict letter of the law. She acknowledges that Shylock has a case that cannot be gainsaid, for he is entitled to his pound of flesh and no one can prevent him from taking it. "The law allows it, and the court awards it." The delighted Shylock is convinced that the clever young lawyer is on his side, and Portia lets him have the full length of the line before she suddenly jerks it tight. For Shylock may have his pound of flesh, but he can have nothing else. If he sheds one drop of blood he breaks the law, for blood was not mentioned in the bond. And by the terms of the law which he loves so well, his goods will then be taken from him by the state.

"Is that the law?" demands Shylock, seeing too late where his insistence on the letter of the law has led him, and Portia is able to show him the exact statute. Shylock wishes to deal with the law no longer, since it is not in his favor, and suggests a compromise. But Portia will not let him off so easily; he has insisted on the letter of the law and now he is liable to it. In the end Shylock has to accept mercy after all, at the hands of the man he hates, and he leaves the courtroom in utter defeat.

> *I pray you, give me leave to go from hence;*
> *I am not well . . .*

The victorious Portia turns to receive the gratitude of Antonio and Bassanio, and she cannot resist teasing her husband a little. Earlier in the proceedings he had excitedly offered the young lawyer everything he possessed if he would save Antonio—"my wife and all the world"—and Portia had remarked dryly at the time, "Your wife would give you little thanks for that."

Now she is going to make him pay for his incautious remark. If Bassanio is so anxious to reward the young lawyer who has saved his friend, let him give up the ring he is wearing. This puts Bassanio in a quandary, as it is meant to do, for his wife gave him the ring and he promised it would never leave his finger. Still, the debt he owes the young lawyer is very great, and he finally agrees.

Back in Belmont, Jessica and her husband are waiting in the moonlight for the return of the mistress of the

house; and since Shakespeare could not bring moonlight
on the stage, he brought moonlight and starshine into the
hearts of his hearers through the loveliness of his lines.

How sweet the moonlight sleeps upon this bank!
Here will we sit, and let the sounds of music
Creep in our ears; soft stillness and the night
Become the touches of sweet harmony.
Sit, Jessica; look, how the floor of heaven
Is thick inlaid with patines of bright gold;
There's not the smallest orb which thou beholdest
But in his motion like an angel sings,
Still quiring to the young-eyed cherubins . . .

Musicians are playing softly in the background, and Portia
comes home to music and the welcoming light of candles
shining through the windows of her hall.

Portia herself is in the mood of an ill-intentioned kitten,
as her unhappy husband discovers all too soon. She greets
her guest Antonio with her usual charm and graciousness
and then the matter of the ring comes up. Portia is sure
that her dear husband would rather part with life itself
than with the ring she gave him, and she plays on that
note with the most unfair and delicate teasing. Then she
relents and admits that she was the lawyer and her maid
was the lawyer's clerk.

The little joke is over, the three married couples are
gay, and the misfortunes of Antonio, the merchant of
Venice, are finally ended.

THE MERRY WIVES OF WINDSOR

THE MERRY WIVES OF WINDSOR is Shakespeare's only domestic comedy, the only play he ever wrote that tells of ordinary middle-class people. The story is about two cheerful women of Windsor who outwit a London knight, and the play is a long, lively game in which they are the delightful victors.

The town of Windsor lies next to Windsor Castle, and the play contains an occasional reference to court life. But it is town life that Shakespeare is describing and he knows it intimately, from the Garter Inn near Peascod Street to the fields near the river Thames where the women of Windsor take their washing. Shakespeare seldom uses a realistic background, but in this play he is as accurate as a photograph.

The London knight who is outwitted by the women of Windsor is named Sir John Falstaff. Shakespeare is reusing here a famous character he invented for one of his history plays, but the fat knight is such a different person in *The Merry Wives of Windsor* that it is easier to think of him as someone else altogether—a comic butt rather than a real human being. It is the women who are real in this play, and they are the ones who make it come to life. The men are mostly fools, and Falstaff is only one fool among many.

The story opens on one of the streets of the town, with a Welsh parson doing his best to act as a peacemaker. Sir John Falstaff has come down to Windsor with several of his disreputable followers and has installed himself at the Garter Inn to be a nuisance to everybody. He and his followers have no money and they have been thieving and lying and starting riots until Justice Shallow, the local justice of the peace, threatens to complain to the Star

Chamber at Westminster. Falstaff admits his sins freely but unrepentantly, and the parson tries to gather together a collection of impartial "umpires"—himself and the host at the Garter and a gentleman of the town named George Page.

Page has a pretty daughter named Anne, and another of the parson's projects is to marry Anne to a cousin of the justice of the peace. The cousin's name is Abraham Slender, a strutting fool with a little yellow beard. He cannot keep up his end of a conversation without his Book of Riddles (which he unfortunately lent to Alice Shortcake just before Michaelmas) and the parson is aware that it will not be easy to persuade Anne to marry him. So he sends a servant of Slender's over to the house of a French doctor in the town, with a letter for the doctor's housekeeper, Mistress Quickly. She has some influence with Anne, or thinks she has, and the parson hopes she will help Slender in his suit.

Falstaff feels no repentance for his past sins. What he chiefly feels is his current lack of money. One of his followers is given a position as a tapster in the Garter Inn, but this is not much help to Falstaff and he decides on a different way to make money. The Page family is well-to-do, and if Falstaff makes love to Mistress Page perhaps she will share her husband's money with him. Since this is so good a plan it ought to work equally well twice. For Page has a friend named Frank Ford, whose wife also "has all the rule of her husband's purse," and Falstaff is quite willing to make love to two women at once. These two women, Mistress Page and Mistress Ford, are the two merry wives who give the play its title. They are delightful, intelligent, honest women and very close friends, and Falstaff makes the mistake of his life when he thinks he can get them to betray their husbands.

Mistress Quickly is a different sort, a blithering old dame who is willing to do any sort of matchmaking and is quite agreeable to the parson's plan for young Anne Page. "Never a woman of Windsor knows more of Anne's mind than I do." It has not penetrated her head, in spite of all Anne's talk about a young London gentleman named Fenton, that this is the man Anne loves, and Mistress Quickly is quite willing to help the foolish Slender. The one who is outraged by the plan is the French doctor, who is hoping to marry Anne himself, and in a rage he challenges the matchmaking parson to a duel.

Falstaff's love letter arrives for Mistress Page, who, as the mother of a grown daughter, is amused to be getting one at all. She reads it through and becomes so annoyed at the fat knight that she thinks there ought to be a law passed against the whole male sex. "I'll exhibit a bill in the parliament for the putting down of men." Her friend Alice Ford arrives with a similar letter, for the lazy old sinner has not bothered to change anything but the name. "I warrant he hath a thousand of these letters, writ with blank space for different names." The two women have one thought in common: "Let's be revenged on him," and they decide that the best revenge is to pretend to lead Falstaff on until he becomes hopelessly involved.

Mistress Ford is taking a risk in deciding to go on with the game, for her husband is a jealous man. Moreover, one of Falstaff's followers tells Ford that Falstaff is in love with his wife, and Ford believes him. Page, on the other hand, refuses to believe that their two wives could be unfaithful. He trusts Mistress Page completely, and his chief interest lies in the duel that is going to be fought between the French doctor and the parson.

The two merry wives send Mistress Quickly to Falstaff with their answers to his letters. Mistress Page sends regrets that she cannot see him immediately, but Mistress Ford says she will be glad to have him visit the house between ten and eleven in the morning, when her husband will be elsewhere.

Falstaff's next visitor is Ford, in disguise and pretending to be a suitor to Mistress Ford. He offers to pay Falstaff if he will report his own success with her, and Falstaff is able to assure him his plans are well advanced. "I shall be with her between ten and eleven; for at that time the jealous rascally knave her husband will be forth." Ford is miserably convinced that his wife is going to be unfaithful to him, since he is almost as much of a fool as Falstaff and knows very little about the lively, honorable woman he is lucky enough to have married.

Meanwhile the French doctor has been dancing about impatiently in a field near Windsor, waiting with drawn rapier for the parson who never comes. The parson has been waiting in another field, near Frogmore, singing songs to himself and rather chilly without his coat but also ready for the fray. The host of the Garter Inn has misled them into going to different fields, and when the antagonists finally meet they become friends in their mutual annoyance at him.

It is nearly ten in the morning, which is the hour set for Falstaff to visit Mistress Ford. Mistress Page, intent on the plan they have worked out together, is hurrying through the streets of Windsor to be there also, when she encounters Ford himself. It seems to Ford that Mistress Page is always visiting his wife. "I think, if your husbands were dead, you two would marry." But what chiefly enrages him is Page's refusal to believe that both wives are faithless. Ford's plan is to re-enter his own house when the clock strikes, and he has invited all his friends to come along with him. "You shall have sport; I will show you a monster."

Meanwhile Mistress Ford has been preparing for the monster's visit in her own way by giving her servants some careful instructions concerning a large basket of wash. As soon as it is full, they are to carry it down to Datchet Mead, a patch of low ground between Windsor Park and the Thames where the townspeople bleach their laundry, and to dump its contents into the ditch there. Its contents will be dirty shirts and stockings and also, if Mistress Ford has her way, Sir John Falstaff.

Falstaff enters with outstretched arms to embrace his jewel and is about to make love to her when Mistress Page knocks at the door. Mistress Ford, pretending to be startled, assures him that her friend is "a very tattling woman" and he had better hide. From his hiding place Falstaff hears the news that Ford is returning to the house in a jealous rage. The two ladies play their parts beautifully, Mistress Page speaking just loudly enough so that Falstaff can hear her, pretending to be very startled when she learns he is in the house, and suggesting the device of the washing basket as the best way for him to escape.

Falstaff is much too fat for the basket, but he is so frightened that he manages to fit himself in somehow and the servants take him away to dump him in the Thames. Ford arrives, convinced that Sir John Falstaff is somewhere in the house, and sends his friends all over the establishment in a useless search. The two ladies gaze after them demurely, for, as Mistress Ford remarks, there is a double charm in the situation. "I know not which pleases me better, that my husband is deceived, or Sir John."

Anne Page, meanwhile, has been obliged to tell young Fenton that her father will not let her marry him. Page is determined that she shall marry the foolish Slender, while Mistress Quickly has promised all three suitors, Slender, Fenton and the French doctor, that she will speed their wooing. "I will do what I can for them all."

Falstaff, much embittered by his ducking in the Thames, nevertheless intends to try once more; this time he will visit between eight and nine and again he tells the disguised Ford all his plans. Mistress Page attends to the schooling of her little son and then she again arrives at the Ford house with the news that the jealous husband is hurrying down the street. This time Mistress Ford disguises her would-be lover as "my maid's aunt, the fat woman of Brainford." Ford has an intense dislike for the old woman and so he beats her out of the house. This time the fat Falstaff staggers away encumbered by skirts and with a well-banged head, but still hopeful.

Ford has been searching wildly through the washing basket, looking for his rival, while his wife eyes him sardonically. "Are you not ashamed? Let the clothes alone." Finally she takes pity on him and tells him the whole story, and Ford humbly begs her pardon. But it seems to Page that the "old fat fellow" deserves to have one more joke played on him, and the two wives agree to ask Falstaff to meet them in Windsor Park at midnight.

In Shakespeare's day there was a great oak in Windsor Park which stood not far from a footpath and was haunted by the ghost of a former ranger named Herne. Falstaff is asked to come disguised as Herne so that no one will suspect him. Near the oak was a pit, formed long ago when chalk and flints were dug from it, and here the rest of the company can hide. Since midnight is fairy time, the Page children and some of the other boys and girls in Windsor will dress up as fairies, in masks and with circlets of tapers on their heads, to give Falstaff a final fright before they let him go.

Anne Page is to be the fairy queen, and her father intends to have Slender spirit her away and marry her at Eton. Her mother intends to have the French doctor spirit her away and marry her at the deanery. But Fenton intends to spirit his Anne away himself and marry her at the church. Anne's father has told Slender she will be dressed in white and Anne's mother has told the doctor she will be dressed in green. So Fenton has arranged to have the postmaster's boy dress in white and another boy in green; and since they are masked they will mislead Anne's two hopeful suitors until she is safely married.

At midnight Falstaff arrives at Herne's oak, with all the conspirators whispering around him in the leafy dark. The parson has been busily organizing the fairies, and as soon as Falstaff throws out his arms to embrace the two wives of Windsor the children are upon him.

> *Pinch him fairies, mutually;*
> *Pinch him for his villany.*
> *Pinch him, and burn him, and turn him about,*
> *Till candles and starlight and moonshine be out.*

This is Falstaff's last punishment, and Mistress Page refuses to carry the joke any further. Falstaff acknowledges his foolishness with resigned good nature, and the two Pages are equally resigned when they learn that Anne is married to Fenton. Mistress Page is quite as ready to welcome her new son-in-law as she is to let Falstaff visit the house.

> *Good husband, let us every one go home,*
> *And laugh this sport o'er by a country fire,*
> *Sir John and all.*

And with this comfortable advice from a happy and intelligent woman, the play ends.

AS YOU LIKE IT

As You Like It is a romantic comedy with a pastoral setting. It belongs to a long literary tradition of escape from
city life, back to a carefree existence in woods and fields.
The countryside of the pastoral is never a real one. It is
idealized make-believe, full of happy shepherds and per-
petual innocence, and Shakespeare made no attempt to
have a realistic Forest of Arden. He put in it whatever he
pleased, including some palm trees and a lion, and he
coupled it with a plot of sunny unreality. But the people
are real, as they usually are in Shakespeare, and the poetry
is some of his loveliest. The play is full of songs, and there
are so many of them that the Forest of Arden is almost
set to music.

> *Under the greenwood tree*
> *Who loves to lie with me,*
> *And turn his merry note*
> *Unto the sweet bird's throat,*
> *Come hither, come hither, come hither!*
> *Here shall he see*
> *No enemy*
> *But winter and rough weather.*

This is a play of green leaves and it opens, suitably
enough, in an orchard. Orlando, the youngest son of a
noble family, is growing restless under the neglect and
contempt that his eldest brother has shown him. His brother
has tried to keep him out of sight because he is so popular and finally decides that he must be killed. He consults
with a wrestler who is going to make an appearance at
court, and the wrestler agrees to try to break Orlando's
neck.

In the court also, a brother has betrayed a brother. The old duke has been banished from his dominions by his younger brother and has gone away to live in the Forest of Arden. Like Orlando, he is much loved and "many young gentlemen flock to him every day, and fleet the time carelessly as they did in the golden world." His daughter Rosalind has not been banished, for she is so beloved by the new duke's daughter, Celia, that they cannot be parted. "Never two ladies loved as they do."

The scene shifts to a lawn before the duke's palace, where Celia and Rosalind are enjoying each other's company and that of the duke's lively jester. The lawn has been chosen as the location for the wrestling match, and when Celia and Rosalind catch sight of the handsome young man who is going to face such a huge and skillful wrestler, they try to persuade him not to risk the match. Rosalind in particular is concerned for his safety, since she has suddenly fallen in love with him. Orlando, who has no difficulty conquering the wrestler, falls helplessly in love in his turn. And he does well to love Rosalind, for she is one of the most delightful of Shakespeare's heroines.

The duke knows that Rosalind is beloved by the people and decides to banish her in the same way he banished her father. Celia refuses to be left behind, and the two friends plan to disguise themselves and make their way to the Forest of Arden. Since Rosalind is the taller, she will dress as a boy and swagger about as effectively as possible with a boar-spear in her hand, while Celia will dress as the boy's sister. Since they are not quite as brave as they appear to be, they decide to ask the court jester to go along with them. "Would he not be a comfort to our travel?" His name is Touchstone, and whether or not his presence is helpful in emergencies there is no doubt that his lively tongue makes him very good company.

In the Forest of Arden, the banished duke has discovered that life in the woods is much happier than the painted and artificial life of the court.

> *Sweet are the uses of adversity,*
> *Which, like the toad, ugly and venomous,*
> *Wears yet a precious jewel in his head;*

> *And this our life, exempt from public haunt,*
> *Finds tongues in trees, books in the running brooks,*
> *Sermons in stones, and good in every thing.*
> *I would not change it.*

Little by little, everyone in the story is drawing near the Forest of Arden. Celia's father is bent on finding the runaways, and Orlando learns that his brother intends to murder him. He leaves home with his faithful old servant and they too arrive in the forest.

Rosalind is there already, together with Celia, who is prettily disguised as a shepherdess, and Touchstone, that reluctant visitor in the land of pastoral. "When I was at home, I was in a better place." Since they have brought jewels and money with them, they are able to buy a shepherd's cottage and settle down gracefully among the olive trees and the sheep, giving Rosalind time to rest her feet and meditate on the woeful state of being in love.

The old duke has been looking through the forest all day for his courtier, Jaques, whose company the duke enjoys because Jaques is such a mournful realist. In his opinion the world has nothing right with it, and the duke likes his conversation for the determined tartness of its flavor. Jaques has encountered Touchstone, the court fool, and is charmed by him, for in Jaques' opinion only the fools are wise and no wise man could enjoy living in such a foolish world. He views all human living with the detached eye of a mildly displeased spectator at a play, and it is Jaques who gives the famous speech that likens the whole world to a theatre.

> *All the world's a stage,*
> *And all the men and women merely players.*
> *They have their exits and their entrances,*
> *And one man in his time plays many parts,*
> *His acts being seven ages . . .*

The duke is amusing himself with Jaques' philosophy and dining in the forest when Orlando rushes in with drawn sword. His old servant is dying for lack of food and Orlando is prepared to fight to get it for him. He finds instead that the outlawed duke is a friend of his dead father's. When Orlando returns, carrying his old servant, they welcome him with music and song and accept him as a member of their well-adjusted company.

Orlando, however, cannot settle down to a placid life in the Forest of Arden. He can think of nothing but Rosalind, in spite of the fact that he has met her only once, and he goes about the forest hanging love notes on the trees and carving the bark in the immemorial fashion of lovers. Touchstone teases Rosalind about the fact that her name is appearing everywhere and so does Celia, and Rosalind is obliged to admit that the unknown gentleman is very thorough. "I was never so be-rhymed since Pythagoras' time, that I was an Irish rat." Celia will not tell her at first who the young gentleman is, but after she has stretched Rosalind's curiosity to the breaking point she finally admits it is Orlando. Rosalind's first reaction is a wail: "What shall I do with my doublet and hose?" But as soon as Orlando himself appears, she promptly thinks of a way both to enjoy his company and to keep her disguise.

Orlando comes in with Jaques who, as usual, is pleased by nothing. He does not wish to have the trees marred with love songs and he does not even like Rosalind's name. As Orlando points out, quite justly, "There was no thought of pleasing you when she was christened," but it remains clear to Jaques that if he had the running of the world things would be in a far better state. It is full of foolishness at present, and the worst foolishness is love.

Jaques takes his departure, quite out of sympathy with love and innocence and the green leaves of spring, and Rosalind and Orlando face each other in the Forest of Arden. Rosalind is enjoying her boy's disguise and has no mind to waste it. She tells Orlando how, as a lad, she was brought up by "an old religious uncle" who uttered many wise precepts on how to avoid the sorrows of love, and she offers to cure Orlando of his love melancholy by giving him lessons in the ways of women. Let him visit the shepherd's cottage among the olive trees each day to practice his love-making on the wise nephew of a wise uncle, and in no time at all he will be cured.

Meanwhile, Touchstone has also caught the infection and decides he will marry a country maiden named Audrey. A young shepherd is less fortunate in his love-making, for he is scorned by a dark-eyed shepherdess. And when Rosalind, who is irresistible in her boy's attire, tries to reprove the shepherdess for her coldness the girl inconveniently falls in love with Rosalind.

Orlando is an hour late in coming for his lesson, and Rosalind, who is a stern teacher, is obliged to reprove him. "Where have you been all this while? You a lover! An you serve me such another trick, never come in my sight more." She then forgives him and continues with the lesson, in a charming scene in which she plays the cheerful traitor to her own emotions. For Orlando swears he is dying of love and his teacher begs leave to doubt it. "The poor world is almost six thousand years old, and in all this time there was not any man died . . . in a love cause. Troilus had his brains dashed out with a Grecian club; yet he did what he could to die before, and he is one of the patterns of love . . . Men have died from time to time, and worms have eaten them, but not for love."

Rosalind is teasing love and teasing herself, and she ends with a final parody of a lovelorn forsaken maid when Orlando says he has to leave and go to dinner: "Ay, go your ways, go your ways; I knew what you would prove, my friends told me as much, and I thought no less. That flattering tongue of yours won me. 'Tis but one cast away, and so, come death!" She then relapses into a more normal tone of voice. "Two o'clock is your hour?"

Orlando promises faithfully to return at two, and Rosalind, left alone, is unable to follow any of her own valuable advice. "I'll go find a shadow, and sigh till he come." But when two o'clock comes, there is no Orlando. Instead the shepherd arrives, bearing an unwelcome love letter from the shepherdess to Rosalind, which, as Rosalind points out, shows a lack of spirit in him. Her second visitor is Orlando's brother and he brings even more unwelcome news. For Orlando has been hurt, trying to save his brother from a lion, and his brother, now full of remorse for all his evil ways, has come to report why Orlando could not be there at two o'clock. Rosalind is quite unable to live up to her masculine attire and faints, although when she recovers she wants Orlando to be told that the whole thing was in jest. "I pray you, tell your brother how well I counterfeited."

Orlando, his arm in a sling, discovers that his repentant brother has fallen in love with Celia and wants to have the wedding celebrated the next day. Rosalind decides that Orlando should be married at the same time. Having already invented a wise uncle, she now invents a magician who taught her all his art, and she assures Orlando that she knows a way to get him his Rosalind in time for the wedding. She promises the shepherd and shepherdess that their problems will be straightened out also. Touchstone concludes that he and his country maid will wed on the same "joyful day," and two pages sing a little song that is well suited to the occasion.

> *It was a lover and his lass,*
> *With a hey, and a ho, and a hey nonino,*
> *That o'er the green cornfield did pass,*
> *In the spring time, the only pretty ring time,*
> *When birds do sing, hey ding a ding, ding,*
> *Sweet lovers love the spring.*

On the wedding day, Rosalind calls to her aid Hymen, the god of marriage. He leads her in before the assembled company in her woman's clothes, and everything is immediately straightened out so that all four sets of lovers can marry each other. As a final solution to their difficulties, another brother of Orlando's enters with the news that the usurping duke, pursuing his exiled brother to murder him, has been suddenly converted by an old hermit. He is resolved to give his brother back his dominions and retire from the world, and Jaques decides to go and bestow his valuable company on the new exile. The old duke returns in triumph to his former estate, the lovers are all united, and the play closes with everything at peace in the Forest of Arden.

MUCH ADO ABOUT NOTHING

MUCH ADO ABOUT NOTHING is a comedy of courtship and marriage, of a quick courtship that nearly comes to disaster and of a slow, reluctant one that is a complete success. The reluctant wooers are Beatrice and Benedick, two of the most delightful people in the history of comedy, and since they are on the stage most of the time they brighten the first courtship along with their own and transform what might have been a melancholy plot into a complete delight.

The other famous characters in the play are a couple of local constables named Dogberry and Verges who have much dignity but no sense. They move with the meditative calm of two well-intentioned tortoises, and in their earnest stupidity they do everything wrong. But it is clear in the end that they have done everything right. For the high-born characters, with their mistaken notions of honor, make mistake after mistake, and it is the efforts of Dogberry and Verges that bring the comedy to its happy ending.

The story takes place in Sicily, in the city of Messina, where the governor is expecting a visit from the prince of Arragon. The prince is returning from the wars, and in his company are two gallant young lords from Italy, Claudio and Benedick. Benedick is already well-known in Messina, for he and the governor's niece have been having a continuous argument, or what the governor calls "a kind of merry war," ever since they first met.

The name of the governor's niece is Beatrice and she does not think highly of the male sex. She feels Benedick is particularly well suited to be a butt for her wit, and since Benedick is an agile gentleman and does not stand still long enough to be a butt for anyone, they have a most enjoyable time trading insults whenever they meet. Beatrice had the last word when Benedick went off to the wars, for she kindly guaranteed to eat anyone he succeeded in killing. The warriors enter, to be welcomed by the governor and his household, and Benedick manages only two sentences before Beatrice is upon him. "I wonder that you will still be talking. Signior Benedick; nobody marks you." Benedick turns on her with the delight of a good swordsman in a worthy opponent, and it is no real regret to him when the hospitable governor invites them all to stay a month.

Claudio has a special reason to be pleased with the arrangement, for he has fallen in love with the governor's daughter, a gentle young lady named Hero. Benedick disapproves of his friend's taste in women, since Beatrice is much prettier, and he disapproves even more of his friend's thoughts of matrimony. For his own part, he intends to remain "the sensible Benedick" forever, heart-whole and a bachelor. "That a woman conceived me, I thank her; that she brought me up, I likewise give her most humble thanks." But there the relationship should end, in Benedick's opinion, and a wise man should entangle himself no further.

Claudio, however, is determined to have Hero for his wife, and the prince, who is an inveterate matchmaker, offers to help him. There are to be masked revels at the governor's house that night, and the prince offers to make love to Hero in Claudio's name and get her father's consent to the match.

The prince has a brother named Don John, who is possessed of a restless sense of evil. He hears of the prince's plan and decides it will be a "model to build mischief on," for he is unhappy himself and would like everyone else to share his unhappiness.

The governor hears of Claudio's plan to marry his daughter and approves of it. He wishes his pretty niece would get married also, but Beatrice shares Benedick's views on matrimony if she agrees with him in nothing else. She is quite undisturbed by the old saying that unmarried women lead apes in hell, for she is sure that the devil will turn her away as soon as she arrives. "So deliver I up my apes, and away to Saint Peter for the heavens; he shows me where the bachelors sit, and there live we as merry as the day is long."

The revelers arrive at the governor's house and the ladies pair off with the masked gentlemen. Benedick gravitates to Beatrice, and since she does not know who he is he feels free to insult her with the information that she got all her wit out of a joke book. Beatrice in her turn tells this unknown reveler exactly what she thinks of Benedick. He is no more than the prince's jester, a low sort of clown who will do anything to get a laugh.

In the course of the evening, Don John manages to persuade Claudio that the prince is wooing Hero for himself. Claudio is gullible enough to believe anything he is told, and when Benedick finds him he is sunk in melacholy. Benedick is not in a cheerful mood himself, for the barb about the court jester has struck deep and he is inclined to brood upon it.

The rest of the company enters and, when the prince presents Claudio with a loving and willing Hero, his sorrow is turned to rejoicing. Beatrice is delighted with her cousin's match, and the prince hopefully offers himself to her as a possible husband. Beatrice refuses him with a tact and charm she seldom bothers to bestow on her suitors, and after she has left the room her uncle adds a further word about her: "She is never sad but when she sleeps; and not ever sad then, for I have heard my daughter say, she hath often dreamed of unhappiness and waked herself with laughing." It occurs to the prince that she would make an excellent wife for Benedick and he thinks of a way to bring the two of them together. Claudio and Hero and Hero's father are willing to do all they can to assist so worthy a cause, and the prince promises to tell them the whole of his plan.

Meanwhile a darker plot is being worked out by the prince's brother, Don John. He intends to thwart Claudio's marriage by persuading him that Hero is untrue, and he and his servant work out a plan. One of Hero's maids, disguised as her mistress, will stand at her bedroom window, and Don John's servant will make love to her there. Don John knows how quick Claudio is to believe whatever he is told, and in this case he will have the additional evidence of his own eyes.

The four affectionate conspirators who want Beatrice

and Benedick to marry close in on Benedick first. He is peacefully walking in the orchard and meditating on the foolishness of love and marriage when the governor and the prince enter with Claudio. Benedick hides himself in an arbor and overhears the three men gravely discussing how madly Beatrice is in love with him. They even invent little circumstantial touches about the way she sits up at night to write him letters and then tears them up into a thousand pieces. Benedick is much moved by the poor lady's plight and manages to convince himself that he has no real reason for remaining a bachelor. In the same spirit of good cheer with which he formerly insulted matrimony he is now ready to embrace it, and, being Benedick, he can easily find a good reason. "The world must be peopled."

The same trick is tried on Beatrice, with a few variations. Hero settles herself in the orchard and sends her to tell Beatrice, in great confidence, that she is being gossiped about. Beatrice hides among the honeysuckles and learns that Benedick is desperate for love of her. He dares not confess his love to her for fear she will mock him, and Beatrice melts as completely as Benedick did. Surely, if he loves her so much, the least she can do is to love him in return.

The other match the prince has been arranging falls upon evil times. Don John suggests to Claudio that he go that night and watch what happens at Hero's window, and Claudio, that most unstable of men, is already half-willing to believe that Hero is untrue to him.

Out in the street the watchmen are being given special instructions, since so many people are assembling for tomorrow's wedding at the governor's house. The instructions are being imparted by two constables named Dogberry and Verges, and since Verges is an old man Dogberry is doing most of the work. Dogberry has a very profound and very English respect for the law, combined with a special chuckleheadedness that is all his own, and the law has a hard time of it in his well-meaning hands. His instructions to the watchmen are a masterpiece of lunatic earnestness, and Dogberry finishes with a warmly gratified pride in his own intelligence.

Now that they have been well and truly instructed, the

watchmen decide to sit on the church bench until two o'clock and then go to bed. They are sitting there in placid meditation when they hear two of Don John's servants discussing the success of the plot against Hero. Much roused, the watchmen manage to arrest them and then send word to Dogberry of their achievement.

Hero is dressing for the wedding, an unaccountable heaviness in her heart, when Dogberry and Verges arrive at the governor's house to tell him of the capture. The governor is far too busy to see the prisoners himself and he tells Dogberry to question them for him. Dogberry is stirred by the heavy responsibility and decides to interview the prisoners at the jail, in as official a manner as possible.

The wedding begins at the church, and Claudio suddenly puts a stop to it by refusing to marry the bride. He describes what he saw at her bedroom window, and the prince, who was there also, confirms the story. Both men are so sure that the woman they saw was Hero that even her own father believes them, and when they leave the church there is desolation behind them.

Only three people are willing to believe in Hero's innocence, the gentle friar who has been performing the ceremony and that lively and kindhearted pair, Beatrice and Benedick. Benedick feels that the governor has been much too quick in condemning his only daughter, while Beatrice is her cousin's passionate defender. The governor finally begins to waver, and the friar makes a suggestion. Hero fainted when the accusation was made, and if it is given out that she died it may be that the sorrowing Claudio will change his mind.

Beatrice and Benedick are left alone, and Benedick tries to woo her in his own fashion. "I do love nothing in the world so well as you; is not that strange?" If he wants to please her, Beatrice has a single answer for him, and it comes out with all the fierceness of her love and loyalty to her cousin: "Kill Claudio."

Benedick has no wish to challenge his best friend to a duel, and Beatrice is furious that she is only a woman and cannot kill Claudio herself. "O God, that I were a man! I would eat his heart in the market-place." Benedick tries to persuade her into a more reasonable frame of mind but she overwhelms him in a torrent of words and he can hardly get a syllable in edgewise. In the end he gives in, partly because he feels that Beatrice is right and partly because he can refuse her nothing.

The scene shifts to the prison cell where Dogberry is solemnly interviewing the two prisoners, with a special stool and cushion for the sexton. The sexton does not think very highly of Dogberry's legal methods and does his best to put things on a more correct footing. He does most of the work and Dogberry does most of the talking, but in the end they manage to get a full confession from Don John's servants.

Hero's father has convinced himself that his daughter is innocent, and he tries to challenge Claudio to a duel. When Benedick enters, Claudio turns to him in relief, expecting to be amused, and Benedick challenges him to a duel also. Then Dogberry and Verges enter, proudly displaying their prisoners, who repeat the confession, and Claudio discovers how cruelly he has wronged Hero. She is beyond the reach of his repentance, since it has been given out that she is dead, but her father offers to let Claudio marry another lady who looks exactly like her.

Benedick goes to report to Beatrice that he has challenged Claudio to a duel, and there is a charming scene of their own special brand of love-making. Benedick has tried his best to write some love rhymes but the art is not in him, nor does either of them see any reason to drop their teasing now that they are in love. As Benedick puts it, "Thou and I are too wise to woo peaceably." They hear the good news of the confession and know that the duel will not be necessary now.

The final scene takes place in the governor's house. It is Claudio's wedding day, and Beatrice and Benedick have decided to be married at the same time to make it a double wedding. Claudio comes for his bride and discovers it is Hero herself, whom he believed to be dead. Then Beatrice and Benedick make their own discovery—that they have been tricked into marriage. Still, whatever the cause, they know very well they are in love with each other and they kiss with a final laugh at themselves. Benedick makes a heartfelt salute to the joys of matrimony with a piece of advice to the matchmaker: "Prince, thou art sad; get thee a wife, get thee a wife." And so a charming comedy of courtship and marriage ends.

TWELFTH NIGHT

TWELFTH NIGHT is perhaps the loveliest of Shakespeare's romantic comedies. It takes place in Illyria, on the shores of the Adriatic Sea, a land of sunlight and laughter and the most beguiling poetry, where no real harm can come to anyone and nothing is damaged except conceit. The world of the play is very much like the festival for which it was named, the twelfth night that comes as a climax to the Christmas holidays when the working world is forgotten in the delight of make-believe. It is one of the most light-hearted of the plays, and the only character who disapproves of laughter—Malvolio—becomes a joke himself.

The story opens in the palace of the duke of Illyria, who is in love. The object of his affections is a beautiful lady named Olivia, who is mourning the death of her brother and will not permit anyone to see her.

On the seacoast of Illyria there has been a violent storm, and another lovely lady comes ashore after a shipwreck to mourn a brother she believes to be lost at sea. This lady is Viola, one of the liveliest and most charming of Shakespeare's heroines, and when she hears of the lovesick duke she decides to disguise herself and become his page.

The household of Olivia is not as grave as it ought to be, in spite of the fact that she herself is in mourning. For her uncle is staying with her, a fat and cheery old reveler named Sir Toby Belch. He has personally chosen a suitor for his niece in the person of Sir Andrew Aguecheek, a limp and well-intentioned knight who knows he is a fool but keeps hoping in a vague way that perhaps he isn't. Sir Toby and Sir Andrew have been sitting up until all hours getting drunk, and Olivia sends her waiting-woman, Maria, to see that they stop it. Sir Toby maintains that he has merely been drinking his niece's health, which is the least any man can do, and he and Sir Andrew end the scene by comparing notes on their dancing. Sir Andrew does not like to boast, but he does feel he is a fine fellow on the dance floor. "I think I have the back-trick simply as strong as any man in Illyria." Otherwise, the knight is feeling a little discouraged, for he is beginning to have his doubts that Olivia will ever marry him.

The duke of Illyria, on the same quest, has decided to send his new page to woo for him. The page is Viola, very charming in her boy's attire, and the duke is sure that so graceful a lad will charm the reluctant lady into accepting his suit. Viola promises she will do her best, but her heart is not in it, for she has fallen in love with the duke herself.

Olivia's household is not an especially orderly one, and her jester has been absent without leave. Maria assures him he will be hanged for staying away, but Feste is undisturbed. After all, "a good hanging prevents a bad marriage." He knows he is safe with his mistress, for Olivia cannot take anyone's offense very seriously and she is sure enough of her own dignity not to feel that a joke will impair it.

Very unlike Olivia is the manager of her household, whose name is Malvolio. Malvolio struts with a lordly gait, completely surrounded with the splendor of his own self-importance. He loves himself so well that he considers Feste an impertinent clown and deplores Olivia's willingness to laugh at his jokes. He says so once too often, and his mistress tells him exactly what is wrong with him. "You are sick of self-love, Malvolio. . . . To be generous, guiltless, and of free disposition, is to take those things for bird-bolts that you deem cannon-bullets." But Malvolio cannot take anything lightly if it affects his dignity, and his dignity cannot be safe unless there is someone to bow to him.

Sir Toby comes lurching in, well fuddled after a night's drinking and blaming it all on the pickled herring. He says there is a young gentleman at the gate, but he is still so drunk that his niece sends him off to cool his head. Everyone tries to dismiss the young gentleman, but even Malvolio cannot stop him. He has a message from the duke and he intends to deliver it.

The young gentleman is of course Viola, come to woo

in the duke's name and quite unperturbed by a cool reception from Olivia's household. Olivia is veiled, and Viola, after starting off on a splendid speech, suddenly interrupts herself. She is not going to waste her speech on the wrong person; Olivia suggests that she shorten it and Viola objects to that too. "I took great pains to study it, and 'tis poetical." Finally Olivia gives in and listens, and Viola tells her the way she herself would behave if she were as much in love as the duke:

> Make me a willow cabin at your gate,
> And call upon my soul within the house;
> Write loyal cantons of contemnèd love,
> And sing them loud even in the dead of night;
> Holla your name to the reverberate hills,
> And make the babbling gossip of the air
> Cry out 'Olivia!'

The argument is all too successful. Olivia does not fall in love with the duke, however, but with his lively and persuasive page, and when Viola leaves she sends Malvolio after her with a ring.

Meanwhile Viola's brother, whom she believes to be drowned, arrives in Illyria, together with the man who rescued him from the sea. The brother's name is Sebastian, and since he is a twin he looks almost exactly like his sister.

It is after midnight in Olivia's house, and Sir Toby Belch is having a splendid time, for he is three-quarters drunk and making the house ring with his joy. He is in the mood for loud and vigorous song, and Feste and Sir Andrew are encouraging him. Malvolio enters, full of outraged dignity, to silence them and can hardly make himself heard over their spirited melodies. His efforts madden Sir Toby and they would annoy even a more placid man, for Malvolio has the sin of self-righteousness and cannot imagine any kind of behavior except his own. As Sir Toby says, "Dost thou think, because thou art virtuous, there shall be no more cakes and ale?" Even Maria, who has been trying to quiet the three revelers herself, finally takes their part against Malvolio and shouts after his departing back, "Go shake your ears."

Maria is really annoyed with Malvolio. She has had enough of his conscious rectitude and his pompous admiration of his own ways, and she decides to play a trick on him. Her own writing is very like Olivia's, and she plans to write a letter that will make him think Olivia is in love with him. Malvolio will have no difficulty believing it, for, as Maria says, he is "so crammed, as he thinks, with excellencies, that it is his grounds of faith that all that look on him love him." And why should Olivia not love him when he loves himself so devotedly?

The duke meanwhile is passing the time by listening to an old song that tells of "the innocence of love" and by describing his emotions at length to his charming page. Viola listens to him, but she knows more about loving than the duke will ever know; she knows how to love in silence.

Maria composes her letter and seals it with Olivia's seal, and then she drops it casually near the garden walk. Sir Toby and Sir Andrew hide behind a tree, along with another member of the household named Fabian, and the three of them watch their enemy come sauntering along. Malvolio is absorbed in his favorite daydream, in which he sees himself married to Olivia, ordering her servants about and lecturing Cousin Toby on his shortcomings. The indignant Sir Toby nearly explodes out of his hiding place with the strain of keeping quiet and listening to him, but he is rewarded when Malvolio stoops and picks up the letter.

Maria has done her work well. It is just the kind of letter a woman in love with her steward might write, cautious and yet adoring. "I am above thee, but be not afraid of greatness. Some are born great, some achieve greatness, and some have greatness thrust upon them." It continues with advice on how best to please her. Let him smile continually: "In my presence still smile, dear my sweet." And let him wear yellow stockings and his garters crossed, for such a costume is most pleasing to her.

Malvolio at last sees his dream coming true. "I will be strange, stout, in yellow stockings and cross-gartered, even with the swiftness of putting on." Practically married to Olivia already, he surges off-stage, leaving Maria to stare after him with meditative pleasure. "He will come to her in yellow stockings, and 'tis a colour she abhors; and cross-gartered, a fashion she detests." What happens then, in Maria's opinion, will be worth seeing.

Viola is again sent by the duke to plead his suit, and this time Olivia receives her willingly. It is clear to all the household that she is in love with the charming page, and Sir Andrew Aguecheek is outraged. He hopes to marry Olivia himself and has been lending money lavishly to Sir Toby on the expectation. Sir Toby points out that he should have come forward as soon as Olivia showed favor to the page and with a few clever jests "banged the youth into dumbness." Since he has failed in this, nothing remains but to challenge the page to a duel—an appalling project for anyone as cowardly as Sir Andrew.

Viola's brother, in the meantime, has been walking about town as a tourist. The friend who saved him from shipwreck cannot accompany him, since he has the reputation in Illyria of being a pirate and dares not show his face. But he loans Sebastian some money, in case there is anything he should wish to buy, and agrees to meet him later in the suburbs.

Olivia is in a melancholy mood because the page does not return her love, and she decides that the solemn and dignified Malvolio will be a suitable companion for her state of mind. She sends for him and he enters on his yellow legs, smiling unendingly in spite of the tightness of the cross-gartering, and greets her in what he feels is an appropriate manner: "Sweet lady, ho, ho." He prances merrily about, refers knowingly to the letter, and calls Olivia sweetheart in a state of gaiety that convinces her she is dealing with a lunatic. Since Olivia is a kindhearted woman, she leaves him to the care of Sir Toby, who treats Malvolio as if he were a demented infant. "We must deal gently with him."

Also in trouble is Sir Andrew Aguecheek, who has finally resolved to fight a duel with the duke's page and has laboriously written out a challenge. Sir Toby sends him off to the orchard to look for Viola, and as soon as she arrives at the house kindly informs her that Sir Andrew is breathing fire. "He is a devil in private brawl . . . and his incensement at this moment is so implacable, that satisfaction can be none but by pangs of death and sepulchre."

Viola has often found her boy's disguise to be an inconvenience, but never more so than at this moment. She hardly knows one end of a sword from the other, and is by no means equipped to fight a duel with the valiant Sir Andrew. Sir Andrew, equally terrified, is hopefully considering the offer of his horse as a bribe if the duke's page will refuse to fight with him. But the two reluctant duelists are finally persuaded into facing each other with their swords in their quivering hands.

At this point Sebastian's friend enters and mistakes Viola for her twin brother. He attempts to interfere with the duel and is arrested by the duke's officers as a pirate. He implores Viola to give him back the money he lent her but she naturally does not know what he is talking about, although she would gladly give him half of what little money she possesses. He is led away by the duke's officers, and then Viola, thinking over what he has said, begins to suspect that her brother is alive.

Sir Andrew can see that the page is a coward and so he recovers his own courage. "I'll after him again and beat him." But unfortunately for him it is Viola's brother he encounters, a vigorous young man who bangs him over the head. Sir Andrew is deeply shocked by such behavior from the page. "I'll have an action of battery against him if there is any law in Illyria. Though I struck him first, yet it's no matter for that." Olivia hears the commotion and asks Sebastian, who she thinks is the page, to come with her to be married; and Sebastian, bewildered but delighted, agrees.

Malvolio has been tied up in the dark to calm his scattered wits, with Feste disguised as a parson to visit the lunatic and persuade the devils to leave him. Feste is very fond of money, and Malvolio finally bribes him into bringing ink and paper so that he can write a letter to Olivia.

In the street before Olivia's house, Viola finds herself wound up in a whole series of predicaments. Sebastian's friend accuses her of ingratitude in refusing to give him back his money; Olivia announces she has just married her; and Sir Andrew Aguecheek accuses her of breaking his head. They have all mistaken her for Sebastian, whose entrance solves the whole problem. The delighted Viola is able to welcome the lost brother she believed to be drowned, and the duke realizes that she is the one he really loves.

Everyone is happy except Malvolio, who gets back his freedom through his letter to Olivia and then finds out how thoroughly he has been tricked. Fabian pleads that it was only a joke, but Malvolio will not forgive such an insult to his dignity. "I'll be revenged on the whole pack of you." He stalks out, an enemy of laughter to the end, and the duke, who wants no one to be unhappy, sends a peacemaker after him.

For no one should be angry in Illyria, and the play closes in joyfulness and a final song.

ALL'S WELL THAT ENDS WELL

ALL'S WELL THAT ENDS WELL takes place in France, in Italy, and in a province called Rossillion in southern France on the Spanish border. The story is an Italian one which Shakespeare read in an English translation, and it has rather a sad plot for a comedy. It tells of an unloved woman who won her husband through a trick, and what brings it to warmth and life is chiefly the relationship between the woman and her mother-in-law. Like so many of the women in Shakespeare's comedies they love each other dearly, and both of them are worth loving.

The story opens in the palace of the countess of Rossillion, who is saying good-bye to her son, Bertram. Bertram is going to the court of the king of France in the company of an old French lord, Lafeu, who is able to give them the latest news of the king's mortal illness.

Also there to say good-bye to Bertram is Helena, the orphaned daughter of a famous doctor, whom the countess has welcomed into her household and brought up almost as her own child. Helena is in love with Bertram, but since she is not of high birth she cannot think of marrying him. He is a "bright particular star" and far above her. Her own social level lies more with a bragging soldier named Parolles who is going with Bertram to the French court; and he and Helena trade outrageous insults on an equality that she cannot feel with Bertram, the count of Rossillion.

Bertram arrives safely at the court of France and is warmly greeted by the sick king. He used to know Bertram's father well, and he also knew of the fame of Helena's father, the great doctor. "If he were living, I would try him." But, as it is, the king is weary of doctors and has resigned himself to death.

The countess discovers that Helena is in love with her

son and calls the girl into her presence. The older woman remembers the ardor of her own youth—"Even so it was with me when I was young"—and she presses Helena very gently until finally she admits the truth.

> *I confess,*
> *Here on my knee, before high heaven and you,*
> *That before you, and next unto high heaven,*
> *I love your son.*
> *My friends were poor but honest; so's my love:*
> *Be not offended, for it hurts not him*
> *That he is loved of me.*

The countess is not in the least offended, for she has already told Helena that she feels like a mother to her. Helena tells her, in her turn, that she would like to go to Paris and try one of her father's remedies on the sick king. The countess, one of the most generous and warm-hearted of women, gives her blessing, and Helena sets off for the French court.

The court is in a warlike state of mind, since most of the young lords are off to the Italian wars. Bertram is longing to go too, and Parolles is encouraging him, but the king feels he is too young.

Helena arrives at court and the king refuses her offer of help; he wants to be left quietly to die. But Helena is willing to stake her life on her conviction that she can cure him, and he is finally willing to let her try, agreeing that if she succeeds she can have any man in the court as her husband.

Helena cures the king after all the learned doctors have failed, and the old French lord, Lafeu, reports the news to Bertram. Lafeu is a thoughtful man, and to him it is a glimpse of the unknown forces that are at work behind the ordinary face of things. "They say miracles are past; and, we have our philosophical persons to make modern and familiar things supernatural and causeless. Hence it is that we make trifles of terrors, ensconcing ourselves into seeming knowledge, when we should submit ourselves to an unknown fear." This sense of the smallness of man's knowledge in the great shadow of the unknown belongs rather to a tragedy than to a comedy, but there is an odd sadness in *All's Well that Ends Well* which carries it several times to the edge of a different world from the bright one of most of Shakespeare's comedies.

Helena is now free to choose a husband from any man in France, and she chooses Bertram. In front of all the assembled court Bertram rejects her because she is not well-born. "A poor physician's daughter my wife!" The king tries to make him give in, for she is "young, wise, fair" and the king himself will add the honors that will make the two of them equal. But Bertram continues to refuse, shifting his ground to the fact he does not love her and has no wish to try, and Helena tries to release the king from the promise he made in his sickness.

> *That you are well restored, my lord, I'm glad:*
> *Let the rest go.*

But by this time the king is furious with Bertram and decrees that the wedding shall take place that night.

Bertram is sure that no one understands him but his dear friend Parolles. Lafeu knows that Parolles is an empty braggart but Bertram is convinced that he is a magnificent soldier and pours out all his troubles to him.

> *O my Parolles, they have married me!*
> *I'll to the Tuscan wars . . .*

Parolles agrees with this plan instantly—"To the wars, my boy, to the wars!"—and Bertram runs away as soon as the marriage ceremony is over, leaving behind him the message that he will never agree to treat Helena as his wife.

Bertram's letter to his mother, which is full of self-pity, is signed "your unfortunate son." But the countess is furious with him and wholly on the side of her new daughter-in-law.

> *She deserves a lord*
> *That twenty such rude boys might tend upon,*
> *And call her hourly mistress . . .*

Bertram's letter to his wife is a single sentence and what she calls a "dreadful" one. "When thou canst get the ring upon my finger, which never shall come off, and show me a child begotten of thy body, that I am father to, then call me husband: but in such a 'then' I write a 'never.' " The conditions that Bertram has set up are impossible, as he meant them to be, and the countess does her best to be comforting. But all Helena can think of is the fact that she has forced Bertram away from the safety of the French court and into the dangers of war, and she decides that, if she runs away from Rossillion, Bertram may be willing to come home again.

Helena sets off as a pilgrim to the shrine of St. Jaques, leaving a letter behind for the countess, who is torn between her love for her son and for her daughter-in-law. She sends Bertram the news that Helena has run away and then there is nothing more she can do except to hope for the best.

In the Italian city of Florence, the women are waiting by the walls for the return of the soldiers from battle. They agree in approving of the French count, Bertram, for his valor, but they also agree in disapproving of his violent and persistent love-making. He has been using Parolles as his go-between in an attempt to have an affair with a reluctant Florentine girl named Diana.

Diana's mother keeps a lodging for pilgrims, and when she sees Helena, newly arrived in Florence in her pilgrim's garments, she stops to speak to her. Since Helena is from France, they talk of the French lord, Bertram. Helena says he is married and Diana says wistfully, "I would he loved his wife."

Bertram is still convinced that his friend Parolles is a fine man and a gallant soldier, and some of his fellow noblemen from France resolve to prove the contrary by playing a trick on Parolles. They will seize him near the enemy lines, where he has promised to go to recapture a lost drum, and will question him after he is blindfolded; and they are sure that Parolles will try to betray everyone to save his own skin.

Meanwhile Helena has decided on a trick of her own to win back her husband according to the terms of his letter.

She tells the whole story to Diana's mother, and Diana agrees to pretend to yield to Bertram, making as the price of her surrender the ring he wears on his finger.

At ten o'clock Parolles is wandering about disconsolately, wondering why he ever boasted he would get back the missing drum. "What the devil should move me to undertake the recovery of this drum? . . . Tongue, I must put you into a butter-woman's mouth . . . if you prattle me into these perils." The French lords and their men leap upon him, shouting sinister gibberish like "Throca movousus" and "Oscorbidulchos volivorco," and Parolles limply allows himself to be captured, promising to reveal everything if they will spare his life.

Meanwhile Bertram has been pleading with Diana to let him into her room at midnight, and she offers to do it in exchange for his ring. Bertram refuses to give her the ring, which for the honor of the family has never left his finger, and Diana points out that he is expecting her to betray her honor too. Bertram gives in and she promises to give him another ring in exchange for his own. So Bertram spends the dark night with a woman he believes to be Diana but who is in reality his own wife Helena.

Bertram gets word that his wife has died on her pilgrimage and a letter from his mother asking him to come home. The wars are over and there is nothing more to keep him in Florence, except the final unmasking of his dear Parolles. As soon as Parolles is brought in blindfolded and surrounded, as he thinks, by the enemy, he lavishly gives away all the military secrets he knows. Then he blackens the characters of everyone there with such a rush of inventiveness that one of the Frenchmen cannot help but be charmed by his ingenuity. "I begin to love him for this."

Bertram returns to Rossillion, where his mother is mourning the death of Helena. The repentant Bertram mourns her also—

> *she, whom all men praised, and whom myself,*
> *Since I have lost, have loved.*

The king arrives and is willing to forgive Bertram's offense until he sees the ring that the young man is wearing.

It is a ring that belonged to Helena, and Bertram had received it in the dark from the woman he thought was Diana. He becomes even more deeply involved in the king's displeasure when Diana herself enters and accuses him of the midnight meeting. She has been asked to do this by Helena, so that Helena can first prove the meeting took place before she reveals that she was the woman involved.

The king is completely confused but doing his best to be just to them all, when Helena herself enters and explains what really happened. She has fulfilled the terms of her husband's letter and he joyfully accepts her as his countess and his wife, so that she is at last able to greet her "dear mother" as the true daughter of the house. The delighted king of France offers to pay Diana's dowry for any man of her choice, and all the sadness and confusion is over. Nothing but happiness remains and, as the king says, it is all the more welcome because of the sorrow that came before.

MEASURE FOR MEASURE

MEASURE FOR MEASURE is one of the most brilliant of Shakespeare's comedies, but the laughter is bitter. It does not deal with people as they would like to be but as too many of them are, and it can be called a comedy chiefly because it has a happy ending.

The story takes place in Vienna, and it opens with the duke of Vienna planning to leave the city. He is entrusting its government to his deputies, an old lord named Escalus and a much younger man named Angelo.

Vienna is riddled with vice, and Angelo, as chief deputy, is determined to reform the city. There are many laws on the statute books but most of them are being ignored, and Angelo is sure that the only way to purify the city is to enforce every law to the utmost of its severity.

His first victim is a luckless young man named Claudio who has been hoping to marry a young girl of Vienna. The actual ceremony was delayed because of difficulty over the dowry, but Claudio has been behaving as her husband and now there is a child about to be born. Under the laws of Vienna, Claudio has committed a crime that is punishable by death, although according to the casual customs of Vienna he has done much less than most of its citizens are doing every day. Still, the law is the law and Angelo is determined to enforce it rigidly. In three days' time, Claudio must die.

In Claudio's eyes, his relation with the girl was a "true contract" and his crime not a serious one. It may be that a petition will save him, and Claudio decides to ask his sister for help. Her name is Isabella and she is about to enter a convent. But Claudio is sure that if she knows the danger her brother is in she will go to Angelo and plead for his life.

The duke, meanwhile, does not intend to leave Vienna at all but to stay within the city in disguise. He has been much troubled by the vice that has flourished during the fourteen years of his rule, and he is hoping that Angelo's stricter nature will succeed where his has failed. On the other hand, Angelo is so cold and precise a man that perhaps he cannot be trusted to deal fairly with the people of Vienna. So the duke intends to remain in the city, disguised as a friar, to see how things work out under Angelo's rule.

A friend of Claudio's arrives at the nunnery to ask Isabella's help. Isabella is a woman of rigid purity, and she feels that her brother has committed a grave sin, in spite of the fact that most people of that day considered a pre-contract to marriage quite as binding as the marriage itself. As the duke himself says later, in a similar case:

> He is your husband on a pre-contract;
> To bring you thus together, 'tis no sin. . . .

But to Isabella, right is right and wrong is wrong, and there are no possible areas of behavior in between. On the other hand, she loves her brother dearly, and she is willing to go to Angelo and plead for his life.

Angelo is a man of complete rigidity, which is a dangerous quality in a magistrate. As the chief deputy of the absent duke, he finds himself with the power of life and death over the people of Vienna, and although his fellow deputy asks for moderation, Angelo is sure that the only way to achieve public virtue is by savage and unremitting punishment.

The underworld of Vienna is swarming with people who have made a profession of vice, gabby and sly and lively and most pitifully human, and Angelo looks at them all with the cold eye of a man who is too righteous to have either imagination or compassion. Such people bore him and he finally leaves them to be questioned by old Escalus, his fellow deputy.

> I'll take my leave,
> And leave you to the hearing of the cause,
> Hoping you'll find good cause to whip them all.

It is his dreadful use of the word "hoping" that betrays Angelo for what he is. He is unfit to have power, and it is his tragedy and Vienna's that too much power has been given to him.

Isabella presents herself before him to plead her brother's case. She is not accustomed to pleading and she is handicapped by her own conviction that her brother has sinned. She is so stiff and formal at first that Claudio's friend, who has come with her, wails reproachfully, "You are too cold." Then she shifts her argument to the high ground that is natural to her and points out that man can only expose his own littleness when he tries to play the tyrant.

> Man, proud man,
> Drest in a little brief authority,
> Most ignorant of what he's most assured,
> His glassy essence, like an angry ape,
> Plays such fantastic tricks before high heaven
> As make the angels weep . . .

Angelo is moved, but not by Isabella's eloquence or by her prayers. He, the man of ice, has fallen violently in love and he tells her to come back the following day. He has in mind a most evil bargain, for now that he is in love he is willing to commit the sin for which he is killing Claudio.

Isabella returns the next day and Angelo offers his bargain. If she will give herself to him for one night, he will spare Claudio.

The horrified Isabella refuses, sure that Claudio would value his sister's honor more than his own life. She goes to the prison to tell her brother what Angelo has suggested, and, as she had expected, Claudio refuses also. "Thou shall not do 't." But Claudio is only human and is worn down with imprisonment and the fear of death. His imagination begins to work on him, and in his terror he suddenly clutches at life on any terms whatever. Isabella tries to tell him that a life of shame would be hateful, but Claudio will not listen to her. He has looked down an abyss.

Ay, but to die, and go we know not where;
To lie in cold obstruction and to rot . . .
To be imprisoned in the viewless winds
And blown with restless violence round about
The pendent world; or to be worse than worst
Of those that lawless and incertain thought
Imagine howling; 'tis too horrible!
The weariest and most loathèd worldly life
That age, ache, penury and imprisonment
Can lay on nature, is a paradise
To what we fear of death.

With an anguished lack of heroism he tries to get her to agree to Angelo's bargain. "Sweet sister, let me live."

Isabella is a woman of no imagination and she cannot understand her brother's cowardice. She would willingly have died in his place, since she herself has never been afraid of death, but she will not commit a sin for anyone. And what Angelo and Claudio are asking her to do is a much greater sin than the one for which Claudio is being punished.

The duke, still disguised as a friar, has come to Claudio's cell and he overhears the whole conversation. He admires Isabella deeply and so he shows her a way out of the dilemma. There is a lady named Mariana, who was betrothed to Angelo until she lost all her dowry and he refused to marry her. She still loves him, and the duke suggests that she can be substituted for Isabella and sent to Angelo in her place. Isabella is only too glad to agree to the friar's suggestion, and she goes to tell Angelo she will meet him that night.

The disguised duke continues his travels about the city. He is deeply shocked by the people of the underworld whom he encounters, since they are cheerfully unable to realize that they belong to the underworld. He is equally shocked by Claudio's cynical friend, who is sure that vice is the natural lot of man and that the duke tolerated its existence in Vienna because he was inclined that way himself.

By this time it is late afternoon, and the duke goes to find Mariana at the moated grange of St. Luke's. Isabella

comes to them with the news that everything has been arranged. Angelo has given her the keys to his garden, which
is enclosed behind a brick wall, and she has promised to
meet him there at midnight. Mariana, as Angelo's betrothed, agrees most gladly to the substitution, since, as
the duke says, the pre-contract she had with him gives her
all the rights of a wife.

The duke, still disguised as a friar, returns to Claudio's
prison to wait for the pardon that Angelo has promised to
send. But Angelo, afraid of possible vengeance from Isabella's brother if he lets him live, sends word to the warden that Claudio is to be beheaded at once. Angelo is
aware that the sentence will be carried out with reluctance,
and to prove that it has been done the warden is to send
him Claudio's head.

There is another man under sentence of death in the
prison, a casual criminal who fears death no more than
"as a drunken sleep . . . insensible of mortality, and desperately mortal." The duke suggests that his head be sent
to Angelo instead of Claudio's, but when the prisoner is
called before them he refuses to cooperate. With that unsinkable self-confidence which characterizes all the more
disreputable people in the play, he flatly declines to be
beheaded. "I will not consent to die this day, that's certain." He goes back with considerable dignity to his
prison straw, with no intention of emerging for the rest of
the day; and the duke, after a moment of outrage at such
unsuitable behavior, decides to leave him alone. Fortunately a notorious pirate died in prison that morning, and
his head can be sent to Angelo instead.

The duke then sends word to Angelo that he is near
Vienna and planning a public return to the city. He wants
Angelo's downfall to be complete and cannot trust the upright Isabella to act a part, and so he lets her think that
her brother has been executed. He is still, as Claudio's
friend once called him, "the old fantastical duke of dark
corners," and he will not do anything in a simple manner if
there is a more complicated and theatrical one available.

The duke comes home to the sound of trumpets, and
his two deputies meet him at the city gate. Isabella has
been told by her friend the friar what to do, and she pre-

sents the duke with a petition, accusing Angelo. She tells the whole story publicly, omitting only the substitution of Mariana, who is also present but veiled. The duke pretends that he cannot believe so preposterous a charge against his noble deputy, and Angelo is relaxing with a smile when Mariana comes forward, unveils and tells the rest of the story. Angelo says the whole thing is an evil plot against him and the women are doubtless the instruments of some enemy. He feels he is safe enough, for it is their word against his, and he has already pointed out to Isabella that she will never be able to accuse successfully a man of his reputation. "Who will believe thee?"

The duke gives orders to have the two women punished for slander, and then he leaves the stage to come back in his friar's disguise. As the friar, he is able to speak in their defense. And he, in his turn, is about to be sent to prison when his disguise is pulled off and he stands revealed as the duke of Vienna.

Angelo realizes he is lost and asks only to be killed quickly, without a long public trial. The duke orders him married to Mariana and then beheaded—"an Angelo for Claudio, death for death." Mariana pleads for his life, and so does Isabella, in spite of the fact she believes he killed her brother. But Angelo himself, rigid in his devotion to the letter of the law, cannot plead against his own sentence. " 'Tis my deserving, and I do entreat it."

But Claudio has not been executed, and therefore Angelo's life need not be taken in exchange for his. Angelo is forgiven for Mariana's sake, and the duke thanks everyone who has helped to further the cause of justice in Vienna. Then he turns to Isabella and asks her to marry him, and the whole company returns to his palace as the story ends.

THE WINTER'S TALE

THE WINTER'S TALE is set in the land of fairy stories, where kings are cruel without cause and bears roam conveniently and sixteen years can be passed over as lightly as drawing breath. The story was popular when Shakespeare was a young man, and in his hands it becomes for the first time worth telling. For some of the people are enchanting and so is the poetry—harsh and strong as winter in the first part of the play, and then as lovely and flowerlike as spring.

The play opens in the land of Sicilia where King Leontes is entertaining his boyhood friend, the king of Bohemia. Two lords, one from each country, are discussing the lavishness of the hospitality and the pleasure the two rulers take in each other, and then the scene shifts to a room of state in the palace and to Leontes himself. His friend, the king of Bohemia, feels he must leave the following morning, and King Leontes is trying to persuade him to stay.

Leontes has a wife, the beautiful Hermione, and she delights in their guest's company because he can tell her of her husband's boyhood. She is sure they must have had a happy childhood together, and the king of Bohemia agrees.

> *We were, fair queen,*
> *Two lads that thought there was no more behind*
> *But such a day tomorrow as today,*
> *And to be boy eternal.*

The queen exerts herself to persuade him to stay a little longer in Sicilia, treating him with the charming ease and familiarity of an old friend, and her husband, looking on, is suddenly possessed by the insane conviction that they have fallen in love with each other.

Leontes makes no attempt to control the storm of jealousy that has suddenly invaded his heart. He turns to the small prince his son, a delightful little boy who has just smudged his nose, and almost persuades himself that his wife has always been unfaithful and that this is not his child at all. The more Leontes lets his anguished mind play with the idea of his wife's infidelity the more completely it gets out of control, and he finally calls in one of his most trusted lords, a man named Camillo, and tells him to murder the king of Bohemia. Camillo is a good man and he does not believe any of the wild accusations of Leontes. Instead he warns the royal guest that his life is in danger and the two of them slip away to Bohemia, leaving Leontes convinced by their flight that all his suspicions are true.

Queen Hermione is soon to have a child and she finds the liveliness of her small son, who is forever talking, almost too much for her. He goes off to exchange teasing conversation with her ladies-in-waiting, and then she calls him back to sit down quietly and tell her a story.

> *Do your best*
> *To fright me with your sprites; you're powerful at it.*

The prince is in a great hurry to tell her a story about goblins and cannot even wait to sit down to begin it.

> *There was a man . . .*
> *Dwelt by a churchyard. I will tell it softly;*
> *Yond crickets shall not hear it.*

Worse than a goblin enters the room. It is Leontes, as crazed by jealousy as a man in a nightmare. He sends his wife to prison, although the guards almost refuse to obey his orders, and closes his ears to the pleas of his lords in her favor. The only concession he makes is to dispatch messengers to the Delphic oracle, to ask for supernatural guidance in judging Hermione.

The wife of one of the noblemen, a gallant and loving woman named Paulina, goes to the prison and finds that the queen has given birth to a baby girl. She brings the baby to the king, sure that the sight of his little daughter will release him from his restless and tormented imaginings. "I come to bring him sleep." But the king is convinced that this child also is not his. He commands Paulina's husband to take the baby "to some remote and desert place" far away from Sicilia and there leave it to die.

Leontes has decreed a public trial for his queen, although he has decided already what the verdict will be. She speaks nobly and patiently in her own defense, and when the messengers arrive from the priest of Apollo at Delphos, they confirm everything she has said. But by this time Leontes is so insane that he cannot believe even the oracle, and he orders the trial to continue.

Tragic news is brought into the courtroom. The little prince, who has been ill with worry over his mother, is dead. Leontes has been a devoted father and he is shocked back into sanity by the news, which he feels is heaven's vengeance on him for scorning the oracle. Hermione faints when she hears of her son's death, and as her ladies take her away the king tells them in anguish to treat her tenderly. He is sure she will recover, but Paulina brings back word that she is dead; and the king, his whole family destroyed by his blind willfulness, dedicates himself to a life of mourning.

Paulina's husband has taken ship to a desert country in far-away Bohemia, so that he can leave the baby princess there as he has been ordered to do. In that wild country he is eaten by a bear, and a young shepherd reports the news to his father in lurid detail. The young shepherd has also watched with fascination while the men on the ship died in the huge waves—"sometimes to see 'em, and not to see 'em; now the ship boring the moon with her mainmast, and anon swallowed with yeast and froth, as you'ld thrust a cork into a hogshead." His father has strange news for him also; he has just found a baby girl and a bundle of gold, and now they are rich for life.

Sixteen years pass, and the scene shifts to the palace of the king of Bohemia. Camillo, the old lord who once saved his life, is longing to go home to Sicilia, but the king of

Bohemia cannot bear to part with him. He leans on him for advice and needs it especially in the case of his son, the handsome young Florizel. Prince Florizel has been spending most of his time in the house of a shepherd who has grown unaccountably rich and who has a most beautiful sixteen-year-old daughter, and the two men decide to go in disguise to the shepherd's house and question him. It is sheep-shearing time, and the shepherd has planned the usual feast. His beautiful foster daughter, who has been named Perdita, has made two dozen nosegays for the shearers and there is to be much singing and dancing. She has sent her foster brother, the shepherd's son, to buy supplies, and his own feeling is that she has overdone it. "Three pound of sugar, five pound of currants, rice—what will this sister of mine do with rice? But my father hath made her mistress of the feast, and she lays it on." He has also been told to buy seven nutmegs, saffron to color the pies and various other commodities. But he buys none of them, because his pocket is picked by a cheerful rogue named Autolycus. Autolycus has come singing down the highway, looking for sheets spread out to dry on the hedges, for he is, as he happily admits, "a snapper-up of unconsidered trifles." Having parted the shepherd's son very neatly from his money, he then decides to attend the sheep-shearing too and goes off down the road, still singing.

On the lawn before the shepherd's cottage, Perdita and Florizel are waiting for the shearers to arrive. Perdita is very conscious of the fact that he is a prince while she is merely a shepherd's daughter, and although Florizel is sure they will be wed eventually she cannot believe it will ever happen. Her old foster father, the shepherd, enters with the neighbors who have come to the feast, and among them are the king and Camillo in disguise. Perdita bids them welcome as though she were the very goddess of the spring.

> *Here's flowers for you;*
> *Hot lavender, mints, savory, marjoram;*
> *The marigold that goes to bed wi' the sun*
> *And with him rises weeping; these are flowers*

Of middle summer, and I think they are given
To men of middle age. You're very welcome.

She has no flowers of the spring, and she longs for them
because they would be the right ones for Florizel—

> *daffodils,*
> *That come before the swallow dares, and take*
> *The winds of March with beauty; violets dim,*
> *But sweeter than the lids of Juno's eyes . . .*
> *The crown-imperial; lilies of all kinds,*
> *The flower-de-luce being one. O, these I lack*
> *To make you garlands of . . .*

She is suddenly abashed by the way she has been behaving,
but in the eyes of the adoring Florizel she can do no
wrong. Whatever she does is set to music by his love.

> *When you do dance, I wish you*
> *A wave o' the sea, that you might ever do*
> *Nothing but that . . .*

Autolycus arrives, complete with false beard and a peddler's pack, and shows a great gift for advertising his
wares. He is particularly successful with the ballads he has
in stock—the naughty one with its refrain, "Whoop, do me
no harm, good man," and the cautionary one about the
moneylender's wife who gave birth to twenty moneybags.
One of the shepherdesses feels this can hardly be true, and
Autolycus defends its veracity indignantly. "Here's the
midwife's name to 't, one Mistress Taleporter, and five or
six honest wives that were present. Why should I carry lies
abroad?"

The only young man who does not buy something from
the peddler's pack is Florizel; and when his disguised
father asks him why, he explains that he has already given
Perdita the best gift he can, his heart and the vow of
marriage. His outraged father doffs his disguise and says
he will never permit his son to marry a peasant girl. He
would kill her rather than permit such a thing to happen,
and he departs leaving a trail of threats behind him.

Perdita gazes after him, knowing that her dream of marrying Florizel is ended but unwilling to abase herself even to a king.

> *I was not much afeard; for once or twice*
> *I was about to speak and tell him plainly,*
> *The selfsame sun that shines upon his court*
> *Hides not his visage from our cottage . . .*

Florizel is determined not to lose her, and they decide to run away together. Camillo suggests they go to Sicilia, for he knows that the king will follow them and that he himself will be able to see his own house again.

Autolycus returns, having sold every ribbon and bracelet in his pack and snipped a great many purses. He agrees to change clothes with Florizel to give the prince a disguise, so that he and Perdita can take ship and sail at once. The shepherd and his son come in, terrified of the king's displeasure and anxious to prove that Perdita is no relative of theirs. Autolycus in his fine clothes convinces them he is a great lord who will intercede for them with the king, but instead he puts them on the prince's boat and they all set sail for Sicilia.

Leontes, the unhappy king of that country, has spent the last sixteen years mourning his dead wife and children, and he has promised Paulina he will never marry again until she herself chooses his bride. Florizel and Perdita arrive at his court, pretending they have been sent by the king of Bohemia; but an outraged message comes from the king himself, who is pursuing them and close on their heels. Leontes is greatly attracted to the two beautiful young strangers, forgives their deception and promises to do what he can for them.

The shepherd and his son have not yet been able to tell Florizel their secret, for the voyage had been stormy and the prince was worried about Perdita. But now that they are on dry land they take their evidence to the palace and present it to the two kings and the assembled court. They show them a royal mantle and letters that identify Perdita as the long-lost daughter of Leontes, and the whole country welcomes the news with rejoicing. The king has everything to make him happy except the fact that his wife is dead, and Paulina offers to take him to her house where she will show him a statue of Hermione. But it is the real Hermione herself, who did not die but has been kept in hiding, and the mother and daughter have a joyful reunion.

And so *The Winter's Tale* ends. At the beginning of the play the little prince had said, "A sad tale's best for winter," and the first part of the story is sad enough. But it ends in a springtime of rejoicing, and the whole court of Sicilia is happy as the play closes.

THE TEMPEST

THE TEMPEST is a story of magic and monsters, and of an enchanted island set in a distant sea. It tells of what happened in three hours on that island, when beauty and nonsense and innocence and terror clash for a time and then quiet into a final peace under the power of a great magician; and to read it is to enter into a wonderful world which is not quite like any other that Shakespeare ever made.

The story opens with the storm that gives the play its name. The king of Naples is returning from the wedding of his daughter in Tunis, and his ship is caught in a tempest. The king and his courtiers come on deck and try to assert their authority, but the sea cares nothing for the name of king and neither does the harried boatswain. He is trying to keep the ship afloat and has no time to give to frightened amateurs. The winds grow fiercer and the ship splits in two. The prayers and the shouting die away, and there is a final resigned comment from one of the passengers. "The wills above be done! But I would fain die a dry death."

The storm is not a natural one. It has been raised by an enchanter who lives on a nearby island. His name is Prospero and he has a fifteen-year-old daughter named Miranda. Miranda is both beautiful and compassionate, and she has watched the wrecking of the ship with horrified eyes. But her father is compassionate too; by his magic power he has made sure that no one will die in the tempest. Instead, they will all find their way to the island, as he gathers them there for a special purpose of his own.

Twelve years ago, Prospero was the duke of Milan. His wicked brother, Antonio, plotted with the king of Naples to overthrow him, and he and his baby daughter were put in an open boat to drift in the seas until they died. But a kind counselor named Gonzalo put in food and drink and Prospero's books of magic, and the boat found its way to an enchanted island. Now, twelve years later, the king of Naples and the duke of Milan have come to this same island with all their households, and Prospero intends to work his magic art upon them.

The magician has a servant named Ariel, a spirit whom he found imprisoned in a cleft pine when he first arrived on the island. Ariel had been fastened there by a witch for refusing to obey her evil commands, and when she died he could not free himself until Prospero released him. The only other inhabitant of the island was the witch's son, the crawling, animal-like Caliban, and Prospero tried to lift him to the level of a human being. He taught Caliban to speak and let him live with them, and in return Caliban tried to attack his daughter. Since then the monster has been kept as a slave, a carrier of wood and water, his fury held in control only by Prospero's power. Caliban is a sullen and vengeful thing of earth while Ariel is a bright spirit of the air, restless only because he must obey commands; and Prospero has promised Ariel freedom within a week if his orders are well carried out.

Ariel has already performed the first of his tasks and brought everyone safely ashore. The ship is safe, the sailors deep in an enchanted sleep, and the passengers wandering about in different parts of the island. The king's handsome young son, Ferdinand, is sitting alone and mourning, for he believes himself to be the only survivor, and Prospero sends Ariel to fetch him.

Miranda is asleep, made so by her father's magic art, and while Prospero waits for the prince he calls Caliban to bring in the wood. Caliban crawls out of his rock cursing them both, father and daughter, for he cannot forget he was lord of the island until Prospero came. He is half a savage and half a sulky, bewildered child in his reproaches.

> *When thou camest first,*
> *Thou strok'dst me, and mad'st much of me; wouldst*
> *give me*
> *Water with berries in 't; and teach me how*

To name the bigger light, and how the less
That burn by day and night; and then I loved thee . . .

Prospero indignantly reminds him of what he tried to do
to Miranda, and Caliban remembers it with a howl of glee.
"Would it had been done!" He would still harm them both
if he could, but he is helpless against his master's enchantment and has no use for the language he has been taught,
except to curse with it.

Ariel comes in singing and behind him is Prince Ferdinand, unable to resist the power of the music. Ariel sings
first of the sea waves and of dancing on the yellow sands,
and then he sings of a king who died.

> *Full fathom five thy father lies;*
> *Of his bones are coral made;*
> *Those are pearls that were his eyes,*
> *Nothing of him that doth fade,*
> *But doth suffer a sea-change*
> *Into something rich and strange.*
> *Sea-nymphs hourly ring his knell:*
> *Hark! now I hear them—Ding-dong, bell.*

Prospero awakens his daughter and she sees Ferdinand
approaching, the first man except her father that she has
seen for twelve years. In her eyes he is as beautiful as a
god, and the prince is equally awed by her loveliness. "O
you wonder!" Prospero pretends to think that the young
man is a spy. He takes him prisoner and threatens to feed
him on roots and sea-water, while Miranda assures him
anxiously that her father does not usually behave in so un-
gentle a manner. Prospero is delighted by the fact that
the two young people have obviously fallen in love with
each other, and now he has a further task for Ariel.

In another part of the island the king of Naples is
lamenting the death of his son, and not even his wise old
counselor can comfort him. This is Gonzalo, who once
saved Prospero's life, and since he is a happy and gentle
old man he points out that the island may yet be kind to
them. The other courtiers tease him for his simplicity and

good will, but Gonzalo is sure that he could govern such an island and keep it as innocent as in the Golden Age.

The invisible Ariel plays solemn music that sends most of the company to sleep. Only two men are left awake, the evil brother of the king of Naples and the evil brother of Prospero. Antonio, who has already plotted his way to a dukedom, points out how easy it would be to murder the sleeping king and rule Naples in his stead. Gonzalo could be killed too, and the rest of the courtiers are weak enough to take orders from anyone. "They'll take suggestions as a cat laps milk." The two conspirators draw their swords to commit murder. Then they hurriedly pretend they thought they heard lions roaring when Gonzalo and the king awaken, roused by Ariel.

Meanwhile another rebellious subject is cursing his ruler, for Caliban can think of nothing but his savage hatred of Prospero.

> *All the infections that the sun sucks up*
> *From bogs, fens, flats, on Prosper fall, and*
> *make him*
> *By inch-meal a disease! . . .*

Caliban feels that the whole island is peopled with tormenting spirits to punish him for being late with the wood; and when a stranger approaches, Caliban falls on his face to escape him.

The stranger is Trinculo, the king's jester, worried about a coming storm and looking for shelter. He is fascinated by Caliban, sprawled at his feet, and only wishes he had him in England to exhibit as a freak. Still, he is not in England now. He is on a very wild island, with the rain threatening to "fall by pailfuls," and there is nothing he can do except crawl under Caliban's cloak for shelter. For, as Trinculo remarks philosophically, "Misery acquaints a man with strange bedfellows."

His friend Stephano enters—Stephano, who in more orderly days back home was the king's butler. He is now gloriously drunk, having floated ashore on a barrel of wine and made himself a bottle from the bark of a tree as soon as he landed. Stephano is under the impression that he has found a most unusual monster, one with four legs, until he laboriously sorts them out and finds that half of them is Trinculo. Trinculo is delighted by the reunion and insists upon dancing with his friend, in spite of Stephano's earnest cautioning: "Prithee do not turn me about. My stomach is not constant."

Caliban has been given a drink from the bark bottle and becomes as tipsy as Stephano. He has found himself a wonderful new master and is quite prepared to kiss the drunken butler's foot and be his servant. He has a vision of being free from Prospero at last and goes off shouting a splendid new song of his own invention:

> 'Ban, 'Ban, Ca-Caliban,
> Has a new master—Get a new man.

Another bearer of logs is Prince Ferdinand, who has been commanded by Prospero to erect a great pile of them by sunset. As soon as Miranda is sure that her father is safely in his study, she steals out to persuade the prince to stop working or to let her carry the logs for him. In the end, neither of them does any carrying of wood. Instead they talk marriage, exchanging vows of love with one another, while Prospero watches them from a little distance and rejoices.

Stephano, meanwhile, is finding it difficult to control his savage new servant, for Caliban loves him extravagantly but hates Trinculo. "Bite him to death, I prithee." Caliban can think of nothing but killing, and he persuades the other two to come with him and murder Prospero while he lies sleeping. They can smash his skull with the nearest log, burn his books and seize his daughter, and then the three of them will be the rulers of the island. Ariel has been listening to them, cloaked in invisibility, and he plays a little tune upon his pipe; but Caliban is undisturbed because he has lived all his life among magic sounds. "Be not afeard; the isle is full of noises."

Ariel flies to the king of Naples and his courtiers, who have wearily been searching the island for the lost prince. A magic banquet is brought to them and then, just as they are about to eat it, Ariel appears in the likeness of a harpy and the table vanishes in thunder and lightning. He speaks to the three men who once tried to destroy Prospero and frightens them with a voice on the winds, bringing justice.

Prospero has prepared a wedding masque for his daughter and the joyful young prince. To the sound of soft music three goddesses descend to earth, Ceres and Iris and Juno. to celebrate the wedding. After a dance they vanish, and the magician who brought them forth speaks words so beautiful that they show Shakespeare to be a greater enchanter than Prospero.

> *Our revels now are ended. These our actors,*
> *As I foretold you, were all spirits, and*
> *Are melted into air, into thin air,*
> *And, like the baseless fabric of this vision,*
> *The cloud-capped towers, the gorgeous palaces,*
> *The solemn temples, the great globe itself,*
> *Yea, all which it inherit, shall dissolve*
> *And like this insubstantial pageant faded,*
> *Leave not a rack behind. We are such stuff*
> *As dreams are made on, and our little life*
> *Is rounded with a sleep . . . .*

Prospero knows that the time is coming when he must leave the island and go back to the ordinary world of men. When he does that, he will leave his magic behind him.

> *I'll break my staff,*
> *Bury it certain fathoms in the earth,*
> *And deeper than did ever plummet sound,*
> *I'll drown my book.*

By a last exercise of his power he is able to thwart the murderous plots that have been hatched on the island, and when everyone has been gathered together in his presence he decides that they have all been punished enough. Caliban goes back to work with the conviction that he has behaved like a "thrice-double ass." Antonio is forgiven and restores the dukedom to his brother. The repentant king of Naples finds his son again and joyfully welcomes Miranda as his daughter. Prospero, now duke of Milan and

a magician no longer, will sail home with them to Naples
to attend the wedding, and Ariel will provide calm seas
for the homeward voyage. Prospero gives his servant a
final and loving farewell, and Ariel goes off to the delighted freedom of which he has already sung.

> *Where the bee sucks, there suck I,*
> *In a cowslip's bell I lie,*
> *There I couch when owls do cry.*
> *On the bat's back I do fly*
> *After summer merrily.*
> *Merrily, merrily shall I live now*
> *Under the blossom that hangs on the bough.*

The Tragedies

TITUS ANDRONICUS

TITUS ANDRONICUS is the first tragedy Shakespeare ever wrote, and it has all the faults that would be natural in an inexperienced and ambitious young playwright. It is not so much a tragedy of blood as a melodrama of butchery, and the mutilations and tortures and beheadings are applied indiscriminately to all the members of the cast. The play was extremely popular in its own day, because it wallowed in the kind of atrocities that are still the mainstay of cheap journalism and cheap fiction, but Shakespeare himself graduated very early from this kind of writing. It was people he cared about, and the ones in *Titus Andronicus* are nothing but cardboard. Nevertheless, there is a curious kind of energy about the play that shakes it to life occasionally, a faint promise of the kind of miracles he was able to achieve later.

The story opens in Rome, where a Roman general named Titus Andronicus is returning in triumph from a victory over the Goths. He brings with him as captives an evil queen of the Goths named Tamora and an equally evil Moor named Aaron. The blood starts flowing immediately when Titus gives orders that the eldest son of Tamora is to be cut to pieces as a sacrifice to grace the funeral pyre of his own sons who have been killed in battle. Tamora becomes his implacable enemy and, with the help of her friend the Moor, she succeeds in turning Rome into "a wilderness of tigers."

By the time Tamora is through with her revenge, there is very little left of Titus except insane grief. His son-in-law has been stabbed and thrown into a pit, two of his sons have been beheaded, his hand has been struck off, and his daughter Lavinia has been raped and mutilated. Since Lavinia's hands have been cut off and her tongue torn out, she cannot tell her father who her attackers were. But she finally manages to write their names in the sand with a stick, and Titus learns that it was that "pair of cursèd hell-hounds," the sons of Tamora.

Then it is the old general's turn for revenge. He kills the two sons of Tamora, with Lavinia standing by and holding a basin to catch the blood, and grinds the bones up into a pie which he feeds to their mother. Then he kills Tamora, who has become the wife of the emperor, the emperor kills him, and his surviving son, Lucius, kills the emperor.

With this action the reign of disorder ceases, for Lucius orders the punishment of the evil Aaron and arranges for the formal burial of the dead. He becomes a "gracious governor" to the city that has been torn with such violence, and the bloody play ends with Rome and her citizens once more at peace.

ROMEO AND JULIET

ROMEO AND JULIET is the first of Shakespeare's great tragedies and the loveliest. It is golden with the light of morning and heavy with the death of all bright things, and the names of Romeo and Juliet have passed into the language as a symbol of youth and love.

The story opens in the Italian city of Verona, which has been troubled by an ancient feud between two noble families, the house of Capulet and the house of Montague. Three times there has been fighting in the streets, and the play opens with a fourth. Two of Lord Capulet's servants deliberately start a quarrel in the public square, and the brawl explodes into a street fight. The two old lords rush for their swords, and it is not until the prince of Verona enters that peace is restored. The prince is weary of the senseless and bloody feud and he decrees that anyone who fights in the streets of the city from that time forward will be condemned to death.

The young heir of the Montagues, whose name is Romeo, has taken no part in the affair. He has been wandering since daybreak in a grove of sycamore trees west of the city. His mother and father are worried about him, since it is not like Romeo to be so sad, and they ask his cousin Benvolio to find out what the trouble is. Benvolio discovers that Romeo is in love with a fair lady named Rosaline who refuses to return his affection. He has been behaving like any proper young Italian lover, spending his days in sighing and his nights in sleepless woe, and it is his cousin's opinion that Romeo ought to go out and look at other young women instead.

The scene shifts to Lord Capulet. He has decided that he is willing to accept the decree of the prince of Verona, for he is an old man and tired of quarreling. With him is a young kinsman of the prince whose name is Paris, and Paris hopes to marry Capulet's beautiful young daughter, Juliet. Her father is reluctant to have her betrothed to anyone, since she is only fourteen, but he is fond of Paris and tells him to approach Juliet during the feast that will be given at the Capulet house that evening. "Woo her, gentle Paris, get her heart."

Lord Capulet has a list of guests, and he gives it to his servant with instructions to go about the city and invite them all. The servant cannot read and is looking for some "learned" man to explain the list to him when he encounters Romeo. Romeo discovers that his dear Rosaline has been invited, and Benvolio challenges him to attend the feast and compare her with the other fair ladies of Verona.

Late that afternoon, Lady Capulet learns that Paris has asked for her daughter's hand in marriage. She wants to know if Juliet favors the match, and sends for the nurse to fetch her.

Juliet's nurse is one of Shakespeare's great comic creations—an earthy, practical, well-meaning old peasant woman with a vast interest in weddings and a special delight in handsome young men. The nurse is a great talker and all her talk is wonderful. Just at the moment her mind is running on the question of Juliet's exact age, and she launches on a long discussion of what Juliet did when she was three years old. It takes some time to haul her away from her reminiscences and back to the present, but the gabby old lady is finally persuaded to stop talking. Lady Capulet asks her daughter about young Paris, and Juliet agrees to look with favor upon him.

By this time the guests are arriving, and some uninvited guests are arriving also. All the guests are masked as they come by torchlight, but two of them have a special reason to be in disguise, for they are Romeo and Benvolio of the enemy house of Montague. With them is a delightful friend of theirs, a kinsman of the prince named Mercutio.

Mercutio, like the Nurse, is one of the world's great talkers. But while he is just as funny as the Nurse he is a gentleman of wit and breeding, and his humor, unlike hers, is intentional. Just at the moment he is highly amused by Romeo, who is in such a state of melancholy that he has decided not to do any dancing, and Mercutio hopes to extricate his friend from the mire of love in which he seems to be sticking "up to the ears."

Romeo is troubled by a sense of foreboding and a warning dream, and this sets Mercutio off on a lively discussion of dreams. In his view they are all caused by a fairy named Queen Mab. She races over people's noses as they lie asleep, in her chariot that is made of half a hazelnut and steered by a "small grey-coated gnat."

And in this state she gallops night by night Through lovers' brains, and then they dream of love . . .

Mercutio is fascinated by this delightful idea and goes on embroidering it with such enthusiasm that his friends have to beg him to stop. For they are already too late for supper at the Capulet house, and the dancing is about to begin.

Within the house the servants are clearing away the tables, and Lord Capulet comes forward to greet his guests. He is a happy man as he bustles about, instructing the musicians and rounding up the ladies for the dance. His own dancing days are over, but he enjoys standing by with an old friend and talking of the days when they were both young.

Romeo, looking for Rosaline, sees Juliet among the dancers, and his heart falls at her feet. She is so beautiful that she makes even the torches seem dim, and he can think of Rosaline no longer now that he has seen Juliet. He tries to find her name from a passing servingman and does not succeed; but he is resolved that as soon as the dance is over he will go and speak to her.

Romeo's question to the servant is overheard by a fierce young Capulet named Tybalt. It was Tybalt who brought such violence to the street fight, for he hates the members of the house of Montague as he hates hell. He sends at once for his rapier, enraged that an enemy should have come to the feast, but his uncle stops him. Old Lord Capulet is not going to have the evening spoiled, and he holds

Tybalt down with one hand, as it were, while he cheers on his guests with the other.

The dance ends, and Romeo is able to make his way to the place where Juliet is standing. He is in the disguise of a palmer—a pilgrim from the Holy Land—and he speaks to her as a pilgrim might who has found the shrine of his saint. But what he really wants is a kiss, and after a charming, half-teasing dialogue, Juliet lets him have his way. Then she is called by her mother and leaves him, and Romeo, questioning the Nurse, discovers that he has fallen in love with the daughter of his father's foe.

The dancing is over and the guests prepare to leave. Juliet, standing by the door to watch them go, pretends to the Nurse that she is interested in several of the young men. But the only one she is really watching is the young man who kissed her, and when the Nurse finds out his name Juliet discovers in her turn that she has fallen in love with an enemy.

Romeo leaves the house of the Capulets but his heart has stayed behind. He reaches the lane that runs by their orchard wall and realizes that he cannot bear to go any farther away from Juliet. He climbs over the wall and leaps into the orchard, and his two friends make a brief, laughing search for him before they go home to bed.

Juliet has been unable to sleep and she comes out of her bedroom to stand on the balcony overlooking the orchard. Romeo, looking up from among the trees, sees her by the window, and for him it is as though the morning had dawned and the sun had risen in the east. "It is my lady; O, it is my love!"

What follows as she leans over the balcony is perhaps the most famous love scene in all literature. Romeo and Juliet speak to each other in the language that all lovers would use if they could, and their lovely words are touched with the magic of the night and the silver of the moon. The hatred that two families bear each other means nothing to them, except as it makes Juliet fear for Romeo's safety. Nothing is quite real to them, in fact, except their love for each other, and their voices reach out in breathless delight, their hearts touching if their hands cannot.

Before they are finally forced to part, they succeed in

making one practical arrangement. Romeo promises to find someone who is willing to perform a secret marriage ceremony, and Juliet agrees to send a messenger to him at nine o'clock in the morning to find out what arrangements have been made. They are too young and too much in love to think of even a day's delay in the wedding.

Romeo goes to the cell of an old priest, Friar Laurence, who has been out in the early dawn to gather herbs. The friar is his friend and confessor, and for a moment he is startled by Romeo's change of heart. But it is clear that this time he is in earnest, and the friar agrees to the secret marriage. For it may be that when the children of the two warring houses are united the parents will forget their hatreds and live in peace.

Benvolio and Mercutio are wandering about the streets that morning, still wondering where Romeo has vanished. They had called at his father's house earlier in the day, but all they found was a letter waiting for Romeo from Tybalt, challenging him to a duel. Mercutio has never liked the arrogant Tybalt and is enlarging enthusiastically on all his failings when Romeo enters and gets Mercutio's cheerful eloquence transferred to him instead. Mercutio enjoys teasing his friend and is delighted to find he has recovered his good spirits and is prepared to tease him back. "Is not this better now than groaning for love? now art thou sociable, now art thou Romeo."

Lacking a lovelorn Romeo, Mercutio looks around for other game and lights on the Nurse. She has just come into view, voluminous in her skirts, and Mercutio is quite unable to resist teasing her. After he has departed, singing a final impertinent song in her honor, Romeo tries to calm the insulted old lady by explaining that Mercutio "loves to hear himself talk." But the Nurse is not appeased. "Afore God, I am so vexed that every part about me quivers." However, she has many things to talk of, including her opinion of Paris and how sweet Juliet was when she was a baby, and Romeo with difficulty manages to penetrate her rambling good will and give her a message for Juliet. The marriage will be performed that afternoon by Friar Laurence in his cell.

Juliet had sent the Nurse at nine in the morning, and

ever since then she has been waiting for her to return. When the old lady finally reappears she is in a most unsatisfactory state of mind, determined to tell her charge all about how her bones ache. Juliet has no real interest in her Nurse's bones at the moment. What she wants is news and what the old lady wants is sympathy, and the scene between them is both funny and charming in its naturalness.

Romeo and Juliet are married that afternoon by Friar Laurence in his cell. The friar is doubtful of the wisdom of so much haste, but Romeo is afraid of nothing, not even death, so long as he and Juliet are united.

It is hot that afternoon while Mercutio and Benvolio are walking about the public square of Verona. Benvolio, a good, temperate soul, is anxious to keep the peace and he tries to persuade Mercutio to go indoors. For hot weather breeds quarrels and he is anxious to avoid any trouble with the Capulets. Mercutio is amused by his pacifistic friend and supplies him with a long and completely unjust account of his warlike ways, to pay him back for suggesting that Mercutio would permit himself to get into an argument.

Benvolio's anxiety is justified; for Tybalt appears, restlessly hunting Romeo to challenge him to a duel. Tybalt has no quarrel with Mercutio, who does not belong to the hated house of Montague, and he brushes him aside as Romeo enters. It is Romeo he has come to seek, and he is determined to kill him.

But Romeo is equally determined, for his part, to be friends with Tybalt, who is Juliet's first cousin and therefore sacred in her lover's eyes. When Tybalt taunts him, Romeo refuses to draw his sword, and Mercutio is outraged that Romeo should refuse to answer such insults. If Tybalt wants a duel, Mercutio is quite prepared to give him one.

Romeo tries to separate the two combatants and his efforts lead to disaster. Tybalt's sword slides in past Romeo's arm, and Mercutio is given a fatal wound. He falls, and the agonized Romeo finds it impossible to believe what has happened. "The hurt cannot be much." The dying Mercutio agrees that it might be worse. " 'Tis not so deep as a well, nor so wide as a church door, but 'tis enough, 'twill serve." And so he meets his death, with a casual gallantry that even lets him make a final pun.

Romeo is driven wild by the thought that Mercutio died for him, and when Tybalt returns he instantly challenges Juliet's cousin to the duel he refused before. Their swords clash, and Tybalt falls dead.

Romeo stands motionless, staring at what he has done. For he has not only killed Juliet's kinsman but has doomed himself to death by the prince's decree. Benvolio hurries him away and then does his best to explain to the prince how the tragedy occurred. But the most Benvolio can achieve is to persuade the prince to change the death sentence to banishment. Romeo must leave Verona by daybreak and never return to the city again.

Juliet is waiting eagerly for night to fall so that her husband can come to her. Instead it is the Nurse who comes, mourning Tybalt's death. At first the horrified Juliet can think of nothing but her murdered cousin, and then she thinks of Romeo instead and forgets everything else in her longing to see him. The Nurse promises to go to Romeo and finds him hiding in the friar's cell, torturing himself with the thought of his banishment and the conviction that Juliet must hate him as a murderer. The Nurse brings him word from his wife, and Romeo learns that at least they will have one night together before he leaves the city.

The night passes, and a bird sings in the orchard below Juliet's window. It is time for Romeo to leave, but Juliet cannot bear to let him go. She is sure it must be the nightingale they heard singing, down in the pomegranate tree, but Romeo knows otherwise.

> *It was the lark, the herald of the morn,*
> *No nightingale. Look, love, what envious streaks*
> *Do lace the severing clouds in yonder east:*
> *Night's candles are burnt out, and jocund day*
> *Stands tiptoe on the misty mountain tops;*
> *I must be gone and live, or stay and die.*

But still Juliet cannot bring herself to let him go. It was

difficult enough to part the night they met, and that was only for a little while. Now it may be forever, although Romeo does his best to comfort her with talk of a happy future.

Desperate with the parting, Juliet turns to encounter her mother. Lady Capulet has entered the room with what she feels is very good news, for Lord Capulet has arranged everything with young Paris and he will marry Juliet the following Thursday.

Juliet has always been a good and obedient daughter, and both her parents are shocked by the intensity with which she fights against their well-intentioned plans. Lord Capulet in particular is outraged by her behavior. He feels that he has been spending years looking for a suitable husband for Juliet and now she refuses the splendid choice he has made for her. The more he thinks about it the more furious he becomes, and Juliet turns in desperation to her mother.

> *O, sweet my mother, cast me not away!*
> *Delay this marriage for a month, a week . . .*

But Lady Capulet will have nothing to do with her either.

After they have left the room Juliet turns to the old Nurse, and the Nurse fails her too. For she is a practical old dame, and now that Romeo is so far away Paris makes a good second choice. It is her candid opinion that Juliet had better forget her absent husband and marry the fine young gentleman her father has selected for her.

> *O, he's a lovely gentleman!*
> *Romeo's a dishclout to him . . .*

Juliet knows there is no one left in her own home to whom she can turn, and her final hope is Friar Laurence. If he cannot help her, then she will kill herself.

Friar Laurence has a plan to offer her, a desperate one but not as desperate as suicide. He has a potion that will give her the appearance of death when she drinks it and keep her in a state of trance for forty-two hours. It is the custom in Verona for the dead to lie uncovered in the family vaults, and Juliet will lie in the Capulet tomb until a letter sent to Romeo brings him back to her. Then her husband will take her to Mantua with him and they will live there safe from Verona's law.

Lord Capulet hears with delight that Friar Laurence has persuaded Juliet to give her consent to the marriage, and his anger melts into warm approval of everyone concerned. Another feast is in prospect, his daughter has given up her strange and unaccountable behavior, and Lord Capulet is a joyful man.

Juliet keeps herself rigidly under control and tries to behave as normally as possible on the night before her wedding. She looks attentively at her wedding finery and speaks with careful naturalness to her mother and to the Nurse. But when they leave, her control breaks for she is very young and desperately alone. She is not even sure that she can trust the friar, for he may have given her poison to hide the illegal ceremony he performed.

In the famous scene that is called the potion scene, Juliet struggles in anguish with the frightening thoughts that come to her. She is close to the breaking point and cannot control her imagination at all. She feels the tomb already pressing down upon her—the heavy air strangling her, the skeletons of her ancestors waiting, the bloody body of the murdered Tybalt lying in its shroud. Driven half insane by her own imaginings, she thinks she sees Tybalt's ghost advancing to kill Romeo, and with a final cry to her young husband she drinks the potion and falls back upon the bed.

The family has been up all night with preparations for the wedding, and at daybreak the Nurse is sent to awaken Juliet and dress her as a bride. She finds her apparently dead, and wailing fills the house. Instead of a wedding the Capulets must prepare for a funeral, and the "poor and loving child" is carried in solemn mourning to the tomb of her ancestors.

In Mantua, Romeo is waiting for news of his family and friends, and especially for news of Juliet. He is in a happy and hopeful mood when his servant arrives from Verona.

How doth my lady? Is my father well?
How fares my Juliet? That I ask again;
For nothing can be ill if she be well.

The servant tells him, as gently as he can, that Juliet is dead, and is frightened by the change in his master's face. Romeo steadies himself as long as the man is there, but when he is alone he turns back to the one thought that is clear in his mind. "Well, Juliet, I will lie with thee tonight." He will not live without her, and he buys poison from an old apothecary before he leaves the city to return to Verona and his dead love.

Friar Laurence has sent the letter to Romeo as he promised, but there was a threat of plague in the city and he learns to his horror that the message was never delivered. Now it is only three hours before Juliet will awaken in the tomb, and since there is no one else he can trust, Friar Laurence decides to go to her himself.

It is night in the churchyard, and Paris comes to mourn at the Capulet tomb under the yew trees. He has brought flowers for the dead girl who was to have been his bride, and he leaves his page to stand guard in case anyone approaches. The page whistles a warning, and Paris stands back to see Romeo, armed with a wrenching iron, come to force open the tomb.

In the eyes of Paris, Romeo is an outlaw whose murder of Juliet's cousin caused her death through grief, and he attempts to capture him. Romeo tries to ward him off. "Good gentle youth, tempt not a desperate man." But Paris will not listen and they fight. Paris falls and has time to make one last request before he dies.

If thou be merciful,
Open the tomb, lay me with Juliet.

No request could touch Romeo more, and he takes the dead man's hand as though it were a brother's. He lays Paris by his lost bride and then bends over Juliet with the beautiful, heartbroken lines that begin, "O my love, my wife!" They have parted from each other before in the night, but this time he will never leave her again. He takes

Juliet into his arms, drinks the poison, and with one last kiss he dies.

Old Friar Laurence, stumbling over the graves, sees the light of a torch burning in the tomb and finds Romeo's servant on guard outside. There is blood on the stones, and he enters the tomb in terror to find Paris and Romeo dead.

It is time for Juliet to awaken and she stirs to find the friar bending over her.

> *O comfortable friar! where is my lord?*
> *I do remember well where I should be,*
> *And there I am. Where is my Romeo?*

Friar Laurence can do nothing but tell her the truth. He tries to persuade her to leave the tomb, for he hears the noise of the watchmen outside. But she will not go, and the frightened old man leaves her alone with her dead husband.

There is no poison left to help Juliet die, but she finds Romeo's dagger. She must be quick, for the watchmen are coming and there is no time for more than one kiss.

> *O happy dagger!*
> *This is thy sheath; there rust, and let me die.*

She falls upon Romeo's body, dead, and the tragic young lovers will not be parted again.

The watchmen capture Friar Laurence and arouse the city. The prince of Verona hears the tale and so do Capulet and Montague, learning that with their hatreds they condemned their children to death. Too late, they offer their friendship to each other, and the story ends as the two old men clasp hands in the brotherhood of a bitter regret.

JULIUS CAESAR

JULIUS CAESAR is a story of politics. It tells of treachery and good intentions and the manipulations of mass emotions, and it rises to the final tragedy of civil war. Shakespeare has taken a page of Roman history and used it to show some disastrous truths about the nature of men and politics, and the result is a masterpiece. The play has not always been admired in periods of relative peace, but in the war-torn twentieth century it has become one of the most popular of Shakespeare's tragedies. For *Julius Caesar* is a mirror in which the present age can see itself.

The story opens in Rome, in the days when Julius Caesar was at the height of his political career, unquestioned master of the city and ruler of most of the known world. He is so much loved by the citizens that they decide to take "a holiday to see Caesar and to rejoice in his triumph," and two of the Roman officials are forced to disperse the cobblers and carpenters who have gathered in the streets to cheer him. For the politicians do not trust the enormous popularity of Julius Caesar. They are afraid he will become too confident of his own power and grow tyrannical in his use of it.

The scene shifts to a public square. Caesar is on his way to the races, with his public officials around him and an adoring crowd following, when someone shouts a warning: "Beware the ides of March." It is March already, and the ides fall on the fifteenth of the month. This is the first shadow of coming disaster, given by a man skilled in reading the future, but Caesar ignores it. "He is a dreamer; let us leave him; pass."

The crowd moves onward, and two men are left behind. One of them is Brutus, a noble Roman of an ancient family which has seen long service with the state, and the other is a brilliant politician named Cassius. Cassius has a plan in his mind—the destruction of Caesar—and he begins, very delicately, to edge Brutus in that direction.

Cassius and Brutus are both old friends of Caesar, and Cassius begins to talk of the days when all three men were equal. He remembers particularly the time that Caesar challenged him to a swimming match and then would have drowned if Cassius had not rescued him.

And this man
Is now become a god, and Cassius is
A wretched creature and must bend his body,
If Caesar carelessly but nod at him.

Cassius also recalls the time Caesar was sick of a fever in Spain, how he cried for water like a sick girl, and how he shook. " 'Tis true, this god did shake." He is still an ordinary man, as he was then, but his political triumphs have exalted him into something almost beyond human control.

The wind brings a shout from the people at the races, and Brutus remarks that he believes some new honor is being given Caesar. Cassius seizes the opening.

Why, man, he doth bestride the narrow world
Like a Colossus; and we petty men
Walk under his huge legs . . .
Now, in the names of all the gods at once,
Upon what meat doth this our Caesar feed,
That he is grown so great? . . .

Rome has always had a tradition of democratic government, and Cassius reminds Brutus it was one of his own ancestors who destroyed a tyrant and helped to found republican Rome. But Brutus will not commit himself, beyond a cautious promise to think over what Cassius has said.

They can speak together no longer, for Caesar is returning from the games. He eyes the gaunt fanatical Cassius, for the control of men is his business, and turns to his close friend, Mark Antony.

> *Let me have men about me that are fat,*
> *Sleek-headed men and such as sleep o' nights:*
> *Yond Cassius has a lean and hungry look,*
> *He thinks too much: such men are dangerous.*

Mark Antony refuses to believe that any danger can come from a man like Cassius, but Caesar knows better.

> *Such men as he be never at heart's ease,*
> *Whiles they behold a greater than themselves,*
> *And therefore are they very dangerous.*
> *I rather tell thee what is to be feared*
> *Than what I fear; for always I am Caesar.*

Caesar in his own mind is above any such ordinary human emotion as fear, for he is beginning to think he is as god-like as the people believe him to be. The god is then obliged to ask Mark Antony to walk at his right side rather than his left, for he is deaf in his left ear.

A friend of Brutus named Casca has attended the games, and Brutus, remembering the shouting, asks him what happened to Caesar there today. "Why, there was a crown offered him . . . He put it by with the back of his hand, thus: and then the people fell a-shouting." Three times he was offered a royal crown and three times he refused it, although in Casca's opinion he longed to possess it and only turned it down to please the people. Finally, Caesar had them all in such a state that they would have shouted for him if he had "stabbed their mothers." "There was more foolery yet, if I could remember it," says Casca, and goes home.

Brutus is shaken in his mind, and Cassius is sure that he has caught him. For Cassius is planning nothing less than the assassination of Julius Caesar, and he needs Brutus on his side if the plot is to be a success. Now that his friend's mind has begun to move in the right direction, Cassius decides to apply a little more pressure. He arranges for some faked propaganda—petitions thrown into Brutus' window in several kinds of handwriting so that it will look like a spontaneous outpouring of appeals from the citizens of Rome.

There is a great storm that night with unnatural lightning blazing in the streets of Rome and wild beasts walking in the Capitol. It is a night full of portent, frightening to men who believe in the supernatural; and Cassius, walking alone, is able to use even the storm for his purposes. He encounters Casca, compares Caesar to the storm and persuades Casca to join the conspiracy.

Brutus has not been able to sleep that night. The talk he had with Cassius has stirred up all the doubts and mistrusts of Caesar that have been slowly developing in his mind, and it has stirred also his profound, selfless devotion to Rome. His family has always served the city, and the tradition is bred in his bones. He cannot let a tyrant destroy his beloved Rome; better to destroy the tyrant instead. But there is no way to destroy the tyrant except by killing him, and Caesar is his friend.

Brutus is roaming restlessly in his orchard when the scene opens, and he sends his serving boy, Lucius, to light a taper in his study. Then he turns to the problem that has been haunting him all night and goes abruptly to the heart of it.

It must be by his death.

Yet how can Caesar's death be morally justified, since he has not yet committed any act of actual tyranny? Brutus has great need to be sure of his moral position, since he is a good man, and he argues with himself that anything is justified if it prevents a future wrong. His boy Lucius brings him the petitions he found lying by the open study window, and Brutus reads what he believes to be a call for help from the citizens of Rome. His ancestor destroyed Tarquin because he was a tyrant; it is the equal duty of his descendant to destroy Caesar.

Still, it is the murder of a friend that Brutus is contemplating, and he has a sense of being trapped in a dreadful, hypnotic, downward pull that leads toward something from which there is no return.

Between the acting of a dreadful thing
And the first motion, all the interim is

Like a phantasma, or a hideous dream . . .

Lucius comes to say there are men at the door, with hats pulled down over their eyes and faces hidden in their cloaks, and Brutus knows they are the conspirators, come to plot murder. He lets them in.

The conspirators do not know if Brutus is one of them, and they maintain an atmosphere of pleasant social intercourse until Cassius is able to take Brutus aside and question him. Then he takes their hands once more, not as a courteous host this time but as a fellow conspirator.

Brutus is determined that their deed shall not be thought of as murder. It is a sacrifice, reluctant but unavoidable, and he only wishes there were some way to kill Caesar's tyranny without also killing Caesar. Since there is not, he is resolved to go through the whole action with a high Roman dignity, and from the first his ideas run counter to those of Cassius. Cassius, as a practical politician, wants them all to take an oath so that there can be no backsliding; but Brutus is convinced that no true Roman needs a formal oath to keep him in the path of duty. Cassius wants Mark Antony to be killed at the same time as Caesar, knowing quite well how dangerous he will be if he is left alive; but Brutus will not permit the thought of further bloodshed since they are "sacrificers not butchers."

The act of assassination will be committed that day, the fifteenth of March at the eighth hour, and one of the conspirators promises to make sure that Caesar will be at the Capitol. By this time it is almost dawn and the men leave. The wife of Brutus sees them go, for she has been waiting to come in to her husband. She has been frightened by his restlessness and his inability to sleep, and since she is the daughter of a Roman statesman she knows how to approach him. In the end, Brutus promises to tell her what has been troubling him, for she has his trust and his love and is very worthy of both.

Caesar also has to deal with a frightened wife. The thunder and lightning have disturbed her sleep and she is fearful of natural omens. She tries to persuade Caesar not to go to the Capitol that day, since she is convinced his life is in danger, but he refuses to hide his head at home.

Cowards die many times before their deaths,
The valiant never taste of death but once.
Of all the wonders that I yet have heard,
It seems to me most strange that men should fear,
Seeing that death, a necessary end,
Will come when it will come.

She finally makes a direct appeal to him, asking him to stay at home for her sake, and Caesar agrees. Then one of the conspirators enters to play upon his vanity and on the idea of yielding weakly to a woman, and Caesar agrees to go to the Capitol.

On the streets leading to the Capitol, two people are waiting. One is a learned man, a teacher, who has found out about the conspiracy and has written on a piece of paper the names of the ringleaders. Caesar will pass that way, and the teacher hopes to fling the paper in his path as he comes along. Also waiting is the wife of Brutus, who knows what her husband intends to do that day and wants Lucius to go to the Capitol for news. She tries to be cheerful and calm, but her nerves are frayed almost to the point of agony. She is convinced she hears sounds from the Capitol until she learns that Caesar has not yet arrived, and then she is afraid she has let slip some word of her husband's intention. She sends the boy off at last to the Capitol, with pitifully vague instructions, and then goes indoors to wait. For there is nothing else she can do. She is only a woman, and politics belong to men.

Caesar passes by along the street, and the learned man urgently tries to give him the list of conspirators. Caesar thinks it is one more petition and rejects it. He enters the Capitol, and one of the conspirators approaches him with a request to let a banished brother return to Rome. Caesar sees himself as one whose decrees are always just and therefore cannot be repealed.

If thou dost bend, and pray, and fawn for him,
I spurn thee like a cur out of my way.
Know, Caesar doth not wrong, nor without cause
Will he be satisfied.

All the conspirators kneel to him, begging him to grant the request, and Caesar scorns them all. "Hence! Wilt thou lift up Olympus?"

But Caesar is not the mountain of Olympus, nor is he a god. He is only a man and therefore mortal. The men who have surrounded him pull out their swords and stab him, and Caesar sees his friend Brutus among them. He gives the anguished cry—"And thou, Brutus?"—which Shakespeare left in the original Latin because everyone in the audience knew it already. *"Et tu, Brute?* Then fall, Caesar!"* He falls dead at the base of Pompey's statue— Pompey whom he had defeated and destroyed—killed in his turn by the men who had been his friends.

One of the conspirators lifts up his voice in the cry that has been used to justify violence in all ages: "Liberty! Freedom! Tyranny is dead!" And Cassius declares with pride that they will be called "the men that gave their country liberty."

Instead, the gift is civil war, and the first seeds of it begin to grow almost at once. Mark Antony enters, the friend of Caesar whom Cassius had wanted to kill until he was overruled by Brutus. Mark Antony finds himself in a difficult position, obliged to smile on Caesar's murderers while he works out in secret his revenge. He asks the right to deliver the funeral oration over Caesar's body and Brutus gives it to him, in spite of the protests of Cassius. Cassius is an experienced politician, and he knows how easily a mob can be swayed by skillful oratory. But Brutus has great faith in reason. He is sure that if he explains carefully to the people of Rome what the motive was for the assassination and if he binds Mark Antony not to attack the good intentions of the assassins, everyone will understand the situation just as clearly as he does and there will be peace and freedom everywhere.

Brutus delivers an earnest speech to the people, carefully worded and as reasonable as the man himself. Then he leaves the citizens of Rome to listen to Mark Antony, and by doing so sets the seal of his own destruction. For Mark Antony is a great orator and a brilliant politician, and he plays on the emotions of the people with almost uncanny skill.

Mark Antony begins his speech faced by two difficulties. He is aware that the people are well disposed toward Brutus and he is also aware that he has promised to say nothing against the conspirators. Brutus has been able to convince the people that the conspirators acted only to save Rome, and they are so unwilling to hear any praise of Caesar that Mark Antony has to shout to make himself heard.

Friends, Romans, countrymen, lend me your ears! I come to bury Caesar, not to praise him.

Beginning on that note, Mark Antony has their attention; and then, with diabolical precision, he begins to work toward the end he has in view. He says, and continues to say, that "Brutus is an honourable man," but little by little he begins to lead his hearers around to the point where they refuse to believe it. There is a low mutter in the crowd, a spark catching here and there, and Mark Antony tends the fire of their growing rage until it begins to crackle and roar. Brutus has murdered their beloved Caesar, the godlike man who loved them so, and suddenly the fire sweeps through them as though they were dry grass. "Revenge! About! Seek! Burn! Fire! Kill! Slay!"

The mob surges through the city of Rome, looking for conspirators to kill, and finds a man who has the same name as one of the assassins. There is nothing else wrong with him, for he is the most harmless of poets, but since he has the same name there is clearly some kind of guilt by association. He cries out pitifully, "I am Cinna the poet, I am Cinna the poet. . . . I am not Cinna the conspirator." But he is torn to pieces.

The same brutality, but more calculating and cold-blooded, is shown by the men who now control Rome. Mark Antony has formed a coalition with Caesar's grand-nephew, Octavius, and with a colorless individual named Lepidus who is willing to carry out orders. The three men plan the destruction of everyone they do not trust, including some of their own relatives, and in the end they murder more than seventy of the senators of Rome. Then they set an army in motion to destroy Brutus and Cassius, although Mark Antony never had any illusions about the viciousness of civil war.

> Blood and destruction shall be so in use,
> And dreadful objects so familiar,
> That mothers shall but smile when they behold
> Their infants quartered with the hands of war . . .
> And Caesar's spirit, ranging for revenge,
> With Até by his side come hot from hell,
> Shall in these confines with a monarch's voice
> Cry 'Havoc!' and let slip the dogs of war . . .

Their enemies, Brutus and Cassius, are each at the head of an army, and Brutus has set up his camp near Sardis in Asia Minor. The two men love each other, but they have wholly different ideas about running the war. Cassius chooses the practical way, even if it should involve occasional financial dishonesty, and Brutus chooses the honorable one. His nerves are rubbed raw in any case, for he has just received the news that his wife has killed herself. She could no longer endure the strain of his absence and the fear of what Mark Antony might do.

Cassius comes to Sardis to bring his disagreement with Brutus out into the open, and there is the famous scene of two highly-wrought men, intelligent and loving friends, quarreling with each other like a pair of children. "I denied you not." "You did." "I did not." They make up with each other finally, but Cassius has seen a side of Brutus he did not know he possessed. "I did not think you could have been so angry." Brutus tells him of the death of his wife, and Cassius is honestly surprised at his own survival. "How 'scaped I killing when I crossed you so?" He wants to talk of the dead woman but Brutus cannot bear to have the subject mentioned, and they fall to a military discussion instead.

Again they cannot agree. Cassius wants to keep their forces where they are and wait for the enemy, and Brutus wants to march forth and meet them at Philippi.

> There is a tide in the affairs of men
> Which taken at the flood leads on to fortune;

Omitted, all the voyage of their life
Is bound in shallows and in miseries.
On such a full sea are we now afloat,
And we must take the current when it serves,
Or lose our ventures.

Cassius gives in, and the meeting is adjourned; for it is very late.

Brutus finds it difficult to compose himself for sleep, and when Lucius tries to soothe him with music the weary child falls asleep over the instrument. Brutus will not wake him, so he turns to a book he has been keeping in the pocket of his gown and starts reading.

The light flickers suddenly, and Brutus can read no longer. He lifts his eyes from the book, and the ghost of Caesar is standing in front of him. He does not recognize the apparition—"Speak to me what thou art"—and the ghost answers: "Thy evil spirit, Brutus. . . . Thou shalt see me at Philippi." He is trying to question the spirit when it vanishes. Lucius stirs in his sleep for he thinks he is still playing his instrument. "The strings, my lord, are false." More is out of tune than the strings of a musical instrument, for nothing now can keep Brutus from the battlefield and his destruction.

On the plains of Philippi there is a parley between the leaders of the two opposing forces, but it ends in insults. There is no escaping the coming battle, but Cassius faces it with a sense of foreboding, for birds of prey have been following as though looking for dead men. He and Brutus leave each other to command their two armies, and Brutus bids his friend farewell.

This same day
Must end that work the ides of March begun;
And whether we shall meet again I know not. . . .

The battle swings back and forth, fiercely fought and fiercely in doubt, and in the confusion Cassius misunderstands what has happened. He thinks the enemy has conquered, and he is determined not to be brought back to Rome a captive. Brutus finds his friend at the foot of the hill, dead with his own sword in his heart, and the same sense of foreboding falls on Brutus in his turn.

O Julius Caesar! thou art mighty yet!
Thy spirit walks abroad and turns our swords . . .

The battle continues into the night, and one after another the friends of Brutus die. The remnant gathers itself together at a rock, and Brutus knows that the time has come to follow Cassius. He asks one of his servants to hold the sword steady, and he runs upon it and dies. His last words are addressed to an earlier and dearer friend than Cassius: "Caesar, now be still."

Mark Antony, the victor, looks down on the dead body of his foe and cannot find it in his heart to hate him. No one could hate a man like Brutus, who meant so well and was so tragically mistaken.

This was the noblest Roman of them all.
All the conspirators, save only he,
Did what they did in envy of great Caesar;
He only, in a general honest thought
And common good to all, made one of them.
His life was gentle, and the elements
So mixed in him that Nature might stand up
And say to all the world, 'This was a man!'

HAMLET

HAMLET is perhaps the most famous of all Shakespeare's tragedies, for it is known all over the world and has exerted a compelling fascination wherever it goes. The hero is so real and his dilemma is so basic to human living that the people of every country recognize him, and he is portrayed with such subtlety and force that he becomes an actual human being in the reader's mind.

Hamlet is not only the most brilliant of the tragedies but one of the saddest, since the hero is not destroyed by any evil in his nature but by a kind of misplaced good. Yet he remains so triumphantly himself that even the violence of his own death has no real power over him. It is only the separation, at last, of the flesh and the spirit, and they have fought each other so long that it is almost better to have them at peace.

The story opens in the cold and dark of a winter night in Denmark, while the guard is being changed on the battlements of the royal castle of Elsinore. For two nights in succession, just as the bell strikes the hour of one, a ghost has appeared on the battlements, a figure dressed in complete armor and with a face like that of the dead king of Denmark, Hamlet's father. A young man named Horatio, who is a school friend of Hamlet, has been told of the apparition and cannot believe it, and one of the officers has brought him there in the night so that he can see it for himself.

The hour comes, and the ghost walks. The awed Horatio tries to speak to it but it stalks away, leaving the three men to wonder why the buried king has come back to haunt the land. It may be because his country is in danger, for there is a threat of war in Denmark; the nephew of the king of Norway is talking of invading it. Whatever the message is that has wakened the ghost, it refuses to share it with them. But perhaps it will speak to Hamlet, and they decide to go and tell the dead king's son what they have seen that night.

Hamlet is in one of the great ceremonial rooms of the castle, somberly watching the behavior of his uncle. His uncle is now king of Denmark, for he has married Hamlet's mother and ascended the throne of Hamlet's father. The new head of the state handles the dignity of his office with practiced ease. He dispatches two courtiers on a peace mission to Norway, gives permission to the son of his lord chamberlain to leave for France, and then turns his attention to his royal nephew. Hamlet is still wearing black in mourning for his father's death, and his uncle chides him gently for what he feels is an undue show of grief. But the king can get no answer from Hamlet, who throws him one brief sentence and then addresses all his remarks to his mother; and it is his mother, the queen, who persuades him not to go back to the university again but to stay at Elsinore.

The royal pair and their courtiers leave the room, and Hamlet is left alone, to face the sick disgust that he has felt all through the conversation.

O God, God!
How weary, stale, flat and unprofitable
Seem to me all the uses of this world! . . .

It is not only his father's sudden death that has plunged Hamlet so deep in melancholy. It is the even greater shock of his mother's marriage, less than two months later, to a man for whom Hamlet has the most savage personal contempt. He cannot keep his sick imagination from playing about the details of their life together, and his sense of anguish and outrage deepens the more his mind dwells on it.

Horatio enters, together with the two officers of the watch, and Hamlet welcomes him delightedly. Horatio has all the qualities that Hamlet lacks, possessing a gentle, easy steadiness for which Hamlet later thanks him from the heart; and his fellow student from the university is the only human being with whom the prince can talk freely. Horatio tells him that the ghost of his dead father has returned to haunt the battlements, and Hamlet is profoundly stirred. "Indeed, indeed, sirs, but this troubles me." He arranges to meet the three of them that night, to watch for the ghost's return, and then waits longingly for the darkness.

The son of the lord chamberlain, a young man named Laertes, makes his final preparations to leave for France and gives his sister a few last-minute instructions before he goes. Her name is Ophelia, and Hamlet has been paying court to her. In Laertes' opinion, she should not pay too much attention to the prince's talk of love for he is heir to the throne of Denmark and not free to marry where he pleases. Ophelia is a gentle girl, very strictly brought up, and she promises to conduct herself carefully at home if he will do the same in Paris.

Their father the chamberlain enters, a pompous, talkative old man whose name is Polonius. He has gathered together a long string of moral maxims to guide his son on his travels, and after Laertes leaves he turns to Ophelia. In the opinion of Polonius also she has been seeing too much of the prince, and although Ophelia maintains that Hamlet has made love honorably and intends marriage, her father gives her an outright order that she is to see no more of him.

Horatio and Hamlet meet on the battlements near midnight. They wait in the cold and darkness, and from below comes the sound of drunken revelry. Hamlet is too civilized to like the kind of brutal carousing that his countrymen indulge in, and he is explaining his objections to Horatio and becoming really interested in the subject when the ghost suddenly enters. Hamlet is jerked into a world that has nothing to do with calm intelligence and careful reasoning, a world of ghosts and goblins and of a forced return from the gates of hell. His father has come out of his grave, and Hamlet searches wildly for words with which to speak to him.

The ghost beckons, and Hamlet's friends try to stop him from following, for it may be an evil spirit that will tempt him to his own destruction. But Hamlet by this time is in a state of almost frenzied excitement, and the three men cannot hold him. His nerves on edge, he follows the steel-clad figure that stalks in front of him, and finally can endure the silence no longer. "Speak! I'll go no further."

The ghost turns and speaks, and it is then that Hamlet receives the full weight of a hideous discovery. For the king his father did not die a natural death. He was poisoned by his brother, who stole his life, his crown and his queen; and a murderer now reigns in Denmark. The dead king has returned from his own torment in purgatory to ask his son to avenge the murder, and to ask him also not to hurt his mother, the woman all three men love. "Leave her to heaven."

The ghost vanishes, leaving Hamlet shaken almost to hysteria by his hatred of his uncle. "O villain, villain, smiling, damnèd villain!" He has not been told what form his revenge ought to take. He only knows that from this time forward it must be the center of his life. He sees himself—that subtle, intelligent, civilized man—as a single rigid instrument dedicated only to vengeance, and when his friends reach him they can make no sense of his conversation. Horatio continues to give his friend the steady, loving sympathy that is so characteristic of him, but even he is disturbed by the prince's "wild and whirling words."

Hamlet is at least clear that secrecy will be vital, and he tries to make the three men swear that they will not reveal what they have seen and heard that night. When they show reluctance, the voice of the ghost beneath the earth echoes Hamlet's command, and the straightforward Horatio is completely bewildered by what is happening. "O day and night, but this is wondrous strange!" Hamlet turns to him almost with a smile.

And therefore as a stranger give it welcome.
There are more things in heaven and earth, Horatio,
Than are dreamt of in your philosophy. . . .

Finally the three men swear on the hilt of Hamlet's sword that they will reveal nothing; and, if he behaves strangely about the court, they will not suggest they know why. Once they have taken the oath, Hamlet remembers

the courtesy that is normal to him, but his heart is heavy
with the burden that has been laid upon it.

> *The time is out of joint; O cursèd spite,*
> *That ever I was born to set it right! . . .*

Polonius, the lord chamberlain, has been puttering about
in his secretive way, making sure that his children obey all
his precepts that have been given them. He sets a servant
to spy on his son's behavior in Paris, in the calm conviction he is doing it only for his son's good, and it is for his
daughter's good that he has ordered her to see no more of
Hamlet. The frightened Ophelia comes in to tell her father
that Hamlet broke in upon her while she sat sewing. With
his face as white as his shirt and the look of a man who
had seen hell, he gripped her wrist, stared at her face as
intently as though he were memorizing it, and then backed
out of the room with his eyes never leaving hers. Polonius,
much shocked by this unforeseen development, decides
that Hamlet has been driven insane by unrequited love.
He deeply regrets he ever told his daughter to spurn the
prince and trots off to tell the news to the king.

The king is already very much aware of the change in
Hamlet's behavior, and extremely worried by it. He has
asked two friends of Hamlet's youth to come to the court
—Rosencrantz and Guildenstern—in the hope that they
can find out what is troubling the prince. The king has at
least the consolation of good news from Norway, for the
prince of that country has given up all thought of invading
Denmark and merely wants safe passage for a military expedition farther south. Polonius enters with a long-winded
explanation of his private theories about Hamlet, and the
queen is inclined to believe them. The king is not so sure,
but he agrees to set a watch on Hamlet's behavior when
he is with Ophelia.

Polonius finds himself alone with Hamlet, who is quietly
reading, and interrupts him with one of his silly and well-
intentioned questions, put to him with anxious solicitude.
Hamlet considers him a "great baby" and amuses himself
for a few moments by playing him as though he were a
fish. Then Rosencrantz and Guildenstern come in, and

Hamlet does not have the contempt for them he does for the lord chamberlain. He lets them see a little of the heaviness of his heart and calls Denmark a prison. The two men protest that it is not, but Hamlet has learned a deeper truth. "Why, then, 'tis none to you; for there is nothing either good or bad, but thinking makes it so: to me it is a prison." They suggest that his difficulty may be ambition and Denmark too narrow for his mind, but Hamlet knows better than that. "O God! I could be bounded in a nutshell, and count myself a king of infinite space, were it not that I have bad dreams."

Hamlet makes the two men admit that the king has sent them, and then gives them an answer to take back: his trouble is only melancholy. He makes a most eloquent speech on the beauty and wonder of the world and why it seems only a heap of grayness to him. Even man, that incredible and intricate piece of creation, is to him only a "quintessence of dust. Man delights not me; no, nor woman either, though by your smiling you seem to say so."

The two men hurriedly explain that they smiled only to think what a poor welcome Hamlet would give to the troupe of traveling actors who have come to Elsinore, and Hamlet is instantly delighted to know that the players have arrived. His quick mind, which leaps at everything, wants to know how they have prospered since he saw them last, and when the players themselves appear Hamlet greets them as old friends. He asks one of them to recite a scene from a tragedy he admires and is so moved that the speech has to be broken off. The actors are taken away by Polonius, who, as lord chamberlain, is responsible for all the entertainments in the castle but who has a frank lack of interest in classical tragedy. Hamlet detains one of the actors for a moment and asks him to present a play called "The Murder of Gonzago" before the king, with a few extra lines to be written into the text by Hamlet himself.

Then Hamlet is left alone, and the courteous, witty, intelligent young prince dissolves into a tormented human being. He has just been watching an actor work himself up into a torrent of tragic emotion over a character in a play.

For Hecuba!
What's Hecuba to him, or he to Hecuba
That he should weep for her? . . .

But he himself, with enough cause to drown an audience
in tears, has done nothing. He starts to rage at his uncle,
and yet he is perfectly aware that he is making a fool of
himself to shout curses when it is action that is required.
Still he cannot be sure what he ought to do. It may very
well be that the ghost was an evil spirit, tempting him to his
own destruction by telling lies, and Hamlet must have
proof of his uncle's guilt before he has a right to take
revenge. Tomorrow night, at the play, a scene of murder
by poison will be presented by the actors whom Hamlet
has trained; and if his uncle turns pale, the dead man's
son will know what to do.

The play's the thing
Wherein I'll catch the conscience of the king.

Rosencrantz and Guildenstern report to the king that
they have not been able to find the real reason for Hamlet's behavior, and the king turns to his second source of
information, Ophelia. Her father sets her out, with a book
in her hand, in a place where Hamlet is sure to come, and
then he and the king hide themselves to watch what will
happen.

Hamlet enters, desperate enough by this time to be
thinking of suicide. It seems to him that it would be such
a sure way of escape from torment, just to cease existing,
and he gives the famous speech on suicide that has never
been worn thin by repetition. "To be, or not to be . . ."
It would be easy to stop living.

To die, to sleep;
No more. And by a sleep to say we end
The heartache and the thousand natural shocks
That flesh is heir to . . .

But Hamlet has never succeeded in deceiving himself,
and he cannot do so now.

> *To die, to sleep;*
> *To sleep; perchance to dream; ay, there's the rub;*
> *For in that sleep of death what dreams may come,*
> *When we have shuffled off this mortal coil,*
> *Must give us pause. There's the respect*
> *That makes calamity of so long life . . .*

No one would endure the weight of human living if he could put a stop to it merely by ceasing to exist. But it may be that a man does not end his torment by suicide but only enters worse territory:

> *. . . the dread of something after death,*
> *The undiscovered country, from whose bourn*
> *No traveler returns, puzzles the will,*
> *And makes us rather bear those ills we have*
> *Than fly to others that we know not of. . . .*

Hamlet will not even be able to kill himself. He has thought too much about it to be able to take any action.

He sees Ophelia, who has been holding some little gifts he gave her in the days when he also gave her his love. She wants to give them back to him, and Hamlet, in his turn, wants nothing to do with any woman. His mother has given herself to a murderer, and everything about the idea of marriage sickens him. "Get thee to a nunnery: why wouldst thou be a breeder of sinners?" He lashes out at Ophelia as wildly as though she has invented the propagation of the human race, so full of pain himself that he cannot stop to be aware of the pain he is causing, and she can only conclude that Hamlet is hopelessly insane.

The listening king is not so easily deceived. He knows that Hamlet has something definite on his mind and is afraid it may threaten his own safety. Hamlet must be sent out of the country, and the king is easily able to think of a political excuse to send him to England. Polonius, a determined old sentimentalist, is still sure that Hamlet is suffering from unrequited love, and the king agrees that after the play the queen should try to discover what is wrong.

Hamlet is very much occupied with his production of the play and is full of advice to the players on the art of acting. It is only to Horatio that he tells his basic purpose, and he asks his friend to watch the king's face during the poisoning scene. The king and queen and all the courtiers enter to see the show, and Hamlet, as restless as a cat, lies down at Ophelia's feet and talks more than he should. "The Murder of Gonzago" begins, and the king grows increasingly disturbed. Hamlet assures him that the whole thing is mere make-believe: "They do but jest, poison in jest; no offense i' the world." The actual scene of the poisoning comes, and the king sees a re-enactment of his own crime. He can endure it no longer. He rises and calls for lights, and the performance ends in confusion. Hamlet is wild with excitement at the success of his plan, and when he receives word that his mother wants to speak to him, he goes with the conviction that now he can be firm in the "bitter business" he has vowed to perform.

The king knows now that his crown and his life are in danger as long as Hamlet remains alive, and he plots with Rosencrantz and Guildenstern to destroy the prince. But the king is no monster, and he is bitterly aware of the magnitude of his sins. He longs for his soul's peace, and is on his knees in prayer when Hamlet passes on the way to his mother's room. It occurs to the prince how easy it would be to plunge a sword into his uncle's back and be done with the whole thing, and then he dismisses the idea as too weak a form of revenge. He must choose some moment when the king is sunk in evil, not in prayer, so that his soul may be damned.

Polonius has gone to the queen's room, since he intends to report back to the king everything that Hamlet says, and he is giving her some final instructions when they hear Hamlet coming. Polonius hides behind the wall hanging, and Hamlet enters the room so tense with fury that the queen thinks for a moment her son intends to murder her. She calls out for help and Polonius echoes her; and Hamlet, thinking it is the king, drives his sword through the tapestry. Then he discovers that he has killed the silly old man instead.

Thou wretched, rash, intruding fool, farewell!
I took thee for thy better . . .

Hamlet has no interest in Polonius at the moment. His whole soul is focused on his mother, intent on making her acknowledge her sin. The bewildered woman can understand nothing in his words except the violence in them, and when he suddenly begins to talk to the empty air she is more convinced than ever that he must be mad. But Hamlet has seen the ghost of his father again, come to force him on in his revenge, and he will not let the unhappy queen go until she is almost in a state of collapse. "O Hamlet! thou hast cleft my heart in twain."

The queen tells her husband that Hamlet has killed Polonius in a fit of insanity, and the king sends Rosencrantz and Guildenstern to find where Hamlet has hidden the body. Hamlet will not tell anyone where he has been able to "lug the guts," as he calls it, and his behavior is so wild that the king has no difficulty in justifying his own plan. For Rosencrantz and Guildenstern bear letters to England demanding the death of Hamlet as soon as he arrives there.

On his way to England, Hamlet encounters the army of the prince of Norway, who is passing through Denmark on his way to Poland. Hamlet is deeply impressed by the fact that so many brave men are prepared to fight and die in a quarrel not their own. It throws him back on his old hopeless problem, his delayed revenge. He knows the real trouble; it comes from "thinking too precisely on the event." And he prays that from this time forward, since he cannot stop thinking, his thoughts will be of blood only.

Her father's death has been too much for the gentle, sheltered spirit of Ophelia, and she wanders through the court singing songs she should never have heard or known. She is insane, and the king and queen can only watch her in helpless pity.

Her brother Laertes, when he hears the news, takes a different course. He is sure that it was the king who murdered his father, and he promptly raises the standard of revolt. The king knows exactly how to handle a hasty young man and has no difficulty in persuading Laertes that

Hamlet should be the object of his rage. It takes the king a little longer to persuade Laertes to murder Hamlet, but he finally agrees to challenge him to a duel and kill him with a poisoned rapier.

The king is obliged to hurry, for Hamlet has slipped out of the trap that was laid for him in England. He sends word to the king that he is coming home, but he knows nothing of what has been happening in his absence. Above all, he does not know that Ophelia is no longer living. She tried to hang a wreath on a willow tree near a brook, and when the branch broke with her weight she made no effort to save herself. Instead she lay in the water, singing her little songs, until she drowned.

Ophelia is to be buried in the churchyard, and two very chatty gravediggers prepare her grave. It was not usual for anyone suspected of suicide to be buried in holy ground, and the realistic diggers decide it must be because she belongs to the "great folk." One of them remains behind to finish the grave, and Hamlet arrives to find him singing to himself, as cheerfully insensitive to death as the clods of earth he is flinging about.

Hamlet is in no special hurry to return to the court, and the gravedigger and the loose bones fascinate him. He finds the skull of a jester he loved when he was a small boy, a man named Yorick, and his quick imagination begins to range over the whole subject of the dissolution of the human body. He has reached the point of conceiving the dust of the mighty Alexander stuffed in the bunghole of a beer barrel when a funeral procession approaches and he lingers to see whose it is.

It is the funeral of Ophelia, attended by all the court, and her brother Laertes is half-crazed with grief. He is enraged that the priest will not permit the singing of a requiem for his sister because she was a suicide, and finally he leaps into her grave, shouting to them to pile the earth over them both until they have reared a mountain. His ranting suddenly puts Hamlet into "a towering passion" and he leaps into the grave to shout even louder than Laertes.

I loved Ophelia; forty thousand brothers
Could not, with all their quantity of love,
Make up my sum. . . .

If there is to be talk of mountains, let "millions of acres" of mountains be piled on them both, for Hamlet can howl rhetoric too.

Back in the castle, Hamlet can feel only the most profound regret for his behavior in the graveyard. "I forgot myself." He resolves to make a special effort to be a friend to Laertes, and when a mincing courtier brings a challenge from him, Hamlet teases the courtier a little but accepts the challenge. He believes it is only a friendly bout, and yet he admits to Horatio that he feels a foreboding. "Thou wouldst not think how ill all's here about my heart." Horatio tries to persuade him to give up the match and offers to make his excuses for him, but Hamlet is able to look at the future with steady eyes. "If it is not to come, it will be now; if it be not now, yet it will come; the readiness is all."

The court gathers to watch the fencing match between the two young men, and only the king and Laertes know that both the rapier and the wine are poisoned. Hamlet begins by offering Laertes his full apologies, with the courtesy that is always his when his shaken soul can give it time to show itself, and the last scene of his life begins.

The end comes quickly. Hamlet scores the first and second hits, and the king tries to persuade him to stop and drink a little wine. Hamlet, intent on the match, puts the cup aside, and the queen picks it up and drinks it. The king, knowing it is poisoned, tries too late to stop her, and she falls dying just as her son and his opponent are both hurt by the poisoned sword. It has changed hands in a close scuffle, and Laertes knows that he deserves his coming death. "I am justly killed with mine own treachery." He manages to gasp out the whole of the plot to Hamlet, ending with the final cry, "The king, the king's to blame."

The dying Hamlet seizes the poisoned sword with his own blood still upon it, stabs the king and then forces the poisoned wine down his throat. The courtiers stand aghast

and he tries to tell them what has happened, for even with
death closing in upon him he can still remember that he
is prince of Denmark and responsible for the welfare of
his country. But he no longer has the strength and he
leaves the task to Horatio, with the final wish that the
prince of Norway is to rule Denmark. He has no more to
say. "The rest is silence."

Horatio gives a last heartbroken farewell to the lonely,
tormented, incomparable human being he loved so much.

Good-night, sweet prince,
And flights of angels sing thee to thy rest.

Four captains carry Hamlet's body away to give it a soldier's burial, and there is a military salute to the dead
prince of Denmark as the play ends.

TROILUS AND CRESSIDA

TROILUS AND CRESSIDA is called a tragedy because it has an unhappy ending; but most of the time it is a comedy, if a rather savage one. It gives a realistic, worm's-eye view of the Trojan war, the most famous conflict of classical antiquity, and portrays the mighty heroes of Homer as squabbling, stupid men. If there is a villain in the play, it is the war itself, a war that has been going on for seven years and is getting nowhere.

The war had begun when Paris, a prince of Troy, abducted Helen, the most beautiful woman in the world. Her husband, Menelaus, gathered together a mighty army to get her back, and for seven years the Greeks have besieged the city of Troy. The "cruel war" has settled down into a long, useless stalemate, and on both sides there is an atmosphere of cynicism and boredom and confusion.

The story opens in Troy. A brother of Paris, whose name is Troilus, has fallen in love with a woman named Cressida and is using her uncle as a go-between to win her favor. The uncle has not been successful, and Troilus is beginning to show his impatience. The uncle is a fretful old fellow (what Troilus despairingly calls "techy") and he decides that Troilus has insulted him. He remarks huffily that he has had "small thanks" for all his hard work and makes a dignified exit. The sound of battle is heard, but Troilus hates the bray of the trumpets. He can think of nothing but Cressida at the moment, and to his mind Helen is not worth a war. "Fools on both sides!"

Cressida's uncle makes one more effort to persuade his niece to accept Troilus as a lover. He finds her in an unsympathetic mood, and when he points out that Troilus has a fine complexion and a dimple in his chin, she only laughs at him. She maintains that even the Greek Achilles is a better man. Her uncle says indignantly that Achilles is "a drayman, a porter, a very camel," and that Troilus is the loveliest man anywhere; and, as soon as Cressida is alone, she admits to herself that she agrees with him. But she is experienced in the handling of men, and she knows how to keep a man hot in his wooing. "Men prize the thing ungained."

The scene shifts to the camp of the besieging Greeks, and to a council of war that is being held before the tent of their general, Agamemnon. It is clear to everyone that the war is going badly. "After seven years' siege yet Troy walls stand." In fact, things are getting worse from the Greek point of view, since the commanders are splitting up into factions. One of the wisest of them, Ulysses, gives a noble and eloquent speech on the importance of order in the universe and emphasizes the importance of accredited authority and a clear chain of command. The root of the difficulty is Achilles, who has not come to the meeting but who lies on his bed and roars with laughter while his favorite companion mimics the behavior of his fellow officers.

> *At this fusty stuff,*
> *The large Achilles, on his pressed bed lolling,*
> *From his deep chest laughs out a loud applause;*
> *Cries, 'Excellent! 'tis Agamemnon just.*
> *Now play me Nestor . . .'*

No discipline can be maintained in the camp as along as Achilles remains in such a state of mind, convinced that he is the most important man in the army and free to do anything he pleases. A solution offers itself when Hector, the mightiest warrior in Troy, sends out a challenge to the Greeks. He offers to engage one of their men in single combat, and the opponent he has in mind is Achilles. But the Greeks decide to use a rigged lottery and have the choice fall on Ajax, who is a "dull, brainless" fool. If Achilles were to be allowed to fight it would only increase his insolence, and the commanders hope it may dampen his pride to have someone like Ajax preferred ahead of him.

Ajax hears that Hector has sent a proclamation to the Greeks and tries to get the text of it from a man named Thersites. Thersites later calls himself "a rascal, a scurvy railing knave, a very filthy rogue." He is all of that. But he is also a bitter realist, hating fools and the damage they succeed in doing in the world, and he particularly hates that greatest of fools, Ajax. He considers him a military ass—"Mars his idiot." Their wrangling is interrupted by Achilles himself who demands, "What's the matter?" Ajax wails that Thersites has been doing nothing but insult him: "I bade the vile owl go learn me the tenour of the proclamation, and he rails upon me." Achilles already knows what the proclamation says, that Hector of Troy has challenged a Greek to combat the following morning, and he graciously adds that the knightly wording is "trash." As for the Greek warrior who is intended to answer it, Achilles is sure that Hector meant the challenge for him. "He knew his man."

Back in Troy, the king of the city and three of his sons are discussing the possibility of returning Helen to her husband and giving up the war. Hector is in favor of the idea.

> She is not worth what she doth cost
> *The holding.*

His brother Troilus disagrees with him. Whatever she may have been worth once, she is worth a great deal now, since she has been bought with so much blood. Moreover, the honor of the city is now at stake. It is the mention of honor that touches Hector and makes him reverse his former decision, and he remembers with delight the challenge he sent into the Grecian camp.

Thersites, meditating on the same subject of war, sees it in a different light. He can detect no gleam of honor upon it. What he sees is disease and stupidity and death, and he itches with a kind of helpless irritation at the blindness of military mankind.

Agamemnon, the Greek general, goes to speak with Achilles, but neither he nor any of his commanders can persuade that childish and sulky hero to emerge from his tent. So they all turn to praising Ajax, telling him what a wise, valiant, modest, wonderful fellow he is, and the delighted Ajax offers to discipline Achilles for them. "With my armed fist I'll pash him o'er the face." They assure him this will not be necessary and that they are all depending on him to be the Greek champion in the coming duel with Hector.

Meanwhile, back in Troy, Cressida's uncle has at last persuaded her to give in to Troilus and manages to bring the two lovers together in his orchard. As soon as Cressida appears Troilus loses his tongue, and the energetic old go-between has to urge him into action. "Come, come, what need you blush? shame's a baby. Here she is now; swear the oaths to her that you have sworn to me." He has fixed a fire for them within the house and everything is in readiness; and Cressida, half smiling, remarks resignedly, "Well, uncle, what folly I commit, I dedicate to you." She tells Troilus that she loves him, and her uncle is charmed by the way Troilus replies to her. "Pretty, i' faith."

Cressida swears to Troilus that she will be faithful forever, and for the moment she really believes it. She does not know that her father, who is in the Grecian camp, has arranged for her to come to him through an exchange of prisoners, and that as soon as she is parted from Troilus by the fortunes of war she will forget all her vows of love.

A handsome young commander is chosen by the Greeks to bring Cressida to her father, and he sets off while the rest of the commanders turn their attention to Achilles. As they pass in front of his tent they all ignore him ostentatiously, and the bewildered Achilles asks Ulysses what they mean by such ingratitude to so great a man. "What! are my deeds forgot?" Ulysses, who has already made one famous and eloquent speech, now makes another.

Time hath, my lord, a wallet at his back
Wherein he puts alms for oblivion,
A great-sized monster of ingratitudes:
Those scraps are good deeds past; which are devoured
As fast as they are made, forgot as soon
As done . . .

The love of novelty is the one touch of nature that "makes the whole world kin."

Then marvel not, thou great and complete man,
That all the Greeks begin to worship Ajax;
Since things in motion sooner catch the eye
Than what stirs not. The cry went once on thee,
And still it might, and yet it may again,
If thou wouldst not entomb thyself alive,
And case thy reputation in thy tent . . .

One of the reasons Achilles has been unwilling to fight is that he is in love with a princess of Troy. But any insult to his reputation rouses him to fury, and he resolves to look at Hector when that mighty hero arrives at the Greek camp for his duel with Ajax. Ajax, meanwhile, has been strutting about the camp and dreaming of his coming triumph while Thersites eyes him with sardonic amusement. "The man's undone forever; for if Hector break not his neck i' the combat, he'll break 't himself in vainglory."

Early the next morning, back in Troy, Cressida parts from her lover after the night they have spent together. A messenger comes with the news that Cressida must be taken to the Grecian camp, and she and Troilus discover that they are faced with a longer parting still. They say farewell with heartbroken vows of fidelity and love, and then Cressida goes off in the safekeeping of the handsome young Greek who has come for her.

She arrives inside the Greek lines in remarkably high spirits for a woman who has just parted from her beloved. She is quite willing to kiss half the commanders in camp by way of greeting, and one of them at least, the honorable Ulysses, does not think highly of her behavior.

Fie, fie upon her!
There's language in her eye, her cheek, her lip,
Nay, her foot speaks, her wanton spirits look out
At every joint and motive of her body. . . .

A trumpet sounds, and Hector appears in full armor for his duel with Ajax. Hector is not anxious to fight Ajax, who happens to be his cousin, and there is only a brief exchange at arms before the encounter dissolves into a general exchange of courtesies. These men are all knights, and it is part of their code that a man must be courteous to his enemies when he is not actively engaged in trying to hack their heads off. The only one who does not behave well is Achilles, and even he succumbs to the general atmosphere.

> Tomorrow do I meet thee, fell as death;
> Tonight all friends.

Troilus has come with his brother Hector to the Grecian camp, and while the warriors feast by torchlight he makes his way to the tent where Cressida is staying. There he sees her with the handsome young Greek who served as her escort, playing exactly the same game that she played with Troilus. "Sweet honey Greek, tempt me no more to folly." When the Greek shows he is in no mood to prolong the game and offers to leave her, she clings to him and, while Troilus watches in agony, she even offers him a gift that Troilus had given.

For a moment Cressida remembers her former lover and tries to take her offering back, but the Greek will not let her. "I will have it. Whose was it?" And Cressida makes the pitiful answer of a light woman.

> 'Twas one's that loved me better than you will.
> But, now you have it, take it.

The watching Troilus can take consolation from one thing only. Tomorrow, in the battle, he will try to kill his handsome Greek rival and ease a little the pain in his heart.

Next morning Hector arms for the same battle, although his wife and sister implore him not to fight that day. Hector in turn tries to persuade his brother Troilus to stay at home. But Troilus is driven on by revenge, as Hector is by honor, and the two brothers go forth together.

The battle, or what Thersites bitterly calls the "clapperclawing," begins. There are honorable men in the battle and brave deeds, but the sum of it is evil. For Achilles is determined to kill Hector and does not care how he does it. Finally he traps the hero when he is standing unarmed, the "day's work done," and has him surrounded and murdered. Then Achilles ties the dead body of Hector to his horse's tail and drags him off the field.

So the great battle ends, not in fair combat but in open butchery, and the speech that closes the play is not on the subject of honor but of disease.

OTHELLO

OTHELLO is a melodrama that is exalted into tragedy through the brilliance of its characterization and the magnificence of its poetry. It tells the story of a strong-hearted, innocent, noble man who lets his mind be poisoned by jealousy until in the end he destroys the thing he loves and then wakens from his madness to destroy himself. It is also a study in evil; for the poisoner, Iago, takes a kind of pleasure in what he is doing, and works at his monstrous design with the intent care of an artist from hell.

The play opens in the streets of Venice, at night, where a conversation is taking place between Iago and a foolish gentleman named Roderigo. Iago, a soldier, is making clear his reasons for hating his general so much. The general is a Moor named Othello, and Iago thought he would be chosen as his lieutenant. Instead Othello has given the honor to a comparatively inexperienced soldier named Michael Cassio, and Iago has become merely the general's standard-bearer.

Iago admits frankly that he is staying in the Moor's service only because he is planning revenge. "I follow him to serve my turn upon him." The path that leads to revenge has already opened up in his imagination, for Othello has been secretly married that night to a young and lovely lady of Venice named Desdemona, and Iago is sure that he can somehow "poison his delight." Roderigo is in love with Desdemona and only too glad to do what he can to spoil the marriage, and Iago finds him a willing assistant in his plans.

Their first move is to rouse Desdemona's father by shouting under his window that a black man has stolen his daughter. Since the father is a senator of Venice, Roderigo is hoping that somehow he will be able to undo the marriage. Iago knows better; for Othello is so brilliant a general that the senate needs his help in the Turkish wars and will not dare to punish him.

It is necessary to Iago's plan that he himself should remain in Othello's mind as a loyal and devoted friend, "though I do hate him as I do hell pains." So he slips away into the night, leaving Roderigo to deal with Desdemona's father, who comes out of his house lamenting. His only daughter has run away with a black man, much older than herself, and she must have had some sort of spell laid upon her to make her do anything so unnatural.

He searches for Othello until he finds him in the streets by night and then he storms out his accusation:

O thou foul thief, where has thou stowed my daughter?
Damned as thou art, thou hast enchanted her . . .

Othello explains with perfect courtesy and dignity that he cannot permit himself to be taken to prison since he is on his way to the council hall. The old senator hears for the first time that the duke has called a meeting, and he goes at once to present his case against his daughter's husband.

The duke and his council are disturbed by rumors that the Turkish fleet is planning an attack on the island of Cyprus, and they are discussing a plan to send Othello there to defend it when Desdemona's father accuses him of witchcraft. Othello asks that his wife be sent for, and while the senators are waiting he describes the way he wooed her. He told her stories of his adventures, of being sold into slavery, of traveling over strange deserts and high mountains, and of all the other terrors he had endured.

She loved me for the dangers I had passed,
And I loved her that she did pity them.
This only is the witchcraft I have used. . . .

Desdemona enters, to stand before the council and choose between her father and her husband. She has been carefully reared to make a suitable wife for some Venetian gentleman, but all her gentleness and love have reached out to an equal love and gentleness in Othello, and it does not matter that he is an older man of an alien race. When she is asked to name the man who is her sovereign lord, she does not choose the father to whom she has always given her obedience but the man she married that night. Her father admits defeat, since there is nothing else he can do, and the talk turns to affairs of state.

The duke puts Othello in command of the defense of Cyprus and is willing to give Desdemona permission to accompany him there. But Othello must set sail immediately, and he entrusts his wife to the care of Iago, who will follow after. Othello has the greatest faith in his standard-bearer. "A man he is of honesty and trust."

The senate adjourns and everyone leaves the room except Iago and the dejected Roderigo. Since Desdemona is lost to him, Roderigo is prepared to go out and drown himself, but Iago laughs at him. "Drown thyself? drown cats and blind puppies." He assures Roderigo that so unnatural a marriage, between a "barbarian and a supersubtle Venetian," will never last, and as soon as he is alone he lays his plans to destroy it. Iago wants to destroy Michael Cassio too, the man who supplanted him as lieutenant, and a brilliant plot comes to him. It is based on Othello's trustfulness—"the Moor is of a free and open nature"—and on his affection for Iago.

I have 't; it is engendered. Hell and night
Must bring this monstrous birth to the world's light.

There is a kind of creeping evil about Iago, a slow inching along that never stops until it has succeeded in destroying a most perfect and loving marriage.

The scene shifts to Cyprus, where the governor of the island is anxiously waiting for news from the sea. There is a rumor, which turns out to be true, that the Turkish fleet has been destroyed in a great tempest, but there is fear that Othello's ship may have been destroyed also. A salute of guns heralds the arrival of a vessel from Venice, and Desdemona comes ashore, with Iago and his wife Emilia who is acting as her maid.

All Desdemona's thoughts are fixed on the rough sea that threatens her husband's safety. But she has been trained, as the daughter of a senator, not to show her feelings, and she spends the time exchanging banter with Iago. She draws Cassio into the conversation, since he is one of her husband's closest friends, and Iago watches with glee as Cassio takes her hand. For Iago's plan is to make Othello think that she and Cassio are lovers, and the small natural courtesies that pass between them are all threads that will help him in the weaving of his design.

A flourish of trumpets announces the safe arrival of Othello and he comes ashore to take his wife in his arms.

> *O my soul's joy,*
> *If after every tempest come such calms,*
> *May the winds blow till they have wakened death . . .*

He sends out a proclamation that there is to be feasting and revelry that night in honor of his wedding, and he leaves his lieutenant Cassio in command of the guard to keep order during the festivities.

Iago comes up to Cassio early in the night and suggests in a friendly way that they drink together to Othello's health, for he wants to make Cassio sufficiently drunk so that Roderigo will be able to pick a quarrel with him. Cassio politely turns him down. "Not tonight, good Iago; I have very poor and unhappy brains for drinking." Iago urges him very gently. "What, man, 'tis a night of revels." He implies that any man who refuses a glass or two of wine is clearly no man at all, and finally Cassio gives in.

Cassio is quite correct about his inability to drink. He grows first sentimental, and then religious, and then full of outraged and rather talkative virtue. "Do not think, gentlemen, I am drunk . . . This is my right hand, and this is my left hand. I am not drunk now; I can stand well enough, and speak well enough." They all assure him that he is certainly not drunk and he wanders off, befuddled and pugnacious, to be baited by Roderigo into a blind rage. The former governor of the island tries to stop them from fighting, and Cassio has the ill luck to hurt him with his sword.

Iago manages to create an added effect of clamor and confusion while pretending to try and stop it, and when

Othello arrives he is faced with a "barbarous brawl" which, as far as he can discover, is wholly Cassio's fault.

> *Cassio, I love thee,*
> *But never more be officer of mine.*

Cassio is left disconsolate, and Iago points out that he can get back into Othello's favor if Desdemona will intercede for him. The general loves his wife so much that he can refuse her nothing, and Desdemona herself is always ready to do anyone a kindness. "She is of so free, so kind, so apt, so blessed a disposition, she holds it a vice in her goodness not to do more than she is requested." Cassio resolves to ask Desdemona for help the next morning, and Iago plans to make it appear to Othello that she is pleading for her lover.

> *So will I turn her virtue into pitch,*
> *And out of her own goodness make the net*
> *That shall enmesh them all.*

Early in the morning, Cassio presents himself at the castle and asks to see Desdemona. She agrees immediately to try and persuade her husband to take him back into favor, and as they talk Othello and Iago enter at a distance. Iago, acting the part of a loyal and worried friend, makes a slight gesture of discomfort when he sees the two of them together, and Othello turns to him. "What dost thou say?" "Nothing, my lord, or if—I know not what." "Was not that Cassio parted from my wife?"

> *Cassio, my lord? No, sure, I cannot think it,*
> *That he would steal away so guilty-like,*
> *Seeing you coming.*

This is the first drop of poison, a small dose and delicately administered.

Desdemona comes over to them to plead Cassio's case, for he is a good man and worthy to be reinstated in her husband's favor. She is so fervent in Cassio's defense that Othello finally gives in to her. "I will deny thee nothing."

Iago now has the situation exactly where he wants it, and as soon as Desdemona leaves he inquires in affectionate and troubled tones if Cassio knew her before the marriage. Othello says that he did and in fact acted as a go-between. Iago becomes even more troubled, giving a perfect picture of a reluctant friend hesitating on the brink of a disclosure that the husband has a right to know. Under Othello's prodding, and apparently with the most bitter regret, Iago is brought to the admission that he suspects Cassio and Desdemona of making love to each other. It is only his great love for Othello that makes him reveal such a thing.

> *I am much to blame;*
> *I humbly do beseech you of your pardon*
> *For too much loving you.*

Two things assist Iago in his slow and delicate injection of poison into Othello's mind. The first is that he is an old and valued friend and Othello has always trusted him. The second is that everyone, including Othello, knows that his marriage is a risky one from the worldly point of view. Nothing holds it together but Desdemona's love for him, and there seems to be no reason why she should love a black man, older than herself, when a handsome young gallant like Cassio is available. Before they left Venice, Desdemona's father gave his new son-in-law a warning:

> *Look to her, Moor, if thou hast eyes to see:*
> *She has deceived her father, and may thee.*

And now Iago makes the same point: "She did deceive her father, marrying you." Othello really knows very little about his young wife; he only knows that he loves her with a helpless, hopeless, devouring passion and that Iago's words have filled him with terror.

Desdemona comes in to remind her husband it is time for dinner, and Othello, trying to wrench away from the desperation of his thoughts, tells himself, "I'll not believe it." But he is incapable of behaving in his usual manner and Desdemona is instantly troubled. "Are you not well?" Othello says that he has a pain in his forehead, and she hopefully tries to bind his brow with a small handkerchief she has. He pushes it away, and the handkerchief falls to the floor between them.

It is a silk handkerchief embroidered with strawberries, the first gift he had ever given her, and she used to kiss it and talk to it when he was away. For some time Iago has been trying to persuade his wife Emilia to steal it from her mistress; and when Emilia finds it lying on the floor, forgotten in Desdemona's worry over her husband, she picks it up and gives it to Iago. Iago has a use for it. He plans to drop it somewhere in Cassio's lodging where that innocent young man will be sure to find it.

Othello enters, and Iago looks with pleasure upon his handiwork. Here is a man who will not sleep again, not even with the aid of drugs.

> *Not poppy, nor mandragora,*
> *Nor all the drowsy syrups of the world,*
> *Shall ever medicine thee to that sweet sleep*
> *Which thou ow'dst yesterday.*

It is doubt that tortures Othello the most. If only he had clear proof that Desdemona is faithless, then at least his agony would be a settled thing. But he cannot be sure, and Iago, seeing him waver, begins to fashion a string of outright lies. He describes how he heard Cassio talking in his sleep, re-living a love scene with Desdemona; and little by little Iago builds a monstrous fabrication that thickens and takes shape before Othello's eyes until it is more real than reality itself. "Damn her . . . O, damn her!" Iago swears to give the wronged husband complete and unswerving service, even if it means Cassio's death, and Othello in turn gives him the place he has been angling for. "Now art thou my lieutenant."

Desdemona is still intent on the promise she has made Cassio and sends him a message of good cheer. "Tell him I have moved my lord on his behalf and hope all will be well." What chiefly troubles her at the moment is the loss of her handkerchief, and she is even more worried when Othello asks her to lend it to him. She says she does not have it about her at the moment, and her husband becomes so violent that she is afraid to say she has lost it. She tries to talk of Cassio, but all Othello can do is to shout, "The handkerchief!" knowing it is in Cassio's hands and convinced that she gave it to him. He had said there was witchcraft in his gift and that the woman who lost it would also lose her husband's love, and Desdemona is almost ready to believe it.

Cassio comes to find out how his suit is progressing, and Desdemona is obliged to admit that she is an unsuccessful advocate. She is out of favor with Othello herself and cannot fathom the cause. Since she is a senator's daughter and accustomed to affairs of state, she is inclined to think it is some political problem that is troubling her husband. Emilia, her maid, is a practical realist and thinks that Othello's trouble is jealousy, but Desdemona is sure that is impossible. As she said earlier,

> *My noble Moor*
> *Is true of mind, and made of no such baseness*
> *As jealous creatures are . . .*

Moreover she has never given him any reason to be jealous. Emilia remarks that jealousy is without reason, a monster that breeds out of itself, and Desdemona, increasingly disturbed, utters a prayer. "Heaven keep that monster from Othello's mind!"

The prayer comes too late. The monster is already there, feeding upon itself and flooding with its poison the mind of its tortured host. And at every point Iago is there also, alert, sympathetic and affectionate, to make the pain worse. By a trick he makes Othello think that Cassio is speaking of Desdemona when he is really referring to a woman of the streets, and finally Othello's agony is such that even pity cannot enter in. "My heart is turned to stone; I strike it, and it hurts my hand."

He has at last made up his mind: Desdemona must die. He lets his mind run on her grace and her sweetness and torments himself with the thought of it, but it does not change his purpose. He will strangle her that night in her bed. "But yet the pity of it, Iago! O Iago, the pity of it, Iago!"

A messenger arrives from Venice and is shocked to discover that a breach has developed between Othello and Cassio. Desdemona hopes that the Venetian gentleman will be able to heal it, since she herself can do nothing. He also brings news that Othello is to be recalled to Venice, with Cassio taking over the government of the island, and Desdemona remarks innocently that she is glad to hear it. Othello can bear no more, and he strikes her.

The Venetian messenger is appalled. The thing is unbelievable. As for Desdemona, she can make only one reply to her husband's brutality. "I have not deserved this."

When the Venetian is alone with Iago, he searches for some sort of explanation.

> Is this the noble Moor whom our full senate
> Call all-in-all sufficient? Is this the nature
> Whom passion could not shake? . . .

And Iago, smiling inwardly at the ruin he has made, agrees gravely that something indeed seems to be amiss. "He is much changed."

Othello tries to force an admission from his wife's maid that Desdemona and Cassio are lovers, but Emilia is steadfast in her denials. Then he sends for Desdemona herself and tries to force the same admission from her. He does not use Cassio's name, and Desdemona still clings to the idea that Othello is enmeshed in some political difficulty. Perhaps the recall to Venice has angered him, and he feels that her father had something to do with it.

> If haply you my father do suspect
> An instrument of this your calling back,
> Lay not your blame on me; if you have lost him,
> Why, I have lost him too.

She is so sure of her own innocence that it is a little while before the savage explicitness of Othello's language penetrates her mind and she realizes of what she is being accused. Even then, there is nothing she can do but deny the charge, with all the lack of skill that innocence has, and to deaf ears.

Emilia comes back to find her mistress in a blurred state, half between sleeping and waking. She is like a child who has been beaten into stupefaction, and for a time she cannot collect herself. Then she decides to send Iago to ask her husband to forgive her for whatever it is that has made him angry.

> *O good Iago,*
> *What shall I do to win my lord again?*

Iago assures her that it is some political matter that is troubling Othello and that it will pass. "Go in, and weep not; all things shall be well." Then, when she has left the room, he sends Roderigo off to murder Cassio. Roderigo will do anything to get Desdemona for himself, and he goes obediently.

It is night and Othello sends Desdemona to bed, with instructions that her maid is to leave her. Emilia is reluctant to let her mistress be alone, but Desdemona insists. "We must not now displease him." Before Emilia goes, she lays out on the bed the sheets that were used on the wedding night and then helps her mistress to undress. Desdemona, bewildered and not really awake, cannot think clearly. An old song is running through her head, sung by a maid of her mother's who lost her lover and died.

> *That song tonight*
> *Will not go from my mind; I have much to do*
> *But to go hang my head all at one side*
> *And sing it like poor Barbara.*

She sings the song to herself while her maid undresses her, but what she is waiting for is a sound at the door. "Hark, who is 't that knocks?"

It is only the wind, and Desdemona goes on with the song. She cannot keep herself from thinking about her husband's accusation, although it seems to her impossible that any woman would do such an evil thing. Emilia says wryly that it is quite possible and sometimes justifiable, considering the way most men treat their wives. But Desdemona will not believe it, and she goes to sleep as a child might, with a light left burning beside her.

Out in the streets, Roderigo stands in hiding with his rapier bared, waiting for Cassio to pass. His quick thrust in the dark does not penetrate Cassio's heavy coat, and Iago is obliged to strike. He wounds him in the leg, Cassio falls, and Othello believes him to be dead. Nothing now remains but to perform his own part in the act of vengeance, and he goes back to the castle and to his bedchamber.

Othello stands for a long time by the bed in which his wife lies sleeping, staring down at her and shaken by his love and his anguish. Finally he cannot prevent himself from kissing her, and Desdemona wakens. "Will you come to bed, my lord?" Othello has stretched his tortured spirit to the high pitch of an act that will not scar her body, and he is determined also that he will not hurt her soul. She must have time to say her prayers before he kills her, and he tells her so.

The terrified Desdemona tries to protect herself with what little skill she has and struggles to make him realize that she is innocent. But she speaks to a madman who cannot listen. Then she learns that Cassio is dead and no one is left who can testify in her defense, and she abandons her useless weapons and pleads only for time. "Kill me tomorrow; let me live tonight!"

Othello does not dare wait. He might weaken. He does not even dare give her the time he promised in which to say her prayers. He speaks the final, terrible line, "It is too late," and then he smothers her.

There is a noise outside—Emilia calling from the other side of the door—and Othello presses harder.

> *What noise is this? Not dead? not yet quite dead?*
> *I that am cruel am yet merciful;*
> *I would not have thee linger in thy pain.*
> *So, so.*

He draws the bed curtains to hide what he has done, and Emilia comes in to say that Cassio is not killed but only wounded. There is a faint sound from the bed, and Emilia finds her mistress dying and barely conscious. The frantic maid tries to find out who committed the murder, and Desdemona has just enough strength left to protect her husband. "Nobody, I myself, farewell."

In a fury of grief and rage, Emilia turns on Othello and he admits that he has killed his wife. He tries to explain his reasons and she sweeps them away. Then he tries to threaten her, but no one can frighten Emilia now.

> *Thou hast not half the power to do me harm*
> *As I have to be hurt. O gull, O dolt,*
> *As ignorant as dirt! thou hast done a deed—*
> *I care not for thy sword, I'll make thee known*
> *Though I lost twenty lives.*

Her cries bring the whole company into the room, and then it is her husband Iago who tries to silence her. "Come, hold your peace." She manages to let Othello know who made her steal the handkerchief, and then Iago stops her with a knife thrust. She dies, remembering the last song she heard her mistress sing. "She loved thee, cruel Moor."

Othello's sword has been seized, but there is another hidden in the room. Always before he has felt safe and confident with a weapon in his hand, but now he has lost all sense of direction. "Where should Othello go?" He has no need to wait to go to hell for he is in it now, and even his attempt to kill Iago is a half-hearted one.

> *I'd have thee live;*
> *For in my sense, 'tis happiness to die.*

Othello asks forgiveness of the wronged Cassio, who gives it freely. And then, with a final return to his natural dignity and control, he sends a message to the Venetian state.

> *When you shall these unlucky deeds relate,*
> *Speak of me as I am; nothing extenuate,*
> *Nor set down aught in malice; then must you speak*
> *Of one that loved not wisely but too well;*

Of one not easily jealous, but, being wrought,
Perplexed in the extreme . . .

Let the senators of Venice also be told that once, when a Turk insulted their city, Othello took him by the throat "and smote him, thus." With that he drives a dagger into his own body and falls dying on the bed beside his wife. "I kissed thee ere I killed thee." And so, kissing her for the last time, he dies.

Cassio pronounces the epitaph of the general he loved. "He was great of heart." Since Cassio is the new governor of Cyprus, it is his task to arrange for the punishment of Iago, that "hellish villain," and so the story of *Othello* ends.

MACBETH

MACBETH is one of the greatest of the tragedies, swift as
night and dark as spilt blood, with death and battle and
witchcraft bound together in wonderful poetry to tell the
story of a man and woman who destroyed themselves.
Macbeth and his wife wanted the throne of Scotland, and
they took it. But the act forced them into a murderer's
world of sleepless torment, always struggling to find safety
and always sinking deeper in their own terror.

The story opens in ancient Scotland during a time of
war. The king has been defied by a band of rebels and he
has sent his trusted captains, Macbeth and Banquo, to defeat them. In thunder and lightning, not far from the place
of battle, three witches meet on a lonely heath. They plan
to meet again at twilight, to speak to Macbeth as he returns from the fighting, and then they vanish into the
storm.

> *Fair is foul, and foul is fair.*
> *Hover through the fog and filthy air.*

The king of Scotland waits for news of the battle, and a
sergeant arrives to tell him of Macbeth's valor. The victorious king also hears of the traitorous behavior of one
of his noblemen, the thane of Cawdor, and decides to give
the title to Macbeth instead. Macbeth is already the thane
of Glamis, but this is a higher honor.

The witches gather again to wait for their victim, chat-
tering to each other in quick, slippery rhyme like evil
children. They sing an incantation to wind up the charm,
and when Macbeth enters his first remark is an echo of
one of theirs. "So foul and fair a day I have not seen."

With Macbeth is his fellow captain, Banquo, returning with him to report the details of the battle to the king, and it is Banquo who first sees the witches. But it is to Macbeth that the three of them speak: "All hail, Macbeth! hail to thee, thane of Glamis!" "All hail, Macbeth! hail to thee, thane of Cawdor!" "All hail, Macbeth, that shalt be king hereafter!"

Macbeth is too startled to answer, and it is the steady and honorable Banquo who inquires if there is any more to the prophecy.

If you can look into the seeds of time,
And say which grain will grow and which will not,
Speak then to me . . .

The witches tell Banquo that he will beget kings and then they vanish, leaving Macbeth protesting that it is impossible that he should ever become thane of Cawdor. The king's messenger arrives to announce that the title has been bestowed upon him, and the new thane of Cawdor is suddenly shaken with a vision of the throne. For a moment an image of evil comes to him—"horrible imaginings" of the one way in which he can fulfill the prophecy and become king—and then he puts the whole thing away from him. "If chance will have me king, why, chance may crown me." When he reaches the palace the king treats him with the greatest courtesy and announces he will pay a visit to Macbeth's castle at Inverness, and again Macbeth is shaken by temptation.

The scene moves to Inverness, where Lady Macbeth is reading the letter her husband wrote her after the battle. In cautious words he tells of the promise made by the three witches, and the mind of his wife leaps, as his has done, to the golden crown that lies waiting. But she knows her husband well. She can guess how he has been playing with the idea of murder and then shrinking back again, and she realizes it will be difficult to force him to take the final step that lies between them and the throne of Scotland.

I fear thy nature;
It is too full o' the milk of human kindness
To catch the nearest way. . . .

A messenger arrives to say that the king of Scotland will be coming to the castle that night, and in a magnificent speech Lady Macbeth calls on all the forces of evil that lie in wait for man to help her to be cruel. When her husband enters she is ready for him and begins to hint at the king's death. "He that's coming must be provided for." Macbeth is evasive—"We will speak further"—and his wife tells him to put on a cheerful and welcoming countenance. "Leave all the rest to me."

The king arrives, accompanied by his sons and by the court, and Lady Macbeth bids him welcome with dignity and grace. Her husband is not by her side, and later, during supper, he finds it unendurable to stay in the same room with the king. He goes outside, to struggle with himself and with the thought of murder.

> *If it were done when 'tis done, then 'twere well*
> *It were done quickly . . .*

But Macbeth cannot face the idea of doing it quickly. He cannot face the idea of doing it at all, for the king is his kinsman and his guest and moreover a good man.

> *I have no spur*
> *To prick the sides of my intent, but only*
> *Vaulting ambition, which o'erleaps itself*
> *And falls on the other.*

His wife has seen him leave and follows him out, to tell him the king has asked for him, and Macbeth gives her his final decision. "We will proceed no further in this business."

Lady Macbeth has a ruthless single-mindedness that her husband can never possess, and she will not admit defeat. Instead, she picks up the two sharpest weapons in her armory and uses them without compunction, telling her husband that he is a coward and that he does not love her. Her contempt brings Macbeth back to the point where she last left him, but he has more imagination than she and it

plays fearfully about the future. "If we should fail—" She
interrupts him before he has finished the sentence.

> *We fail!*
> *But screw your courage to the sticking-place,*
> *And we'll not fail . . .*

Lady Macbeth has thought of everything. The king will
sleep soundly after his long journey, and she will make his
guards drunk so that they will sleep too. The king can be
murdered with the daggers of his guards, and when they
are found, drunk and bloody, no one will dare deny that
they have done it. Macbeth is convinced in spite of himself
that the thing is possible and the crown of Scotland really
within his grasp, and they plan the murder for that night.

It is after midnight, but Banquo is too restless to sleep.
In the courtyard, by torchlight, he encounters Macbeth,
as restless as himself, and tries to talk with him about the
three witches. Macbeth puts him off, and Banquo says
good night.

Macbeth is waiting for the signal from his wife, the bell
that will tell him the guards are drunk and asleep, and as he
waits his imagination begins to act upon him and produces
a phantom in the air.

> *Is this a dagger which I see before me,*
> *The handle toward my hand? Come, let me clutch thee.*
> *I have thee not and yet I see thee still. . . .*

There is blood on the dagger, and Macbeth tries to wrench
his mind away from what he knows to be a creation of his
own imagination. "There's no such thing." His thoughts
roam over the evil things of the night, wolves and witchcraft and murder moving like a ghost toward its prey, and
when the bell rings he answers the summons as though
he were himself a thing of the night. "I go, and it is done."

At the foot of the stairs, in the darkness, Lady Macbeth
waits while her husband commits the murder. She has done
her part and now there is nothing left except to listen to the
sounds of the night. Lady Macbeth is not as strong as she

thought she was. She is made of flesh, not iron, and her thoughts begin to get out of control as she remembers the scene she has just left.

> *I laid their daggers ready;*
> *He could not miss them. Had he not resembled*
> *My father as he slept, I had done 't.*

Macbeth comes down to her, the murder completed, and there is the terrible whispering scene between the two of them, first the short, broken sentences of conspiracy and then Macbeth's gathering agony as he looks at his bloody hands. As he crept downstairs, someone stirred in his sleep in one of the rooms and said a little prayer, and Macbeth, listening, had tried to say Amen. He could not, and it troubles him. His wife implores him not to think about it, but he cannot stop himself.

> *But wherefore could I not pronounce Amen?*
> *I had most need of blessing, and Amen*
> *Stuck in my throat.*

His wife tells him they dare not let their minds move in that direction. "It will make us mad." But Macbeth cannot control his own imagination, and the man who saw a "dagger of the mind" has also heard a voice crying through the castle.

> *Methought I heard a voice cry, 'Sleep no more!*
> *Macbeth does murder sleep!'* . . .

Lady Macbeth does not know what her husband means, but the voice that haunts him goes on.

> *Still it cried, 'Sleep no more!' to all the house.*
> *'Glamis hath murdered sleep, and therefore Cawdor*
> *Shall sleep no more; Macbeth shall sleep no more.'*

Macbeth is almost in a state of trance with the horror of what he has done, and his wife tries to jerk him back to a more practical and matter-of-fact state of mind. She tells

him to go and wash his hands and to put the daggers into
the hands of the sleeping guards, but Macbeth shrinks from
going back to the place of so much blood.

> *I am afraid to think what I have done;*
> *Look on 't again I dare not.*

His wife snatches the daggers from him and goes back to
do it herself, leaving Macbeth to stare at his hands.

> *Will all great Neptune's ocean wash this blood*
> *Clean from my hand? No; this my hand will rather*
> *The multitudinous seas incarnadine,*
> *Making the green one red.*

His wife returns, her hands like his, for she has used
the dead king's blood to smear his innocent guards. There
has been a knocking at the south gate but Macbeth is
powerless to move, and his wife gets him off to bed, talking
to him reassuringly.

> *A little water clears us of this deed;*
> *How easy is it, then! . . .*

The castle porter has heard the knocking, but he is
drunk and sleepy and slow to answer. He would rather
amuse himself with the idea of how hard he would work
if he were the porter at the gate of hell. "But this place is
too cold for hell. I'll devil-porter it no further."

The knocking has been done by two noblemen, arriving
early to visit the king, and when Macbeth enters to greet
them he is in full command of himself. One of the noblemen, whose name is Macduff, goes in to see the king and
finds him dead, and the whole castle is thrown into an
uproar. Macbeth quickly kills the two guards before they
can explain the bloody daggers on their pillows, and justi-
fies the deed on the plea that he could not endure to have
such evil murderers alive.

Both he and Lady Macbeth play their parts well, but
the sons of the dead king are not deceived. They know
their own lives are in danger—"There's daggers in men's

smiles"—and they steal away in the night and leave Scotland. The act makes them appear guilty of having planned the murder, and since Macbeth, thane of Cawdor, is next in line to the throne, he is made king.

The scene shifts to the royal palace on the day of a great feast. Among the invited guests is Banquo, the man who knows the new king better than anyone else and has the strongest reason to suspect him of murder. Macbeth inquires carefully where his old friend will be during the day, and Banquo answers that he and his son will go riding, returning just in time for the banquet. Macbeth cannot feel safe on the throne as long as Banquo is alive, and he persuades two lawless men to kill him. His son must die too, for the three witches promised the throne of Scotland to Banquo's descendants, and Macbeth is resolved that this last part of the prophecy must never be fulfilled.

Neither Macbeth nor his wife has been sleeping well, and they are both tortured by "terrible dreams." Macbeth can almost find it in his heart to envy Duncan, the king whom they killed.

> *Better he with the dead,*
> *Whom we, to gain our peace, have sent to peace,*
> *Than on the torture of the mind to lie*
> *In restless ecstasy. Duncan is in his grave;*
> *After life's fitful fever he sleeps well;*
> *Treason has done his worst: nor steel, nor poison,*
> *Malice domestic, foreign levy, nothing*
> *Can touch him further.*

They have managed to convince themselves that if Banquo and his son were dead they would at last find peace, and as night falls the murderers that Macbeth has sent move to their place of ambush.

Banquo and his son leave their horses and walk toward the palace gate, talking of the weather and with the boy carrying the torch. When the murderers attack, Banquo shouts a warning and his son escapes. The cutthroats know they have done only half their task, and one of them goes to report to Macbeth.

Macbeth sees the murderer standing by the door just as

the company is sitting down to the banquet, and he goes over to speak to him. "There's blood upon thy face." For a moment he permits himself the hope that the crime has been a complete success and then learns that the son is still alive and the task only half done. "But Banquo's safe?" Banquo is safe enough, dead in a ditch with twenty deep gashes in his head, and Macbeth turns back to the feast. Banquo, at least, will trouble him no more.

He looks for the empty seat that should be waiting at the table, but it seems to be taken. "The table's full." He stares at his empty seat, and the ghost of the murdered Banquo stares back at him, with blood in its hair.

Before his bewildered guests, Macbeth speaks to the man he killed. "Thou canst not say I did it." His wife reminds him in a fierce whisper of the dagger he once saw, which he also thought to be real. But nothing can unfix her husband's desperate attention until the ghost vanishes, and even then he cannot shake his thoughts loose again.

> *The times have been,*
> *That, when the brains were out, the man would die,*
> *And there an end; but now they rise again . . .*

His wife reminds him of his guests and Macbeth at last recollects himself. For he is a host, and a good one.

> *Give me some wine, fill full.*
> *I drink to the general joy o' the whole table,*
> *And to our dear friend Banquo, whom we miss . . .*

He should not have spoken Banquo's name. The corpse returns again that should be safe in a ditch, and the bloody image drives Macbeth half-crazed with fear. He is a notable warrior and can fight anything that is alive, but he cannot war with shadows. The ghost vanishes again but the feast is ruined, and Lady Macbeth gets rid of the guests as quickly as she can.

Macbeth thought he could get what he wanted by murder, and now he has found that no amount of killing can keep him safe. His wife returns to find him in the grip of

a terrible truth. "It will have blood, they say; blood will
have blood." But almost at once he forgets it, for he is a
practical man and must consider the problem of Macduff.
Macduff has refused to come at his bidding, and from the
spies he has planted in that nobleman's house Macbeth
knows there is danger from him. At once, and seeing it
as the obvious solution, the murderer's thoughts go back to
murder again. As for the ghost he thought he saw that
evening, the whole thing can surely be explained by lack
of sleep. When he and his wife are a little more accustomed
to killing, things will go more smoothly and easily for them.

Macbeth decides to consult the three witches again, since
they were the ones that started him on his course. Hecate,
moon goddess and goddess of ghosts, prepares a special
answer for the new king which will destroy Macbeth
through hope. For, as she tells the three witches,

> *You all know security*
> *Is mortals' chiefest enemy. . . .*

The witches prepare a special brew for their boiling cauldron, pouring into it things of poison and evil and torment
that turn it into a "hell-broth" while they sing incantations
around it.

> *Double, double, toil and trouble;*
> *Fire burn and cauldron bubble.*

Macbeth enters and the witches agree to show him the
future. There is a sound of thunder and three apparitions
rise up from the cauldron. The first tells him to beware of
Macduff, the second says that Macbeth will never be harmed
by anyone born of woman, and the third assures him
that he will not be conquered until Birnam wood comes
to the hill of Dunsinane. To Macbeth all this spells security, but he cannot keep himself from asking one thing
more. He cannot forget the earlier promise made to Banquo, that his descendants should rule Scotland, and he
must know if it is still true. The witches show him a vision
of a long line of kings, with a bloody Banquo smiling as

he exhibits them, and Macbeth gives way to furious rage at the witches who have betrayed him.

> *Infected be the air whereon they ride,*
> *And damned all those that trust them!* ...

Macbeth learns that Macduff has gone to England to ask for help from the dead king's elder son, and in revenge he sends murderers to the nobleman's castle to slaughter his wife and children. A messenger comes to warn of danger, but Lady Macduff does not know what to do. "Whither should I fly?" There is no time in any case, for the murderers are already in the castle, and she and her brave little son are killed by them.

Macduff, in England, finds that the king's elder son is unwilling to trust anyone in Scotland; for Macbeth, who was once "thought honest," became a traitor and the rest may too. But finally, after a long conversation, the two men convince each other of their good faith, and then the news comes to Macduff that his family has been murdered. The prince talks of revenge, but the anguished father sees no adequate way he can revenge himself on Macbeth. "He has no children." Only one hope is left him for the future: to go back to Scotland and find the murderer at the other end of his sword.

Macbeth goes out to gather the soldiers together, leaving his wife alone in the castle. As long as they were together they could derive strength from each other, but now that Lady Macbeth is alone she feels the powers of darkness closing in. She can control herself by daylight, for her will is very strong, but she is helpless at night. She keeps a light beside her always, to ward off the dark; but she cannot escape from her dreams and lately she has begun to walk in her sleep. Her disturbed waiting-woman has called in the doctor, and the two of them are watching together in case Lady Macbeth walks that night.

This is the famous sleepwalking scene, one of the most brilliant pieces of writing in the history of dramatic literature. For Lady Macbeth is re-living the murder of the king, the thing she has tried so hard to push into the back of her mind and forget. Her mind is choking and drowning in blood, and all the advice she whispered to her husband that night, all her dreams of power and safety, are blurred by the persistent image of what the two of them did. "Who would have thought the old man to have had so much blood in him?"

All this while, she has been moving her hands against each other, over and over again, trying to wash them. The woman who once thought that "a little water" could do away with all the evidence of murder now rubs endlessly at the spots she thinks are there, murmuring to herself, talking of Banquo, of the king, of Macduff's wife, all dead and all coming back to her in the broken, wavering images of sleep. Then she slides back in her memory to the knocking at the gate and reaches out to a husband who is no longer beside her. "Give me your hand. What's done cannot be undone." She goes back to bed, and the horrified doctor says that she has more need of a priest than of a physician. "God, God forgive us all!" And indeed Lady Macbeth has great need of forgiveness.

The English and Scottish soldiers, led by the dead king's elder son, march toward Dunsinane, and Macbeth within the castle listens to the reports of their advance. His own men are deserting him, and Macbeth curses the cowards by whom he is surrounded. He buckles on his armor before he needs it, but there is no real security in anything. Even the doctor who has come to cure his wife can do nothing, and Macbeth asks him a question out of his own desperate need.

> Canst thou not minister to a mind diseased,
> Pluck from the memory a rooted sorrow,
> Raze out the written troubles of the brain,
> And with some sweet oblivious antidote
> Cleanse the stuffed bosom of that perilous stuff
> Which weighs upon the heart?

The doctor admits that he cannot, and the weight upon the murderer's heart continues.

Outside, in the country near Birnam wood, the invading force pauses and the prince sends out an order. Each soldier is to cut down a green bough and carry it in front of him, so that no one can tell how many men there are, and in that formation they advance upon the castle of Dunsinane.

Within the castle Macbeth waits. He is sure the thick walls can withstand a siege and that famine and sickness will destroy his enemies before they can destroy him. Yet one enemy has already made an entrance, for the wailing of the women tells him that his wife is dead. It seems to Macbeth that there is very little sense to human living.

> *Tomorrow, and tomorrow, and tomorrow,*
> *Creeps in this petty pace from day to day,*
> *To the last syllable of recorded time;*
> *And all our yesterdays have lighted fools*
> *The way to dusty death. Out, out, brief candle!*
> *Life's but a walking shadow, a poor player*
> *That struts and frets his hour upon the stage,*
> *And then is heard no more. It is a tale*
> *Told by an idiot, full of sound and fury,*
> *Signifying nothing.*

A messenger comes with the news that Macbeth never thought to hear, that Birnam wood is moving toward Dunsinane. The prophecy of the three witches is coming true, and for a moment Macbeth almost does not care. "I 'gin to be aweary of the sun." But at least he can die like a soldier, and perhaps he will not die after all. For the witches made him another prophecy: that no man born of woman could ever harm Macbeth.

His soldiers refuse to follow him and they give up the castle to the invaders, but Macbeth, shouting defiance, fights on alone. He hesitates when he sees Macduff, for enough of that family has been slaughtered already, but Macduff's sword is out and they fight. Macbeth exults in the fact that he is untouchable, and Macduff reveals that he was not "of woman born" but ripped from the womb. Macbeth realizes in despair that the witches have mocked him and that there is no hope left. But he goes on fighting, and he dies like a warrior if he could not live like a man.

The young prince becomes the new king of Scotland and announces the end of "this dead butcher and his fiend-like queen." But Macbeth and his wife were more than that. They were violent human beings who took a wrong turning, for Shakespeare could make even murderers real. Their deaths were not a tragedy but their lives were, and, with their passing, peace came again to Scotland.

KING LEAR

KING LEAR is the most titanic of the tragedies, a huge, shattering almost superhuman play whose very shapelessness is part of its strength. It is a story of poison and insanity and murder, of the sins that are committed through lust of possession and of the cruelties that the young are willing to inflict upon the old. It wrenches apart the normal world to show its terrible underside, and yet it is not a story of despair for there is no weakness in it. It is as unreasoning as a storm, but with all a storm's strength and magnificence, and if Shakespeare had written nothing but *King Lear* he would still rank as one of the world's greatest playwrights.

The story takes place in ancient Britain and opens in the palace of King Lear. Lear is an old man now and he has decided to give up his kingdom and divide it among his three daughters. His eldest daughter, Goneril, is the wife of the duke of Albany; his second, Regan, is the wife of the duke of Cornwall; and his youngest, Cordelia, is being wooed by a French duke and the king of France. Lear has not yet decided which of Cordelia's two suitors he approves, but there is no question about his feeling for Cordelia herself. She is his "joy" and he loves her best of his three daughters.

King Lear is a very old man and to the willfulness of age has been added the unchecked self-indulgence of a rich and powerful king. He is accustomed to adulation and to getting his own way in everything, and instead of dividing the kingdom in an orderly fashion he decides to make the act an open test of his daughters' love for him. Whichever loves him the most will be given the most land.

The eldest, Goneril, protests her undying devotion and is given a third of the kingdom. The second, Regan, does

181

the same and gets another third, but the youngest, Cordelia, is checked by a stubborn honesty. She does not love her father to the exclusion of everything else in the world. She loves him dearly, as a daughter should, but she will not wallow in superlatives for all the land in Britain. She knows quite well why her sisters spoke as they did, but she will not open her mouth in an easy lie that will bring her land and power.

King Lear reacts like a spoiled child whose toy has been snatched away just as he was going to show his possession of it. He divides the rest of the land between Goneril and Regan, and in an open fury casts his youngest daughter from him. "Hence, and avoid my sight!"

Lear has a good and loyal subject, the earl of Kent, and Kent is moved to protest. He is so shocked by Lear's behavior that he does not speak to him in the words that should be used to royalty but as one human being to another. "What wouldst thou do, old man?" He calls the king both blind and mad to treat Cordelia so, and out of the furious depths of his rage Lear banishes Kent from the kingdom.

The French duke who has been wooing Cordelia refuses to marry her now that she is landless and forsaken, but the king of France accepts her gladly as his bride. They leave together for France, and Cordelia tearfully commits her old father to the care of her two sisters. The arrangement is that he will live one month with one daughter and then one month with the other, accompanied by the hundred knights that make up his retinue, and both Goneril and Regan are displeased with the plan. They discuss the matter with each other, using words like "unruly waywardness" and "infirm and choleric" that they would not have dared use before. But the kingdom is theirs now, and they have less need for caution.

Another father falls victim to his own haste and lack of judgment. It is a good friend of Lear's, the old earl of Gloucester, who has two sons. The illegitimate son, Edmund, has cast a covetous eye on his father's lands but he cannot inherit them as long as the legitimate son, Edgar, is alive. So he forges his brother's handwriting on a paper that plots against their father's life. Gloucester believes it, for he has always loved Edmund dearly, and the vicious Edmund warns his innocent brother to go armed.

Since Goneril is his eldest daughter, Lear pays his first visit to her and his presence angers her from the start. She is a harsh, impatient woman and she cannot endure the fact that her father behaves as though he were still the king.

> *Idle old man,*
> *That still would manage those authorities*
> *That he hath given away! Now, by my life,*
> *Old fools are babes again . . .*

Lear returns from hunting, and in his daughter's absence orders his dinner with all the assurance of a man accustomed to instant obedience.

While Lear is waiting for it he acquires a new servant. It is the banished earl of Kent who has returned in disguise so that he can watch over his beloved master. He promptly shows his worth by tripping up Goneril's insolent steward and calling him a "base football player," and King Lear is delighted with his new servant. The only kind of insolence he will tolerate is the affectionate fooling of his own jester, and the jester can tell him truths that he will listen to from no one else. "Thou hadst little wit in thy bald crown when thou gavest thy golden one away."

Goneril comes in frowning, to lecture her father on his behavior. She also wishes him to reduce his household to fifty knights, and while she suggests it respectfully enough, her purpose, as Lear's fool says, is clear. She wants to "make an obedient father." King Lear, old, magnificent, lively and the least obedient man on earth, flies into one of his sudden rages.

> *Darkness and devils!*
> *Saddle my horses, call my train together.*
> *Degenerate bastard, I'll not trouble thee;*
> *Yet have I left a daughter.*

He plans to go instantly to Regan, his second daughter, who will surely take him in. Goneril's husband, the duke of

Albany, is a gentle man, and he tries to make peace between his wife and his father-in-law. But Lear storms off with his followers, leaving Goneril to point out to her husband how rational her behavior has been.

Lear is trying to behave in a rational manner also, but with little success. "O, let me not be mad, not mad, sweet heaven. Keep me in temper; I would not be mad." He sends his servant, the disguised Kent, ahead of him with a letter to Regan and her husband, the duke of Cornwall, and at the same time Goneril sends her steward with a letter to Regan.

Gloucester's illegitimate son, Edmund, learns that Regan is planning to visit his father's castle, and he uses the news as part of his plot to destroy his brother Edgar. He convinces his father that Edgar intends murder, and the young man escapes into the night just as Regan and her husband arrive at the castle. Regan attempts to put the blame for Edgar's unfilial behavior on Lear's knights, who must have corrupted him; for she, like her sister, is determined to get rid of her father's retinue and the last remnants of his power.

The disguised Kent arrives at the castle at the same moment as Goneril's steward and promptly recognizes him as the man he tripped up in Goneril's palace. He attacks him again with wholehearted zest and is put in the stocks by Regan and her husband. Their host, the earl of Gloucester, protests that Lear's messenger should not be treated in such a fashion, but Kent is philosophical about his enforced stay. "Some time I shall sleep out, the rest I'll whistle."

Lear arrives to find his servant in the stocks and cannot believe that Regan and her husband could have done such a thing. "They could not, would not do 't; 'tis worse than murder." He demands to see them both, and they send back a message that they are weary from their travels. Lear says they must see him,

> Or at their chamber-door I'll beat the drum
> Till it cry sleep to death.

His sardonic fool encourages him in his own fashion. "Cry to it, nuncle, as the cockney did to the eels when she put 'em i' the paste alive; she rapped 'em o' the coxcombs and cried, 'Down, wantons, down!' 'Twas her brother that, in pure kindness to his horse, buttered his hay."

The duke and duchess of Cornwall finally consent to see Lear, and he starts to explain to his "beloved Regan" how badly he has been treated by her sister. Regan remarks coldly that she is sure her sister behaved correctly, and she adds that Lear is an old man who should let himself be guided by others. She suggests that her father should apologize to Goneril, and Lear inquires bitterly if this is the speech he should deliver:

> 'Dear daughter, I confess that I am old;
> Age is unnecessary; on my knees I beg
> That you'll vouchsafe me raiment, bed and food.'

He is still sure that Regan will be kind to him; and even when Goneril arrives and Regan takes her part against him, he struggles to be patient and adjust himself.

> I can be patient, I can stay with Regan,
> I and my hundred knights.

But Regan will not have him on those terms. She is sure that he does not need a hundred knights; twenty-five should be sufficient. In fact, it is doubtful if he really needs any attendants at all.

Lear cries aloud for patience. What he ought to feel is fear, but what actually possesses him is rage.

> You unnatural hags,
> I will have such revenges on you both
> That all the world shall—I will do such things,—
> What they are yet I know not, but they shall be
> The terrors of the earth. You think I'll weep;
> No, I'll not weep. I have full cause of weeping,
> But this heart shall break . . .
> Or ere I'll weep. O fool! I shall go mad.

The king and his fool go out into the stormy night, leaving Goneril and Regan to justify their conduct to each other.

The house is not large enough to entertain their father properly, and if he is foolish enough to go out into the storm he has only himself to thank. The earl of Gloucester, their host, is deeply troubled, but Regan's husband tells him to leave the whole matter alone. "Shut up your doors, my lord, 'tis a wild night."

It is a night of wind and darkness and rain, and not even the wolves are abroad. But King Lear rages through it, the storm within him more violent than the storm without, and he shouts back at the tempest with a fierceness to match its own.

> Blow, winds, and crack your cheeks! rage! blow!
> You cataracts and hurricanoes, spout
> Till you have drenched our steeples, drowned the cocks!
> You sulphurous and thought-executing fires,
> Vaunt-couriers to oak-cleaving thunderbolts,
> Singe my white head! . . .

The faithful fool has no rage to carry him through the storm, and his plaintive prose breaks in on Lear's violent and magnificent poetry. "Good nuncle, in, and ask thy daughters' blessing; here's a night pities neither wise man nor fool."

The king pays no attention to him. He is obsessed by his own agony and he shouts back at the storm with a thunder to match its own.

> Rumble thy bellyful! Spit, fire! spout, rain!
> Nor rain, wind, thunder, fire are my daughters:
> I tax not you, you elements, with unkindness;
> I never gave you kingdom, called you children . . .

Kent finds his master raging through the night and tries to persuade him to take refuge in a little hut where he can keep warm in the straw. Lear hears him pleading, and it penetrates his mind that his fool is shivering. "How dost, my boy? art cold? I am cold myself." When he reaches the hut, however, he refuses to go in, for the storm is his refuge.

This tempest will not give me leave to ponder
On things would hurt me more. . . .

Lear does not think of those things. "That way madness lies." Still, he decides to enter the hut, gently letting the fool go ahead of him, and his thoughts turn to the helpless poor, who have to endure such storms as this because they have no money to pay for shelter. He had never thought about such matters as long as he was king, safe and sheltered and warm, but now he knows the pain of the poor and wishes he had known it earlier.

The fool comes running out of the hut to say there is "a spirit" inside. It is Edgar, the son of the earl of Gloucester, who cannot escape abroad because all the ports are guarded. He has disguised himself in the filthy rags of a "Tom of Bedlam," one of the lunatics who roamed through the villages of England, pursued by the devils in their own minds and begging for bread. Edgar comes out of the hut whining the madman's prayer. "Who gives any thing to poor Tom? whom the foul fiend hath led through fire and through flame, through ford and whirlpool, o'er bog and quagmire . . . Do poor Tom some charity, whom the foul fiend vexes."

Lear stares at him. "Have his daughters brought him to this pass? Couldst thou save nothing? Didst thou give them all?" He is kin to the madman now that his own wits are leaving him, and he tries to tear off his fine clothes to match Tom of Bedlam's rags. For the garments of man cover what is really only a "poor, bare, forked animal," and Lear has no more use for his clothes than he has for the comfortable illusions that have been sheltering his mind. He inhabits now the loneliness and the wild realism of insanity.

The earl of Gloucester enters with a torch. He has been told by his evil guests, Regan and her husband, not to look for Lear, but he cannot leave him helpless in the storm. He knows a farmhouse where Lear can go for shelter, but the king will not leave without his new friend, the Tom of Bedlam, and to quiet him they let Edgar follow. Kent is profoundly grateful to Gloucester for his help, but Lear is wandering in a world of his own, haunted by his daughters. In his mind they are on trial in a formal court of law, and the tattered madman is a "robed man of justice" with the fool his fellow judge. Kent may join the commission if he wishes, and the stool in the corner of the farmhouse is clearly Goneril. Then Lear thinks he hears the dogs at the gate, his own dogs, barking at him, and the madman offers to protect him. "Tom will throw his head at them. Avaunt, you curs!" Lear's mind slips to Regan, and he feels the doctors should dissect her to find out "what breeds about her heart" and makes it so hard. Kent implores him to lie down and rest, and Lear agrees at once. "Make no noise, make no noise; draw the curtains; so, so, so. We'll go to supper i' the morning."

Gloucester tells Kent that the king must be taken away at once, for Regan is plotting against his life, and the only safety lies in getting him to Dover. This is the seaport that leads to France, and the French army, led by Cordelia's husband, will land there to win the old king back his throne. Kent and the fool take Lear away but Edgar, the disguised madman, stays behind. His own misfortunes seem to him "light and portable" compared to the king's.

Edgar's father, the earl of Gloucester, returns to his castle, but the news that he has helped Lear to escape arrives there before him. Regan and her husband have the old earl bound to a chair and try to force him to tell everything he knows about the king's escape and the French invasion. They gouge out one of his eyes, and a servant of Regan's husband is so horrified by what his master is doing that he attacks him. He manages to injure him and then is killed by Regan, who runs him through with a sword. Then Gloucester's other eye is put out, and he cries aloud for his loved son, Edmund, to help him. He is told it was Edmund who betrayed him, and then the triumphant Regan orders her servants to turn the blinded earl from the castle.

> Go thrust him out at gates, and let him smell
> His way to Dover. . . .

An old man leads him the first part of the way, and then Gloucester asks to be left alone. The old man protests that he will not be able to see his way, and the earl replies,

I have no way, and therefore want no eyes;
I stumbled when I saw. . . .

He feels there is nothing left but suicide and he plans to go
to Dover and throw himself over the high cliff that plunges
down to the sea. He asks Tom of Bedlam to lead him
there, not knowing that the disguised madman is really his
son. Edgar can hardly endure to go on playing his part
once he sees his blinded father, and yet he knows that he
must for a little while.

The news of the French invasion has reached Goneril,
but she has difficulty in persuading her gentle husband, the
duke of Albany, to arm. She hates him for what she calls
his cowardice, and he hates her for what he knows is her
cruelty. Goneril's idea of a desirable man is Edmund, who
is the new earl of Gloucester now that his father has been
dispossessed and blinded and his brother has disappeared.
Goneril wants Edmund for her lover, but when she hears
that Regan is now a widow she fears that her sister will
want him too.

At Dover, the French king finds himself called back to
France and leaves a marshal in charge of the troops he has
brought to Britain at his wife's request. All Cordelia's
thoughts are for her father, who wanders through the high
grass in the fields around the town, with nettles and hem-
lock in his white hair. The doctor can suggest nothing that
will help his crazed mind except rest, and Lear cannot rest.

The blinded earl of Gloucester and his son arrive in
Dover, and Edgar pretends to lead his father to the top of
the cliff. In lines so vivid that they are almost dazzling in
their realism, Edgar describes the sheer drop of the cliff
on which he says they are standing and the little figures far
below. Gloucester throws himself forward, expecting to be
killed, and Edgar pretends to be a passer-by who has picked
him up at the foot of the cliff. Gloucester is convinced
his life was saved by a miracle, and he is willing to shoulder the burden of staying alive since it has been forced
upon him.

Lear comes wandering by and mistakes Gloucester for
Goneril. But his mind is chiefly on the days of his king-

ship and the lies his subjects told him to make him think he was not a mortal man. "When the rain came to wet me once, and the wind to make me chatter, when the thunder would not peace at my bidding, there I found 'em, there I smelt 'em out. Go to, they are not men of their words; they told me I was every thing; 'tis a lie, I am not ague-proof."

Lear is mad, but like the blinded Gloucester, he knows more than he once did. He knows now on what a frail and reasonless basis the world punishes, and how little right those in authority have to be the punishers. If the criminal and the judge should change places, no one would know which was which. "Handy-dandy, which is the justice, which is the thief?" All the outward show on which Lear has built his life has gone, and in its place there comes a queer, wild wisdom. "A man may see how this world goes with no eyes."

The king's attendants take him away, talking to him soothingly, and the earl of Gloucester and his son Edgar are left alone. Goneril's steward comes stealing up, to get credit with his mistress by murdering the old earl, and Edgar kills him in defending his father. In the steward's pocket he finds a letter that Goneril had written to Edmund, suggesting that her dear Edmund kill her husband and take her as his wife; and Edgar saves the letter so that he can show it later to Goneril's intended victim.

Within a tent in the French camp, Lear has at last fallen asleep and his daughter Cordelia waits until the doctor says it is safe to waken him. With a prayer for his recovery she kisses her father, and the old man opens his eyes. He does not know her at first, but the doctor is reassuring. "He's scarce awake; let him alone awhile." Lear can perceive it is daylight and he has a vague stirring toward sanity.

> *I am a very foolish, fond old man,*
> *Fourscore and upward; not an hour more nor less;*
> *And, to deal plainly,*
> *I fear I am not in my perfect mind.*
> *Methinks I should know you and know this man;*
> *Yet I am doubtful . . .*

His eary mind gropes a little further and then he recognizes his daughter, who is weeping.

> *Be your tears wet? yes, faith. I pray, weep not;*
> *If you have poison for me, I will drink it.*
> *I know you do not love me, for your sisters*
> *Have, as I do remember, done me wrong:*
> *You have some cause; they have not.*

"No cause, no cause," says Cordelia, who has never ceased to love him, and she persuades her father to walk from the room. He goes with her as trustingly as a child. "Pray you now, forget and forgive: I am old and foolish."

The day of battle arrives, and the French forces are defeated. Cordelia and Lear are taken prisoner, and the triumphant Edmund has them sent away under guard. Goneril's husband, the gentle duke of Albany, is head of the army and he intends to use them kindly, but Edmund has no intention that he shall. Cordelia is afraid of prison only for her father's sake, and Lear does not fear it at all. He will be with his darling, and they will both be safe from the rise and fall of fortunes at the court. They will be able to take upon themselves

> *the mystery of things,*
> *As if we were God's spies; and we'll wear out,*
> *In a walled prison, packs and sects of great ones*
> *That ebb and flow by the moon.*

Edmund tells the duke of Albany what he has done with the prisoners, and the duke is displeased by his arrogance. Regan enters the argument on Edmund's side, announcing she intends to have him as her husband, but Goneril knows that her sister is dying for she has given her poison. The evil Edmund is proclaimed a traitor, on the evidence in the letter which Edgar has delivered to the duke, and then Edgar appears in full armor and vanquishes him in a duel.

As Edmund lies dying, the bodies of Goneril and Regan are brought in; and Edmund derives a kind of twisted satisfaction from the fact that they both died for love of him.

Edmund was beloved:
The one the other poisoned for my sake,
And after slew herself.

This curious twilight comfort brings remorse, and Edmund remembers the order he has given to have Cordelia hanged in prison. The duke sends Edgar to have the order changed but he is too late; Lear comes in with the dead body of his daughter in his arms.

The old king has always been a fighter, and in his final agony he fights still. He denies his own tragic words— "She's gone forever"—and struggles to believe that she still lives. There is a final flash of his old warrior spirit before the darkness begins to close in, and then his clouded mind and burdened heart weaken under the weight that has been laid upon them. He apologizes pitifully for his bad eyesight when he finds that he cannot recognize the people who have gathered round him. He tries to be courteous as a king should, but he cannot understand what they say. The girl in his arms is all he can understand, and her death drags from him a final cry of pain.

No, no, no life?
Why should a dog, a horse, a rat, have life,
And thou no breath at all? Thou'lt come no more,
Never, never, never, never, never!

Lear's heart breaks and he dies. The people assembled there know that death has come as a kindness to him for he could endure no more, and the pitying duke of Albany speaks the final words as the tragedy ends.

TIMON OF ATHENS

SHAKESPEARE found the story of Timon of Athens in the same book in which he found the account of Mark Antony's funeral oration over Caesar and his later love for Cleopatra of Egypt. Shakespeare turned both of these into masterpieces, and perhaps for a time he saw equal possibilities in the story of Timon. But the anecdote of a man's hatred for his fellow men was not real enough or human enough to interest Shakespeare for long. The play is less a play than a parable, and the characters are types rather than human beings. *Timon of Athens* is a little like the painted wall hangings that were so popular in Shakespeare's day, when worthies from the past were shown in characteristic attitudes and stood for moral positions. In this case the subject is ingratitude, and while it is handled with force and vigor there is no sense of any permanent human reality about it.

The story opens when Timon, a wealthy citizen of Athens, is at the height of his prosperity and is lavishing gifts and gold on all his friends. A poet dedicates his work to him, a painter does his portrait, and a jeweler comes with a precious stone. The senators of Athens flock to Timon also in a "great flood of visitors," and as he enters to the sound of trumpets his suitors press about him with special favors to ask. Timon grants them all, for he has a loving and considerate nature and gets real pleasure out of doing good.

The only Athenian who will accept nothing from Timon and who eyes him with a kind of sardonic pity is a cynic named Apemantus. In his opinion the fawning Athenians are nothing but knaves.

The strain of man's bred out
Into baboon and monkey.

193

When Timon asks him where he is going, Apemantus says that he plans "to knock out an honest Athenian's brains," and when Timon says that he will be executed for it, Apemantus disagrees, for the law will not execute a man for doing nothing.

Timon gives a great banquet and only Apemantus refuses to take part in it. "I scorn thy meat, 'twould choke me; for I should ne'er flatter thee. O you gods, what a number of men eat Timon, and he sees 'em not! It grieves me to see so many dip their meat in one man's blood . . ." Equally troubled is Timon's steward, who loves his master and who knows that the fortune he is giving away so lavishly will not last much longer. The steward has warned Timon about his money just as Apemantus has warned him about his false friends, but Timon will not listen to either of them. He has a happy, confident nature and he refuses to look for evil anywhere.

The creditors begin to gather, demanding the money that Timon owes them, and Timon's steward is finally able to convince his master that he is deeply in debt. He tells Timon how worried he has been,

When all our offices have been oppressed
With riotous feeders, when our vaults have wept
With drunken spilth of wine, when every room
Hath blazed with lights and brayed with minstrelsy . . .

The steward is convinced that Timon's friends are summer flies who will disappear with the first storm, but Timon is sure they do not love him only for his wealth. He sends messengers to all the Athenians to whom he has been kind, asking them to lend him some money.

He sends one of his servants to his friend Lucullus, "nothing doubting" his willingness, and Lucullus is highly amused. "La, la, la, la! 'nothing doubting,' says he?" It seems to Lucullus that Timon has a fundamental flaw in his nature. "Every man has his fault, and honesty is his." Another friend is more tactful in his refusal but his answer is the same, and none of Timon's disturbed and sympathetic servants can find an Athenian who will lend money to him.

Timon's creditors press him more violently, wringing from him the cry: "Creditors? devils!" He decides to give one final banquet to his false friends. "I'll once more feast the rascals." The Athenians come flocking, having decided that Timon was only testing them and must be rich after all, and they hungrily eye the covered dishes that are set out so lavishly before them.

Before the dinner starts, Timon gives a bitterly ironic prayer of thanks to the gods and then he shouts to the assembled guests, "Uncover, dogs, and lap." The covered dishes are filled with nothing but lukewarm water which Timon hurls in their faces, following it with the dishes themselves and an hysterical flood of invective.

> *Live loathed, and long,*
> *Most smiling, smooth, detested parasites . . .*
> *You fools of fortune, trencher-friends, time's flies,*
> *Cap-and-knee slaves, vapours and minute-jacks! . . .*
> *Burn, house! sink, Athens!'henceforth hated be*
> *Of Timon man and all humanity!*

The guests scramble for the hats and gowns that their host has torn from them in his fury and hasten as quickly as they can out of the house of that once-happy man. "Lord Timon's mad."

Timon is indeed mad, with a rage that eats into his heart and dissolves the loving kindness he once possessed in the bitter acid of hate. He does not hate his false friends only. He hates the whole of Athens, and through it the whole world. He utters a savage curse against the city and leaves it forever, to live in the woods among the beasts of prey. But his servants love him still, that "poor honest lord, brought low by his own heart," and his steward in particular is resolved to take care of him.

Timon, digging for roots by his cave near the sea, finds gold instead and in savage glee offers it to a captain who is marching to conquer Athens. The captain is himself an Athenian, thrown out of the city by the ingratitude of the senators, and he is as eager to destroy the city as Timon is to have him do it.

Sick with rage and seeing the whole world as diseased as

his own fortune, Timon tries to ease his heart of its weight of loathing in a flood of magnificent, tortured rhetoric. Apemantus comes to visit him, and Timon looks at that professional man-hater with a kind of bewilderment.

> *Why shouldst thou hate men?*
> *They never flattered thee.* . . .

The news spreads that Timon has found gold and is giving it away, and two thieves come to steal it from him. Timon welcomes them, for now he sees all men as thieves. For a brief moment he is touched by the faithfulness of his old steward—

> *You perpetual-sober gods! I do proclaim*
> *One honest man* . . .

but his final advice to his anxious servant is still on the same bitter theme he has learned so well. "Hate all, curse all, show charity to none."

Now that Timon has gold again, his former suitors rush out to the cave to do him honor and the senators of Athens ask his help against the captain who is besieging them. Timon says he will do his countrymen one kindness: there is a tree near his cave which he is planning to cut down, but before it is felled anyone who wishes may come out from Athens and hang himself on it.

The senators have nothing left to do except to abase themselves before the besieging captain. They appeal to his sense of justice, and he promises to destroy only the guilty. Then the news comes that Timon has died in his cave and written a final epitaph, carrying with him to his grave his unrelenting contempt for the human race. Shakespeare found the text of the rhymed epitaph in the old story and gives it as he found it, but he characteristically ends the play with Timon's "faults forgiven" and peace in the city of Athens.

ANTONY AND CLEOPATRA

ANTONY AND CLEOPATRA tells the story of rulers so mighty that they divided the world among them and of a love so gigantic and so tempestuous that it dragged armies and navies after it like toys. It is one of the most magnificent of the tragedies, a glittering, golden piece of work whose people and whose poetry are worthy of the theme, and it is dominated by that most enchanting and outrageous of women, Cleopatra, queen of Egypt.

The story opens in a room in Cleopatra's palace in the city of Alexandria. The great Roman general, Mark Antony, is in Alexandria, helplessly in love with the queen and ignoring all messages from Rome. Since the death of Julius Caesar, Mark Antony is one of the three men who rule the Roman empire among them. He is the strongest and most experienced of the three and is needed at home. Moreover, Antony is married, and there is everything to draw him away from Egypt. But Cleopatra is in Egypt and so he remains.

Two of his friends are discussing the matter when Antony and Cleopatra enter followed by their trains. Cleopatra has been teasing Antony, suggesting that he does not really love her, and when messengers from Rome are announced she redoubles the attack. No doubt Antony's wife has sent him some message of reproof, or perhaps young Octavius Caesar, his fellow ruler in Rome, has sent strict orders that must be obeyed. The natural result is that Antony refuses to hear the messengers from Rome and bends his energies to placating the ruffled queen of Egypt. They leave the room together, planning what they will do that night to amuse themselves, and the messengers wait unheeded.

In another room in the palace, Cleopatra's attendants

197

are listening to a fortuneteller when the queen enters, looking for Antony.

> *He was disposed to mirth; but on the sudden*
> *A Roman thought hath struck him. . . .*

It is the Roman side of Antony—vigorous, warlike and driven by duty—that Cleopatra dreads even more than she dreads his wife, and she fights it in her own way. When she sees him coming, deep in conversation with one of the messengers from Rome, she retreats, since she prefers to choose her own ground, and Antony and the messenger are free to talk together at last.

Antony hears bad news, of armies gathering on the march against the Roman power and of the death of his wife. He thought he wished her dead until he heard the news, but now he deeply regrets it. "She's good, being gone." As for the enchanting queen who holds him fast in Egypt, Antony knows that the time has come when he must break away from her and he calls his friend Enobarbus to tell him they are leaving at once.

Enobarbus is an easy and amused realist and it entertains him to consider the effect Antony's departure will have on the queen. "Cleopatra, catching but the least noise of this, dies instantly. I have seen her die twenty times upon far poorer moment." Antony knows only too well what Cleopatra's behavior will be and he remarks bitterly, "Would I had never seen her," but Enobarbus feels that she is something no tourist should miss. "O sir! you had then left unseen a wonderful piece of work, which not to have been blest withal would have discredited your travel."

Cleopatra is planning a campaign against Antony and his "Roman thought" and she sends her attendant, Charmian, to find out what his current mood is.

> *If you find him sad,*
> *Say I am dancing; if in mirth, report*
> *That I am sudden sick . . .*

Charmian suggests that the best way to keep a man is to fall in with his moods and not to cross him in anything, but the highly experienced Cleopatra dismisses the suggestion. "Thou teachest like a fool; the way to lose him." At least, whatever else may be said for Cleopatra's lovers, they will never be bored.

Antony comes in briskly, his face alight, and Cleopatra promptly decides that she is gravely ill. This is chiefly because she is sure that the message he has just received came from his wife.

> *What says the married woman; you may go?*
> *Would she had never given you leave to come!*
> *Let her not say 'tis I that keep you here;*
> *I have no power upon you; hers you are.*

In an eloquent flow of language, the heartbroken and betrayed queen repudiates the false traitor, and it is extremely difficult for Antony to get a word in edgewise through the brilliant drama she is staging for his benefit. He finally succeeds in explaining that political matters call him back to Rome, where civil war is brewing, and then he adds what he should have said first: that his wife is dead. Even so, Cleopatra does not forgive him easily or in a moment, and when she finally does and is at her most charming, Antony's heart is at her feet. Under such circumstances, and with his wife safely dead, Cleopatra is content to let him go.

Back in Rome, the two other rulers of the empire, Lepidus and young Octavius Caesar, are discussing plans for defense against the invading Pompey. Caesar is youthful and rigid and unforgiving and he talks in deep disapproval of the absent Antony, who turns back all the Roman messengers and loses himself in riot in Egypt. He does not know that Antony has already left Alexandria, where Cleopatra is restlessly trying to fill in the vacant time by writing him floods of letters. The invading Pompey is in Sicily, and there he receives the unpleasant news that Antony is on his way to Rome.

The meeting between Caesar and Antony is a difficult one at first, in spite of the earnest efforts of Lepidus to act as a peacemaker. Caesar has a long list of all the offenses Antony has committed, and Antony has no real answer for any of them. With the casual dignity of a great man, he is willing to apologize within reason but he has no intention of humbling himself. Caesar is well aware of Antony's strength and how dangerous it is for the two of them to quarrel, and he is finally willing to offer his sister to Antony as a wife. Antony is equally aware of the political danger of such a quarrel and, moreover, he is far from Egypt; and so he accepts the offer.

*After the three rulers leave the room, Enobarbus is welcomed back to Rome by the friends who missed him while he was in Egypt. They are particularly anxious to hear about Cleopatra, who has been much talked of; and Enobarbus, in poetry that is worthy of its subject, describes the way she looked the first time she met Antony, when she came up the river Cydnus in her barge.

> *The barge she sat in, like a burnished throne,*
> *Burned on the water; the poop was beaten gold,*
> *Purple the sails, and so perfumèd that*
> *The winds were lovesick with them; the oars were silver,*
> *Which to the tune of flutes kept stroke, and made*
> *The water which they beat to follow faster,*
> *As amorous of their strokes. . . .*

He goes on to describe the meeting in full, and many other things about Cleopatra, and one of his friends remarks that Antony must leave her now that he is marrying Caesar's sister. But Enobarbus knows better.

> *Never; he will not.*
> *Age cannot wither her, nor custom stale*
> *Her infinite variety; other women cloy*
> *The appetite they feed, but she makes hungry*
> *Where most she satisfies . . .*

Back in Alexandria, Cleopatra waits, searching for something to pass the time and able to think of nothing but Antony. A messenger arrives from Rome and she flies at him, barely giving the man time to speak as she tries to drag out of him the news she wants to hear. When he does manage to deliver his message it is the worst news she could have had: Antony's marriage to Caesar's sister. Cleopatra is a demon when she is angry, and she harries the unfortunate messenger with her unforgiving and feminine rage until she teaches him what it is to be the bearer of bad news to a great queen. After he has fled from the room, she realizes that she has behaved in an outrageous fashion and tells her attendant to call him back. "I will not bite him." But as soon as he returns she behaves as badly as ever, under the impression that if she alternately cajoles and threatens him he will somehow be able to change the news he brings. But even the queen of Egypt must bow before an accomplished fact. The frightened messenger escapes a second time and she sends after him, but this time she merely wants to know the color of her rival's hair.

The three men who govern Rome meet with the rebel, Pompey, and agree to a settlement. Everyone believes there will be peace except Enobarbus, who is sure that Antony's marriage will never last. For his new wife is "of a holy, cold and still conversation," and Antony has known something more gay and strange and magnificent in Egypt. The marriage that was intended to bind Antony and Caesar together will in the end separate them, and Antony will return "to his Egyptian dish again."

Pompey gives a great feast on his galley to celebrate the peace settlement, and a vast amount of wine is absorbed by all the guests. Lepidus has a difficult time keeping pace with the others—"I am not so well as I should be"—and Antony launches into a long and valuable description of the nature of the crocodile. "It is shaped, sir, like itself, and it is as broad as it has breadth." Pompey, who is more nearly sober, is tempted by one of his friends to kill his three guests and thus become the sole ruler of the world. His honor does not permit him to murder them, but he has a fleeting regret that his friend did not do it first and ask permission afterwards. He returns to find Lepidus, dead drunk, being borne from the fray. The rest join hands under the direction of Enobarbus in a drinking song, and finally Caesar, his tongue blurred by wine, brings the party to a conclusion and the rulers of the world stagger ashore.

Antony's soldiers win their usual successes in the field of battle, and Antony himself departs for Athens. He takes his wife with him, and Caesar bids his sister an emotional farewell. She is also the cause for emotion in Egypt, where Cleopatra is trying to discover what Antony's new wife looks like. Or rather, she is trying to convince herself that she does not have a serious rival in Octavia, and she questions the Roman messenger closely. At first he answers, honestly enough, that the lady is not as tall as Cleopatra and that she is low of voice. Cleopatra promptly translates this as "dull of tongue and dwarfish," and inquires about her posture. Even a messenger can learn in time, and he assures her that Octavia has a very poor posture. Moreover she has an unattractively round face, dull hair and a low forehead, and Cleopatra is delighted with him.

> *There's gold for thee:*
> *Thou must not take my former sharpness ill . . .*

Cleopatra can see that the messenger is a good and intelligent man. "I repent me much that so I harried him." And as for Antony's marriage, it will surely be a failure in the end. "All may be well."

The marriage has already begun to fail. In Athens, Antony informs his wife that her brother has displeased him in many things, and she offers to act as an intermediary between them. For warfare between the two men would mean disaster.

> *Wars 'twixt you twain would be*
> *As if the world should cleave, and that slain men*
> *Should solder up the rift.*

But Octavia cannot heal the breach. Caesar does not really wish to share power or obey instructions, and he has deposed Lepidus, made war on Pompey and refused to divide his conquests with Antony. Antony for his part has returned to Egypt and from there he declares war on his brother-in-law.

Cleopatra has triumphed, for she has Antony back again.

But she makes it very difficult for him to carry on the war, since her presence in the camp takes his mind from military matters. She has a brisk argument with Enobarbus on the subject, and even Enobarbus cannot persuade her to leave. Then she interferes disastrously with the strategy of the war, for Egypt is a sea power and Cleopatra persuades her lover to fight not by land but by sea. Enobarbus points out to Antony that his soldiers are landsmen, veterans of the only kind of war they understand, but Antony will not listen. One of the soldiers pleads with him also, but an officer tells him he pleads in vain.

Our leader's led,
And we are women's men.

The sea fight is even more disastrous than the soldiers feared. Cleopatra suddenly loses her enthusiasm for the war and orders her ships to flee; and Antony, incapable now of doing anything without her, turns and follows. Since the battle is lost, the kings of the East who have followed Antony yield to Caesar, and so do most of his men. One of the few who refuses to leave him is Enobarbus, although his reason tells him that there is no longer anything left in Antony worth following.

Even in defeat and disgrace, Antony is a hero still. He knows he is ruined—"I have lost my way forever"—but his chief concern is for the safety of the men who have been faithful to him. There is a ship laden with gold in the harbor, and he asks them to take it and make their peace with Caesar. Then Cleopatra enters to try and make her peace with him.

O my lord, my lord,
Forgive my fearful sails! I little thought
You would have followed.

The old magic works and Antony takes her to his heart again. As long as the two of them are together, nothing can conquer them.

Yet Caesar is clearly the conqueror and he may set what

terms he pleases. He sends word to Cleopatra that she will be permitted to live in peace if she will drive Antony from her dominions, and Antony is infuriated beyond the point of reason. He decides to challenge Caesar to single combat; for that young man must obviously be a coward, hiding behind all his ships and his legions, not daring to face his enemy in a fair fight. Then the tortured Antony finds a messenger from Caesar kissing Cleopatra's hand. He orders the man to be savagely beaten and turns on Cleopatra in almost equal anger for having encouraged him.

But Cleopatra knows how to shift the current of Antony's rage, and she manages to turn it into fierce plans for rebuilding his shattered army and fighting at its head. Before he goes to battle, the two of them will have one last "gaudy night" together, and Cleopatra rises joyfully to his mood.

> It is my birthday:
> I had thought to have held it poor; but, since my lord
> Is Antony again, I will be Cleopatra.

Enobarbus has been watching with horror their complete inability to face the facts, and he knows that the time is coming when he must leave Antony. It is no longer safe to be in the service of a man whose valor is stronger than his reason.

The night before the battle Antony makes a last farewell to the men who have followed him, and even the practical and rational Enobarbus is shaken to tears. In the morning Antony arms himself, with Cleopatra helping. He is in the happy mood of a man who is at a trade he understands and he looks forward to the coming battle with a boy's joyfulness. Even when he finds that Enobarbus has betrayed him and gone over to Caesar, he generously concludes that the fault has been his own. He sends all his friend's possessions after him, with a gentle and loving letter wishing him good fortune.

Enobarbus, in Caesar's camp, is already in a state of agonized remorse at what he has done, and when a mule train arrives at his tent with all the treasure that Antony has sent after him, it is a mortal blow to his heart. "I will go seek some ditch, wherein to die." Enobarbus cannot bear to go on living with himself, and he dies in the night, crying out with his last words to the man he betrayed.

Antony's soldiers fight for him with a fury that nothing can withstand, and he and his army return to Alexandria in triumph, to the sound of trumpets and tambourines and with Cleopatra hanging upon the neck of her hero. But the next day Antony tries to fight Caesar by sea and again he finds that the Egyptian fleet cannot be trusted. It yields to the enemy and Antony is convinced that Cleopatra has betrayed him into the hands of Caesar.

The witch shall die;
To the young Roman boy she hath sold me . . .

His fury is as colossal as the man himself, and Cleopatra once again treads the measures of the dance she has performed so long and so skillfully. She sends word by one of her attendants that she has killed herself, and then goes to hide in the huge funeral monument that would have held her body.

The news is brought to Antony while he is still threatening to kill her, and at once a kind of stillness comes over him.

The long day's task is done,
And we must sleep. . . .

Everything is forgotten except his love for Cleopatra, the glory that outweighed empires and made everything else in the world worthless. He asks Eros, his friend, to run him through with his sword, and Eros, pretending to obey, kills himself instead. For it is easier to die than to kill his master.

Antony falls on his own sword, but even his death is a failure. For he still breathes, and he cannot find anyone to kill him. He pleads with the guards.

I have done my work ill, friends. O, make an end
Of what I have begun.

But none of the sorrowing guards will run him through with a sword. Then Antony learns that Cleopatra is alive and has only pretended death, and a curious patience takes possession of him. He asks his men to render him one final service and carry him to the monument where she is hiding.

> Take me up;
> I have led you oft; carry me now, good friends,
> And have my thanks for all.

The men carry him to the monument and lay his limp body before it while Cleopatra cries out, "O Antony, Antony, Antony!" Antony takes a fierce pride in the fact that he took his own life instead of having it taken from him by Caesar, but he refuses to die until he has held Cleopatra in his arms again.

> I am dying, Egypt, dying; only
> I here importune death awhile, until
> Of many thousand kisses the poor last
> I lay upon thy lips.

Cleopatra dares not leave the monument for fear that she may be captured by Caesar, but she and her maids manage to draw the dying man up into it. Antony's mind is chiefly on her safety and he tells her the one man she can trust of all those about Caesar. Then, in her arms, he dies and leaves desolation behind him.

> O! withered is the garland of the war,
> The soldier's pole is fall'n; young boys and girls
> Are level now with men; the odds is gone,
> And there is nothing left remarkable
> Beneath the visiting moon.

What Antony has done, Cleopatra can do also. It is no sin to "rush into the secret house of death," and if he has killed himself, so can she.

We'll bury him; and then, what's brave, what's noble,
Let's do it after the high Roman fashion,
And make death proud to take us. . . .

But Cleopatra, although she is many things, is not a
Roman, and she puts off for the moment the matter of suicide. She remains in her monument and sends Caesar a
message asking what he intends to do with her. Caesar
sends the Roman that Antony told her she could trust
with orders to take Cleopatra alive, and he captures her
through a trick. The queen, in a furious rage, tries to stab
herself. She has no intention of facing "the sober eye of
dull Octavia" or of being hooted at by a mob while she
is carried a prisoner through the streets of Rome.

Caesar himself enters, and Cleopatra kneels to the young
emperor in a sudden shift of mood. He is the "sole sir o'
the world" and she is his obedient servant. As a token of
her submission, Cleopatra presents him with an itemized
account of all her money and jewels, calling upon her treasurer to witness that it is a full list. The treasurer states,
quite honestly, that she has kept most of it back, and
Cleopatra attacks him with the same fury she showed
when she was monarch of her world instead of a helpless
prisoner. "Slave, soulless villain, dog!" She then admits
to Caesar that she may have kept back the mention of a
few things, but they are "lady trifles" and "toys." Her
captor assures her that she may keep them all. "Caesar's no
merchant."

But Cleopatra knows well enough in her heart what
Caesar intends for her. She is a notable prize and she will
be exhibited through Rome, a plan which is, in the eyes
of that great queen, "most absurd." She has no intention
of letting it happen and she has already been parted too
long from Antony. She knows very well the full truth of
what her maid has told her.

Finish, good lady; the bright day is done,
And we are for the dark.

But if Cleopatra must go down into the dark, she will do
it like a queen, and she calls for her crown and her robes
of state. Then she gives audience to an old countryman

who has with him a basket of figs. Hidden within it is a snake, the serpent of the Nile. Cleopatra does not intend to hurt herself more than is necessary, and she has already found out from her doctor the most painless way to die. It is through the bite of the asp, and the snake waits beside her as her maids robe her for the last time and give her scepter and diadem.

One of the women falls dead of grieving, and in a flash of jealousy Cleopatra can picture her reaching Antony first.

> *He'll make demand of her, and spend that kiss*
> *Which is my heaven to have. . . .*

She cradles the snake in her arms, utters a final word of contempt for that "ass" Caesar, and in her own strange and magnificent fashion she dies.

Her attendant Charmian says good-bye to her dead mistress.

> *Fare thee well.*
> *Now boast thee, death, in thy possession lies*
> *A lass unparalleled. . . .*

Then she goes to her own death, living only long enough to answer the guard's reproachful question, "Is this well done?"

> *It is well done, and fitting for a princess*
> *Descended of so many royal kings. . . .*

Caesar enters to find that his captive has escaped him, and he stands gazing at her. "She looks like sleep." He gives orders that she and Antony are to be buried together, for never will any grave on earth hold another such pair of lovers, and so the story of Antony and Cleopatra ends.

CORIOLANUS

CORIOLANUS is the most perfectly shaped of Shakespeare's tragedies, and the one most nearly classical in its form. It is a technique that matches the subject, for the hero is a Roman who is as rigid and unyielding as a sword. He has all the Roman virtues carried to excess and in the end they destroy him.

In the first part of the play the hero is called Caius Martius, which is his family name. During the course of the action he captures the city of Corioles and is given the honorary name of Coriolanus, and it is by this name that he is generally known.

The story opens in the streets of Rome during a famine. Corn can be bought only at high prices and the citizens are starving. They are sure the rulers of the city are to blame and plan an attack upon the Capitol. An old man named Menenius, who is a close friend of Coriolanus, tries to stop them, arguing that it was the gods and not the senators who caused the famine.

> *You slander*
> *The helms o' the state, who care for you like fathers,*
> *When you curse them as enemies.*

The angry citizens retort that the senators are trying to destroy them. "They ne'er cared for us yet. Suffer us to famish, and their store-houses crammed with grain; make edicts for usury, to support usurers; repeal daily any wholesome act established against the rich, and provide more piercing statutes daily to chain up and restrain the poor. If the wars eat us not up, they will."

Menenius is arguing with them, tactfully and on the whole patiently, when Coriolanus enters and calls them all curs. He has nothing but contempt for the citizens of Rome and their talk of hunger, and he had hoped the senate would let him use his sword against them. Instead, the senate has yielded to the people and allowed them to choose five tribunes to represent their interests; and Coriolanus is furious.

News comes that the Volscians, a warlike tribe in Italy, are planning an attack on Rome, and Coriolanus is happy again. He delights in war, the one occupation he has been trained for and really understands, and he feels it has the further advantage of putting to use the surplus population —"our musty·superfluity." He goes to the Capitol to receive his orders, and two of the tribunes who have been appointed to represent the people stay behind to discuss him. Both these tribunes are clever politicians, very skillful at rousing and channeling the emotions of the populace, and both of them hate Coriolanus for his arrogance.

When the leader of the Volscians hears that three men are to command the Roman army against him, he is well pleased that one of them is Coriolanus. For he is a warrior himself, and as eager to fight with Coriolanus as the Roman hero is to fight with him.

Of the same mettle is the mother of Coriolanus, a Roman matron named Volumnia. She reared her son to be a fighter and sent him to the wars when he was hardly more than a boy, keeping always before his eyes the image of a heroic and unbending Roman and taking a fierce pride in his wounds because they brought him honor. Her daughter-in-law, Virgilia, is a gentle girl, fearful of war and bloodshed. "O Jupiter! no blood." As the two women sit sewing, Volumnia gives her daughter-in-law a lecture on the proper behavior of a warrior's wife, the kind of behavior she practices herself. A lively friend of theirs arrives with the news that Coriolanus is besieging Corioles, and she wants them both to go out with her for the afternoon. "Prithee, Virgilia, turn thy solemnness out o' door, and go along with us." But Virgilia is too frightened for her husband's safety to enjoy herself while he is away, and she cannot feel the happy and militant pride that comforts his indomitable mother.

Before the walls of the besieged city of the Volscians, Coriolanus shows himself to be the true son of his mother. When the Roman soldiers turn and flee, he forces them back furiously into the battle, and almost single-handed he wins the city. Then, bleeding and exultant, he rides off to help the rest of the Roman army, a mile away. "Where is the enemy? Are you lords o' the field?" Again he leads the attack, and the Volscians are routed. He refuses to take any special reward for his services, having as fierce a contempt for rewards as he has for weakness. His general dares praise him only in his absence, but he does prevail upon the conqueror of Corioles to take a new title, the name of Coriolanus. Even this is not accepted with much grace.

> *I will go wash;*
> *And when my face is fair, you shall perceive*
> *Whether I blush, or no; howbeit, I thank you.*

Back in Rome, his friends and his enemies wait for his return. His wife is terrified he may be hurt, but his mother takes a contrary point ot view. "He is wounded, I thank the gods for 't." Volumnia knows exactly where he was injured, in the shoulder and the left arm, and she remembers with equal pride the hurts he endured before. "He had, before this last expedition, twenty-five wounds upon him." The trumpets sound to usher in her son, and she rejoices. "Before him, he carries noise; and behind him, he leaves tears." But they will never be her tears, not even if he should die of his wounds, for she cares more for her son's honor than for his life. At the beginning of the play, one of the rioting citizens said that Coriolanus did not fight "for his country; he did it to please his mother." And she is well pleased.

When the hero enters, crowned with a garland, his first act is to kneel to her. His wife is weeping and incapable of speech, which amuses Coriolanus a little.

> *Wouldst thou have laughed had I come coffined home,*
> *That weep'st to see me triumph? . . .*

Only one thing is needed to make his mother completely happy, that he should become consul.

In order to become consul, the candidate must stand in the market place, in a gown of humility, to explain his qualifications and beg the Romans for votes. The two tribunes of the people, who hate Coriolanus, are sure he will never submit himself to this, and even the Romans who admire him admit that "he's vengeance proud, and loves not the common people." He will not admit to a love he does not feel, even though it is for his own advantage. He is willing to accept the consulship from the senate but most unwilling to go through the ceremony of asking the people for it. To be "supple and courteous to the people" seems to him to be an unbearable humiliation, and although he finally consents to make his appearance in the regulation way in the forum, he is not in a mood that is likely to win him many votes.

The people of Rome are quite willing to forget his past contempt for them and make him their consul. "If he tell us his noble deeds, we must also tell him our noble acceptance of them. Ingratitude is monstrous." But Coriolanus hates boasting and was not even willing to linger in the senate house while his achievements were being described. It is torture for him to stand in the market place like a merchant, announcing his qualifications to people he wholeheartedly despises, even though his old friend Menenius reminds him it is nothing but a custom. "The worthiest men have done 't."

Coriolanus asks one citizen what is the price of the consulship, and the citizen replies, quite truthfully, "The price is, to ask it kindly." But Coriolanus cannot twist his tongue to that sort of kindness, and although he forces himself to say the right words, he is enraged in his heart at having to bow in this fashion to "Hob and Dick." The people give him their vote, but their tribunes talk to them afterwards and have no difficulty in persuading them they have been mocked. Some of them noticed at the time that there was "something odd" about the way Coriolanus treated them, and it does not take the tribunes long to fan their doubts into rage.

The tribunes, since they represent the people, go to tell

Coriolanus that he will not be consul after all. To him this
is a clear sign that the rabble is trying to overrun the state
and destroy all reasonable authority. The two tribunes,
maneuvering for his ruin, accuse him of treason. One of
them even tries to arrest him, but Coriolanus shakes him
off violently.

> Hence, old goat! . . .
> Hence, rotten thing! or I shall shake thy bones
> Out of thy garments.

Menenius tries to keep the peace but Coriolanus draws his
sword and to prevent civil war his friends hurry him away.
Menenius argues with the triumphant tribunes in an effort
to find some sort of compromise, and they finally agree to
a parley in the market place.

Everyone wants to keep the peace, except Coriolanus on
the one hand and the two tribunes on the other. Even his
mother advises him to wait at least until he possesses the
power of a consul before he angers the people. Coriolanus
cannot understand her—"Would you have me false to my
nature?"—and she tries to explain that everyone must
bend a little sometimes. "You are to absolute." All his
friends work upon him, and he finally agrees to go to the
market place and flatter the people.

Coriolanus means well, but he cannot do it. The two
shrewd politicians on the other side know exactly how to
anger him and then to trap him in his anger. In spite of all
the efforts of the peacemakers the contest flares up again,
with Coriolanus raging in contempt and fury, and the
people bent on showing him that their power is greater
than his. They banish him from Rome, and Coriolanus
hurls the sentence back in their faces.

> You common cry of curs, whose breath I hate
> As reek o' the rotten fens, whose loves I prize
> As the dead carcasses of unburied men
> That do corrupt my air, I banish you . . .

As far as the people are concerned he has become their

open enemy, and they follow the banished man to the gates of the city, rejoicing in his overthrow.

Outside Rome, Coriolanus says good-bye to his wife and mother with all the dignity that is normally his. "Bid me farewell, and smile." But in his heart there burns an unresting fire of hatred for the city that tried to destroy him, and he turns toward the one man who will understand how he feels. This is his great enemy, the leader of the Volscians, who lives as he does in the blunt, simple world of sword and camp and by the same rigid code. The leader of the Volscians is outraged that such ingratitude should have been shown to a great warrior and offers to share his command with him; and the two men, together, march on Rome.

Within the city, the tribunes are congratulating themselves on having rid the state of an ambitious and insolent man and achieved peace. A rumor comes that Coriolanus and the whole Volscian army are advancing, and the terrified tribunes refuse to believe it. Eventually the whole city hears the news, and each man is sure it was no fault of his. "Though we willingly consented to his banishment, yet it was against our will." "I ever said we were i' the wrong when we banished him."

Coriolanus and his army pitch their tents before the city, and his friends in Rome go out to plead with him. They find him as cold as steel, and as unyielding. Old Menenius is sure that Coriolanus will listen to him, and as a practical man approaches him after dinner. He boasts to the Volscian guards how close his friendship is with the great general, but Coriolanus turns him away.

There is only one thing left to try. The wife of Coriolanus, his mother and his little son dress in mourning and go out to present themselves to him. When he receives them, he is inwardly desperate, for it was "with a cracked heart" that he sent Menenius away. The old man had been almost a father to him. But Coriolanus has made a vow to the Volscians, and his honor will not permit him to break it. Now he is faced with the three human beings he loves best in the world, and above all he faces his mother, to whom he has always given obedience. When she enters, Coriolanus kneels to her as he always has, and

she shakes the foundation of his world by kneeling in turn
to him. As he says, it is as unnatural as if the pebbles on
the beach should rise up and strike the stars.

Volumnia pleads with him, and he fights for his honor
and his oath against his love. Everything he has been taught
tells him that what he is doing is correct; but his mother,
who taught him, now tells him he is wrong and that true
honor lies in mercy. She speaks of his blasted reputation in
the eyes of posterity if he destroys the city, of his duty
to her, and then, when she thinks she has failed, she takes
defeat like a Roman.

> *We will home to Rome,*
> *And die among our neighbours . . .*
> *I am hushed until our city be a-fire,*
> *And then I'll speak a little.*

But she has already won. Her son has always obeyed her
in everything, and he cannot withstand her in this. He
agrees to her suggestion of a compromise peace, although
he knows that he has destroyed himself in doing so; for he
is the sworn servant of the Volscians, and he must return
to face them with what they will consider an unprofitable
treaty.

In Rome there is hysterical rejoicing over the city's
deliverance. "The shouting Romans make the sun dance,"
and Volumnia is hailed as the woman who has saved them
all. But her son returns to a different city, Corioles, and
the conspiracy that is waiting for him there. The leader of
the Volscians cannot risk any longer the presence of a man
who overshadows him in military glory and who has al-
tered the purposes of the expedition. Because of the tears
of the Roman women,

> *which are*
> *As cheap as lies, he sold the blood and labour*
> *Of our great action: therefore shall he die.*

But even in the city of the enemy Coriolanus is loved
and admired, and there are many who would have spoken
in his defense. So the leader of the Volscians strikes quickly.

The Roman hero is surrounded by a gang of conspirators
and killed. But his dead body will be treated with honor
and given fitting burial as a great warrior, and it is acknowledged that even in the city of his foes he will possess "a
noble memory."

CYMBELINE

CYMBELINE is listed among the tragedies in the First Folio; but it has a happy ending, in spite of many misfortunes and much bloodshed, and should really be called a tragi-comedy. Its world is not that of real men and women but rather the land of fairy tales, and most of the plot is too complicated, with its wicked stepmother and kidnaped children, to arouse very much emotion. Yet it is a beautiful play of its kind. It has some of the most lyrical of Shakespeare's poetry and one of the loveliest of his heroines.

The story opens in the palace of King Cymbeline, ruler of ancient Britain. The king has married again, and he has been hoping that his daughter Imogen will marry the foolish Cloten, son of the new queen. Instead the princess has secretly married a gentleman of the court named Posthumus, and she loves him with all the devotion of her loyal, steadfast heart. Imogen's two brothers were stolen from the nursery twenty years ago and she is the sole heir to the kingdom. Her father is furious with her for having married without his consent, and his anger is fed by the new queen, who pretends to be sympathetic to the princess but actually hates her.

Posthumus is banished from the kingdom, and he and Imogen exchange gifts as a pledge of their love. She gives him a diamond ring and he slips a bracelet on her arm. Then he leaves her, to set sail for Rome, and Imogen turns to face the full measure of her father's wrath. But she has the spirit to defend herself, and his violence leaves her unshaken.

A servant of her husband sees the young exile off to his ship, and Imogen questions him closely about every move that Posthumus made, even to the waving of his handkerchief. It troubles her that her father interrupted the last words they were speaking to each other:

> *I did not take my leave of him, but had*
> *Most pretty things to say; ere I could tell him*
> *How I would think on him at certain hours*
> *Such thoughts and such, or I could make him swear*
> *The shes of Italy should not betray*
> *Mine interest and his honour . . .*
>   *. . . ere I could*

> *Give him that parting kiss which I had set*
> *Betwixt two charming words, comes in my father,*
> *And, like the tyrannous breathing of the north,*
> *Shakes all our buds from growing.*

It is not the "shes of Italy" who come between Imogen and her husband. It is a mischievous Italian named Iachimo who persuades the young Briton, in the course of a casual conversation, to place a wager on Imogen's faithfulness. Posthumus means no harm. He is convinced that Imogen will be true to him and he is so sure of it that he is even willing to wager the ring she gave him. But Iachimo is equally convinced that he can win the bet, and he sets sail at once for Britain.

Imogen makes him welcome at the British court, since he carries a letter of introduction from Posthumus. Iachimo at once tells her a series of lies about her husband—how the "jolly Briton" is reveling among the ladies of Rome and never thinks of his forsaken wife. He then adds he would be glad to console her for her husband's faithlessness by taking his place, and Imogen, suddenly understanding his drift, shows that she has something of her father's temper. She tells him exactly what she thinks of his "beastly mind" and is ready to have him turned away from the court when Iachimo assures her hastily that he only told the story to test her love for her husband. He makes quick amends by describing how popular Posthumus is with everyone in Rome, and Imogen forgives him completely.

Since Iachimo cannot win the wager by a direct assault, he shifts to a trick. He tells Imogen that he has a trunk full of jewels and silver which he and Posthumus and several Roman lords are planning as a gift to the emperor, and asks her if she will keep it safe for him. The unsuspecting Imogen agrees willingly, and it is arranged that she will keep the trunk in her room overnight, since Iachimo is sailing in the morning.

That night Imogen lies reading in bed until almost midnight. Then she folds down a page in her book, leaves her taper burning and goes to sleep. Iachimo steals out of the trunk where he has been hiding and makes note of everything in her bedroom, from the carved chimney piece on the south side of the room to the silver andirons, shaped like cupids, on the hearth. Then he slips the bracelet, her husband's gift, from her arm, makes special note of a mark on her body, and hides himself again. He goes back to Italy, armed with enough evidence to convince Posthumus he has spent the night with her.

Cloten, the son of the evil queen, is still hoping to marry Imogen and has been paying court to her. The following morning he waits impatiently outside her room, to follow the advice he has been given on his wooing. "I am advised to give her music o' mornings; they say it will penetrate." Cloten is a stupid young man and in the end a wicked one, but the morning song he offers her is one of the loveliest ever written,

> *Hark! hark! the lark at heaven's gate sings,*
> *And Phoebus 'gins arise,*
> *His steeds to water at those springs*
> *On chaliced flowers that lies;*
> *And winking Mary-buds begin*
> *To ope their golden eyes;*
> *With every thing that pretty is,*
> *My lady sweet, arise:*
> *Arise, arise!*

When Imogen finally appears, Cloten is wholly unsuccessful in his wooing. He informs her that Posthumus is a base and beggarly wretch, and Imogen retorts that the least of her husband's garments is worth more than the whole of

Cloten. She is particularly short with him because her worried thoughts are focused on the loss of her bracelet.

> *Last night 'twas on my arm, I kissed it;*
> *I hope it be not gone to tell my lord*
> *That I kiss aught but he.*

The bracelet has gone to Rome to do exactly that. In a brilliant scene, Iachimo uses his information with such skill that Posthumus believes him and is engulfed in a murderous rage. He hates his wife with the same violence he loved her before, and he is ready to kill her for the crime he believes she has committed against him.

An ambassador from Rome arrives in Britain with a demand for tribute to be paid the Roman emperor, and King Cymbeline refuses. The whole court, however, treats the ambassador with the greatest courtesy, and even Cloten manages to behave with dignity in the presence of a foreigner.

Also from Rome comes a letter from Posthumus, which has been sent to his servant with orders to murder Imogen. He has sent his wife a letter telling her to meet him at Milford Haven, far to the west in Wales, but he does not intend to be there himself. It is merely a device to give his servant an opportunity to kill her. Imogen, full of joyful excitement, is sure that if anyone else can get to Milford Haven in a week, she can get there in a day, and her husband's servant, with a heavy heart, helps her to steal away from the court.

The scene shifts to the mountains of Wales, where for the last twenty years a courtier named Belarius has been hiding. In revenge for an unjust sentence of banishment that the king had passed on him, Belarius had stolen Cymbeline's two sons from the nursery and brought them up as his own children. They are young men now and restless with a desire to see the world instead of spending all their time in a cave in the mountains.

> *What should we speak of*
> *When we are old as you? when we shall hear*
> *The rain and wind beat dark December, how*

In this our pinching cave shall we discourse
The freezing hours away? We have seen nothing. . . .

Belarius sends them up into the mountains to hunt game, but he is nevertheless proud of the young princes for refusing to be content any longer with the narrow life they have lived for the past twenty years.

Not far away, Imogen and the servant have left their horses and are continuing on foot, because, as Imogen understands it, they are near the place where Posthumus is waiting for them. Instead, the unhappy servant is obliged to show her the letter he had from Posthumus, with instructions for her death. Imogen cannot bring herself to hate her husband, although she is human enough to hate the Italian women who she thinks must have stolen her husband's love and tempted him to murder. As for death, it is welcome to her since she has lost him.

Come, fellow, be thou honest;
Do thou thy master's bidding. . . .

The frantic servant hurls the sword away from him, and then explains piteously that he has not had a wink of sleep since the letter arrived with its order to kill her. Imogen shows a wry kind of sympathy for him: "Do 't, and to bed then."

The servant finally manages to convince Imogen that he will never obey his master's command. Instead, he has a plan for her, and finally she is willing to listen. He will send word to Posthumus that she is dead, while she herself goes to Milford Haven and takes refuge there with the Roman ambassador. He has brought along doublet and hose so that she can disguise herself as a page, and he has also brought along a little box that the queen once gave him. The queen told him it was a restorative, but she believed it to be poison. The doctor who gave it to the queen knew her too well to trust her with "a drug of such damned nature" and had substituted another drug that would give the appearance of death but not kill.

Back at the court, King Cymbeline has declared war on Rome but has guaranteed safe conduct to the ambassador as far as Milford Haven. The queen is delighted that the princess has disappeared, since she can now order the kingdom to her own liking, but her son Cloten is enraged. He discovers that Imogen went to Milford Haven to meet Posthumus there and he decides to follow them, to kill the husband and possess the wife. He plans to dress in his rival's clothes, for he still remembers what Imogen once said to him. "She said upon a time—the bitterness of it I now belch from my heart—that she held the very garment of Posthumus in more respect than my noble and natural person." So it is a pleasure to Cloten to don the garments of Posthumus as he goes out to his revenge.

Imogen is making her slow way to Milford Haven, sleeping on the ground at night and growing increasingly weary. She finds a cave in the mountains and enters it, hoping for food and drawing her sword in spite of the profound mistrust she feels for any weapon. The two young princes and Belarius find her there, and they are enchanted by the beautiful boy. She says that her name is Fidele and that she is on her way to meet a kinsman at Milford Haven, and they invite her to stay with them.

By the next morning the two brothers are devoted to their young guest. She has done the cooking for them, and they leave her with great reluctance to go out hunting. They feel that one of them should stay behind, since Fidele is obviously not well, but she is cheerfully reasonable about it.

> I am ill; but your being by me
> Cannot amend me; society is no comfort
> To one not sociable. I am not very sick
> Since I can reason of it. . . .

Left to herself, Imogen takes the drug that has been given her as a restorative and lies down on the floor of the cave with her head on a cushion.

Cloten, looking for Posthumus, arrives in the mountains and is challenged by one of the young princes. They fight, and the prince cuts his head off. Belarius recognizes the dead man, although it is a long time since he has seen him, but the young victor is quite unperturbed at having killed the queen's son and has already planned what to do with the head.

> *I'll throw 't into the creek*
> *Behind our rock, and let it to the sea,*
> *And tell the fishes he's the queen's son, Cloten . . .*

His brother enters the cave, carefully removing his shoes so as not to waken their beloved guest, and finds her stretched out on the floor lifeless. She has the appearance of death, and in deep sorrow the two brothers prepare her grave. They have only a few flowers to give her, but their dirge is one of the most beautiful of laments.

> *Fear no more the heat o' the sun,*
> *Nor the furious winter's rages;*
> *Thou thy worldly task hast done,*
> *Home art gone, and ta'en thy wages;*
> *Golden lads and girls all must,*
> *As chimney-sweepers, come to dust. . . .*

After they have gone, Imogen awakens and finds the headless body of Cloten beside her. It is dressed in the clothes of Posthumus, and the vague confusion with which she wakens turns to anguish when she believes she recognizes her husband. "O! my lord, my lord." The Roman ambassador finds her there and takes her as his page. He is on his way to Milford Haven to meet the Roman legions that are under his command.

The war breaks out, and Belarius and the two princes leave their mountain cave to fight for Britain. Posthumus is back from Italy and he does the same, since he longs for death now that he has ordered the death of Imogen. The four men, fighting like heroes, hold a country lane against the Roman legions and turn what would have been a British defeat into a victory.

Posthumus is captured by Cymbeline's men because he is believed to be a Roman, and imprisoned. In prison he sees a vision of the future happiness that will be his, but when he is taken out to be hanged he goes with his jailer gladly. "I am merrier to die than thou art to live."

Then the orders are changed, and Posthumus is taken instead to the king. In a long final scene, Cymbeline learns of the death of his wife and how much she hated him, finds his two sons again and forgives Belarius for stealing them, discovers that the page of the Roman ambassador is his daughter Imogen, receives the confession of the villainous Iachimo, listens to the remorse of Posthumus and sees his daughter reunited with her husband. In conclusion, he makes friends again with the Roman ambassador, explaining that the refusal to send tribute had been on the advice of the dead queen. Rome and Britain will be "friendly together" and from the royal line of Cymbeline peace and plenty will come again to the land.

The Histories

NOTE ON THE HISTORY PLAYS

Shakespeare wrote ten history plays, and eight of these form a continuous story. They deal with the events that led up to England's first great civil war and then describe the conflict itself.

In writing these plays, Shakespeare had nothing to help him except the standard history books of his day. The art of the historian was not very advanced in this period, and no serious attempt was made to get at the exact truth about a king and his reign. Instead, the general idea was that any nation which opposed England was wrong, and that any Englishman who opposed the winning side in the civil war was wrong also.

Since Shakespeare had no other sources, the slant that appears in the history books appears also in his plays. Joan of Arc opposed the English and was not admired in Shakespeare's day, and so in his play about her she is portrayed as a somewhat comic character who wins her victories through witchcraft. Richard III fought against the first of the Tudor monarchs and was therefore labeled in the Tudor histories as a vicious usurper, and he duly appears in Shakespeare's plays as a murdering monster.

Shakespeare wrote nine of these plays under Queen Elizabeth, the last and greatest of the Tudor line. She did not encourage historical truthfulness but what she did encourage was patriotism, an exultant, joyful, intense conviction that England was the best of all possible countries and the home of the most favored of mortals. And it is this patriotism, which Shakespeare felt also, that breathes through all the history plays and binds them together. England's enemy is not so much any individual king as the threat of civil war; and the history plays come to a triumphant conclusion when

227

*the threat of civil war is finally averted and the great
queen, Elizabeth, is born.*

*These plays of Shakespeare are not to be taken as
accurate history. He was a playwright, not a historian,
and even when his sources were correct, as in the
matter of dates, he would sometimes juggle his information for the sake of effective stagecraft, Shakespeare
was not interested in facts; he was interested in swiftly
moving action and in people, and as a result some of
his characterizations seem more real than history itself.
Shakespeare's bloody and superb king seems much
more convincing than the real Richard III, merely because Shakespeare wrote so effectively about him; and,
for that matter, a complete act of the imagination like
Sir John Falstaff seems more real than any of the
English royalty. Shakespeare moved in a different
world from that of the historian, a world of creation
rather than of recorded fact, and it is in this world that
he is so supreme a master.*

KING JOHN

KING JOHN tells the story of a medieval king of England who had an unhappy and bloody reign. The play does not mention the chief event of John's reign, the signing of the Magna Carta, for the audiences of Shakespeare's day had been trained to respect kings rather than to respect the people who tried to limit their power. It was not until the following century that the subject of constitutional government became important to Englishmen, and it is doubtful that Shakespeare had ever heard of the Great Charter. What he knew about King John was the average information of his own day, and he wove it into an effective and vigorous story.

The play opens when King John is receiving an ambassador from the king of France. The French king is convinced that the throne of England belongs rightfully to John's nephew Arthur, and he is supporting Arthur's claim with enough enthusiasm to be willing to go to war on the subject. King John lacks the strength to be a really evil man, but his actions are guided by his dominating mother, Queen Elinor, who is determined that he shall keep the throne. Equally determined on the other side is her daughter-in-law, Constance, who has been pressing the claim of her little son Arthur and has finally won the king of France to her support.

King John dismisses the French ambassador and is working on plans to finance the coming war when two brothers present themselves before him to settle an argument. One of them is the most delightful character in the play, the cheerful, chatty, irrepressible Philip Faulconbridge. He is being sued for all of his father's lands, which his younger brother claims because he says Philip is illegitimate, and they have agreed to bring their case to the king. The king realizes that Philip has a close resemblance to his own great elder brother, Richard Coeur-de-Lion, and offers him the choice of getting the land or of claiming that mighty monarch as his father. The young man has no real wish to be related to his skinny brother, for whom he has a brisk contempt, and he is quite willing to shift fathers and agree to be illegitimate. Queen Elinor accepts the lively young gentleman, now called the Bastard of Faulconbridge, to serve under her colors in the wars in France, and the English side gains not only a redoubtable fighter but a most charming and effervescent talker.

Outside the French town of Angiers, which is currently held by the English, the French king greets the duke of Austria, who has come with his forces to help Arthur win the crown. King John arrives also, and there is a parley between the opponents whose dignity is somewhat marred by a violent quarrel between Elinor and Constance. Elinor tries to persuade her grandson Arthur to leave his mother for her. "Come to thy grandam, child." Constance retaliates by using the same nursery tone to her son in bitter mockery.

> Do, child, go to it grandam, child;
> Give grandam kingdom, and it grandam will
> Give it a plum, a cherry, and a fig:
> There's a good grandam.

Poor little Arthur, who is not long out of the nursery himself, is embarrassed almost to the point of tears. He has no wish to have any wars started on his behalf, but the arguments of the adults rage about him and he can do nothing to prevent them.

The king of England and the king of France finally appeal to the citizens of Angiers. Let them acknowledge the true king of England, whether it be Arthur or John. But the canny citizens merely announce that they are the true subjects of the king of England, whoever he may be, and retreat inside their fortified walls. The two armies fight each other inconclusively and then decide to attack the town and discuss kingship afterwards. The anguished citizens suggest a truce; let Queen Elinor's niece marry the

French king's son and unite the two kingdoms. The kings agree, and peace is declared.

The Bastard of Faulconbridge is a fascinated onlooker to these convolutions of royalty, while he carries on his own private and impertinent warfare with the haughty duke of Austria. To Arthur's mother, Constance, the agreement between the two kings is a tragedy; for now she will never win the throne for Arthur, her beautiful boy who means more to her than anything else in the world. She becomes hopeful, however, when an envoy arrives in France from the Pope. The Pope has decided to excommunicate King John because of a disagreement over the authority of the church. The French king has a brief struggle with his conscience, decides he does not dare to be friendly with an enemy of the Pope and breaks off his alliance with King John.

The two armies fight again and John is victorious. Arthur is his captive now, and he plans to take the boy back with him to England. He assures Arthur he will be safe there—"Thy grandam loves thee"—but in his heart King John knows that his throne will never be secure as long as Arthur is alive. He tells his nephew's keeper, a man named Hubert, that he wants the boy killed as soon as they are back in England. Then he and his forces sail from France, leaving Constance half mad with sorrow at losing her son.

> *Grief fills the room up of my absent child,*
> *Lies in his bed, walks up and down with me,*
> *Puts on his pretty looks, repeats his words . . .*

Meanwhile, in England, King John has sent word to Hubert that he wants Arthur's eyes put out with hot irons, and with a heavy heart the man goes to carry out the order. Arthur is too innocent to know why Hubert has come and wonders why his friend and keeper looks so sad.

> *Are you sick, Hubert? you look pale today:*
> *In sooth, I would you were a little sick,*
> *That I might sit all night and watch with you:*
> *I warrant I love you more than you do me.*

Arthur is most anxious for everyone to be happy, and once, when Hubert's head ached a little, he used his best handkerchief to help make it better. But the pain is no longer in Hubert's head but in his heart. He has sworn to obey the king, and after he has shown his prisoner the warrant, he gives the signal to the attendants. They come in, armed with rope and irons, and Arthur is terrified of them.

> I will not struggle; I will stand stone-still.
> For heaven's sake, Hubert, let me not be bound!
> Nay, hear me, Hubert: drive these men away,
> And I will sit as quiet as a lamb;
> I will not stir, nor wince, nor speak a word,
> Nor look upon the iron angerly. . . .

Hubert sends the men away and tries to use the iron on Arthur himself. But he finds that he cannot hurt so dear a child, in spite of his sworn duty to the king, and he goes to give John the false report that Arthur is dead.

King John has just permitted himself to be crowned a second time, to make his title to the throne doubly secure. He has yielded to the entreaties of his nobles to give Arthur his liberty, when Hubert brings the news the boy is dead. His nobles are sure it was John who killed him and they depart in anger, leaving that uncertain tyrant to meditate upon his mistakes. "There is no sure foundation set on blood." A messenger comes with more bad news, that France is invading England with a huge army. John does not understand how so great a force could have entered England without his mother's knowledge, and the messenger tells him that Queen Elinor is dead.

The Bastard of Faulconbridge arrives, as alert and cheerful as ever, and King John sends him to try and win back the nobles to his side. Then Hubert reveals to the repentant king that Arthur was not killed after all, and John sends him out to tell the nobles the good news.

It is too late. Arthur tries to make his escape from the castle, disguised as a ship's boy, and leaps down from the high wall. He dies at the base of the castle, broken on the stones, and the nobles find him there. They conclude that Hubert has killed him, and Hubert escapes with his life only because the fair-minded Faulconbridge protects him. The nobles are convinced, however, that King John is implicated somehow and they go to join forces with the army of the king of France.

King John is making his peace with the envoy from the Pope when Faulconbridge comes in with the news that his nobles have forsaken him. The king takes the news with limp resignation, and the Bastard of Faulconbridge, who is never limp, tries to rouse him to action. The king gives him command of the army, and the young man is in his element now. He sends a lively and delighted challenge to the enemy and almost single-handed holds back the French might. In the end the French lose their reinforcements, and the English nobles, informed of an intended treachery by a dying Frenchman, return to their own king.

But King John is dying too, burning with fever and carried outdoors by his attendants so that his soul, at least, can have "elbow room." He cannot rest—"Within me is a hell"—and no one can give him ease. He dies, leaving the kingdom to his son, and all the lords vow fealty to the new king.

All through the play there have been threats of sedition and of division within the kingdom. But the Bastard of Faulconbridge has always been loyal to the monarchy, and he is therefore well suited to pronounce the last, proud words of patriotism in the play.

> *This England never did, nor never shall,*
> *Lie at the proud foot of a conqueror,*
> *But when it first did help to wound itself. . . .*
> *Nought shall make us rue,*
> *If England to itself do rest but true.*

RICHARD THE SECOND

RICHARD II is the first of a series of linked plays that carry England to civil war and back to peace again. It tells of the deposition and murder of a king, and this is a tragedy upon which all the later action of the series depends. But the play can stand equally well by itself as an isolated work of art, both through the brilliance of its poetry and through the remarkable portrait of King Richard. That unwise and unsteady young man was really cast by fate to be an actor, and it was his misfortune that he was a king.

King Richard ruled in England toward the end of the Middle Ages, and he occupied an uneasy throne. His grandfather, the mighty and warlike King Edward, had many sons and two of them were still alive. These were the duke of Lancaster and the duke of York, and it was the struggle of their descendants for the crown that finally brought England to civil war. Another son, the duke of Gloucester, was killed with Richard's consent, and the young king has already succeeded in making himself unpopular with the people of England. He has spent lavishly, taxed ruinously and bestowed his favors on worthless hangers-on.

The story opens as King Richard is talking to the oldest of his uncles, the duke of Lancaster. This duke was always called John of Gaunt, from the English way of pronouncing his birthplace, Ghent, and Richard treats him with the respect due an elderly and powerful man. The duke's son, Henry Bolingbroke, has had a fierce quarrel with the duke of Norfolk and accused him of treason, and King Richard is prepared to listen to the rights of the argument between the two men. Henry is his first cousin, but Richard sees himself as an impartial and almost godlike king and does not doubt his own ability to be the best and most upright of judges. What he calls "the unstooping firmness of my upright soul" is his honest opinion of himself, although it is a judgment few of his nobles would have cause to share.

In this case, King Richard cannot persuade the two men to make peace with each other, and he sets a time and a place for them to fight a duel. The duel is about to begin, in all its glittering array of heralds and trumpets, when Richard suddenly changes his mind and has the whole thing stopped. Instead, he sends the two men into exile. It is a bitter sentence to them both, but especially to Henry Bolingbroke. He deeply loves England and is loved by all Englishmen in return, and his proudest title is that he is a "trueborn Englishman."

Richard is delighted to get rid of his cousin, for Henry's popularity is a threat to the throne. He has practised a "courtship to the common people . . . wooing poor craftsmen with the craft of smiles," and the king does not approve of it. Richard himself is on his way to Ireland to put down a rebellion there, and he does not feel himself bound by any scruples in the way he raises funds. He is willing to force money out of his subjects if he cannot get it by legal means, and when he hears that his uncle, John of Gaunt, is on his deathbed, he is chiefly pleased at the thought of the vast Lancastrian estates he can seize and turn over to his own use.

Old John Gaunt is dying with his heart full of fear for England. He is convinced that his beloved land is being destroyed, and he expresses his love for his country in some of the most famous lines ever written about England.

This royal throne of kings, this sceptered isle,
This earth of majesty, this seat of Mars,
This other Eden, demi-paradise,
This fortress built by Nature for herself
Against infection and the hand of war,
This happy breed of men, this little world,
This precious stone set in the silver sea . . .
This blessed plot, this earth, this realm, this England . . .
This land of such dear souls, this dear, dear land . . .

This most loved of countries is now being infected from within, although it could not be conquered from without.

> *England, that was wont to conquer others,*
> *Hath made a shameful conquest of itself . . .*

King Richard enters the room of the dying man, and John of Gaunt tries to reprove him for his bad government. Richard is furious and calls his uncle a "lunatic, lean-witted fool." When the old man dies he at once seizes all his property for the crown, and Richard's other uncle, the duke of York, is appalled. By right and by law the money and lands of the dead duke of Lancaster belong to his exiled son, Henry Bolingbroke. But Richard will not listen to his uncle's warning and refuses to be turned from his course.

The nobles of England are equally shocked when they hear the news of what Richard has done. They have been growing increasingly restive under the young king's erratic tyranny, and when they hear that Henry is returning to England they go to enlist under his banner.

During Richard's absence in Ireland he has left the country under the government of his uncle, the duke of York, and the excitable old man has no idea what to do with the rebellion he suddenly finds on his hands. He has no money, no carts for the armor, no way of raising troops. The old man does his best to comfort Richard's woeful young queen, who loves her husband devotedly, and the king's unpopular favorites scatter to do what they can against the approaching army.

The duke of York goes out to parley with the rebels, and Henry greets him as "my gracious uncle." The old duke is not pleased.

> *Tut, tut!*
> *Grace me no grace, nor uncle me no uncle:*
> *I am no traitor's uncle . . .*

Henry maintains that he is not a traitor but has only come to England to win back his right to the estates of his dead father; and his uncle admits there is no army to oppose him. The muddled old man does not know what he ought to do, caught between his sworn duty to the king and the fact that he is helpless to fulfill it, and he finally decides to retire peacefully as "neuter."

King Richard lands on the coast of Wales, aware of the existence of the rebellion but convinced that Heaven would never permit an anointed king to be destroyed.

> *Not all the water in the rough rude sea*
> *Can wash the balm from an anointed king . . .*
> *For every man that Bolingbroke hath pressed*
> *To lift shrewd steel against our golden crown,*
> *God for his Richard hath in heavenly pay*
> *A glorious angel . . .*

This was a doctrine that was believed by most men in Shakespeare's England. All kings were chosen by God, and if the kings were evil it was up to God, not to men, to destroy them. But Richard takes the doctrine and surrounds himself with it like a golden frame, in which he stands and postures. His loyal but unhappy nobles would like him to be a little more practical, on the basis that Heaven helps those that help themselves, but they cannot stir Richard from his exalted and self-conscious position.

The news comes that twenty thousand Welsh soldiers have deserted the army, thinking the king is dead, and for a moment Richard's picture of himself is shaken. Then he becomes the invincible monarch again, with a God-protected glory. Further news comes that all England is flocking to Henry's banner, even old men and children, and that Richard's worthless favorites have all been executed. The king abandons his former role of exalted confidence and becomes instead, with the emotional suddenness that is characteristic of him, a mourning philosopher.

> *For God's sake, let us sit upon the ground,*
> *And tell sad stories of the death of kings:*
> *How some have been deposed, some slain in war,*
> *Some haunted by the ghosts they have deposed,*
> *Some poisoned by their wives, some sleeping killed;*

> All murdered. For within the hollow crown
> That rounds the mortal temples of a king
> Keeps Death his court . . .

This grim view of kingship is quite as exaggerated as the golden one that went before, but Richard can do nothing by halves. His friend suggests that he show a little more courage, and the king grows hopeful again; it will be "an easy task" to overcome the rebellion. Then the final news comes that his uncle, the old duke of York, has yielded to the enemy, and Richard clutches grief to his heart as though it were a fair lady. He will go to Flint Castle and "pine away," taking a melancholy and artistic pleasure in the depth of his woes.

Henry arrives at Flint Castle, apparently prepared to make a respectful submission to the king if he can have the Lancastrian estates back again. Richard is in a regal mood again, threatening all traitors with supernatural punishment from the walls of the castle. But when he is alone with a friend, he lapses into tears, for it seems to him a pitiful thing that he should be prepared to hurl his whole kingdom away and be buried in oblivion.

> . . . my large kingdom for a little grave,
> A little little grave, an obscure grave . . .

When Richard comes down from the castle walls to greet his cousin Henry, he is a king again. He is gravely courteous to his foes and wholly cooperative—a model monarch in defeat and quite prepared to accompany the victorious Henry back to London.

The scene shifts to the garden of the old duke of York, where Richard's queen is trying to escape her fears. She has no heart for dancing or storytelling and turns instead to listen to a gardener who is giving instructions to his men. He is a good gardener, careful to give support to the loaded boughs of the apricot trees and keep the flowers unchoked by weeds, and he only wishes the king of England had treated his kingdom as well as he himself treats his garden. For he has just heard the news that Richard is being deposed and Henry is taking the crown. The horri-

fied queen steps out of the shadow of the trees to ask him
where he heard such news, and the gardener assures her
regretfully that it is true. He can do nothing for the unhappy lady, but when she is gone he sets out a bank of
rue, the herb of sorrow, to commemorate the place where
her tears fell for her husband.

In London, in the great hall at Westminster, the parliament of England has gathered together to give Henry the
crown. No one speaks against his claim except the loyal
and spirited bishop of Carlisle, who prophesies that the
end will be civil war if Richard is deposed and Henry
enthroned.

> *If you crown him, let me prophesy,*
> *The blood of English shall manure the ground*
> *And future ages groan for this foul act . . .*
> *Disorder, horror, fear and mutiny*
> *Shall here inhabit, and this land be called*
> *The field of Golgotha and dead men's skulls. . . .*

The bishop is placed under arrest, and Henry sends for
Richard so that he can formally surrender his crown in
the full view of all.

Richard is in one of his moods, and in spite of his very
real agony he cannot resist so large an audience. His performance confuses Henry, a blunt and practical man who
has been given to understand that Richard is ready to
relinquish the crown and cannot understand why he takes
so long about it. But Richard is an actor at heart, and
this is his best scene. "Now mark me, how I will undo
myself." It is done in the grand manner, this dethroning
of himself, and ends with a suitable flourish.

> *God save King Henry, unkinged Richard says,*
> *And send him many years of sunshine days!*
> *What more remains?*

One more thing remains, that he should make a full
confession of his crimes. They have been neatly written
out for him on a piece of paper, so that everything will
seem legal, but this is something Richard cannot do. It is

not fair to ask it of him, and his mood shifts to that of the tortured martyr. That is, of course, what he is, except that he has a curious ability to stand off and admire the picture he makes. He even calls for a looking glass in which he may study his own face, and then, in a dramatic gesture, breaks the glass.

> A brittle glory shineth in this face:
> As brittle as the glory is the face . . .

His practical cousin remarks that the glass showed only the shadow of his face, and Richard picks up the word "shadow" and plays with it as he has already played with his grief. But it is true grief, for all that, and his words are simple at the end. He leaves the hall, a king no longer, and the time of Henry's coronation is set for the following Wednesday.

Richard is to be lodged in the Tower of London, where state prisoners were usually kept, and his wife stands waiting in the street to give him a last farewell. Then the earl of Northumberland, who has been Henry's greatest ally, comes with changed orders: Richard is to be sent to the castle of Pomfret instead. Richard goes, because he must, but he never swerves from his conviction that he is the true king of England and Henry is a seditious usurper.

The new King Henry discovers soon enough that the seeds of violence and of civil war are easier to sow than they are to gather up again. Some of Richard's supporters plot against Henry's life, and among the conspirators is the son of the old duke of York. The duke finds out about it and goes to warn the king, and the duchess of York sends her erring son after him in the hope that he will arrive before his father. King Henry is full of worries about his own son, Prince Hal, who takes no interest in the new dignities that have been thrust upon him and spends his time in drinking and riot. The perturbed father is ready to be kind to his uncle's son, especially when his aunt entreats him; but he knows, nevertheless, that as long as Richard is alive such plots against his own life will continue to breed.

King Henry does not actually order Richard to be killed.

But he speaks to one of his knights in terms that make his wishes clear enough, and the knight goes to Pomfret Castle to murder the one-time king.

Richard in his dungeon has been alone with his thoughts, those roving, speculative thoughts that make him unfit to be a king but are not steady enough to make him a philosopher. He sees no one except the man who brings him his food, until a faithful groom who once worked in his stables gets permission to visit him. Many people loved Richard, and the groom speaks in a way for them all, although his talk is chiefly of horses. "What my tongue dares not, that my heart shall say."

The groom leaves, Richard's last friend on earth, and the murderers enter. Richard defends himself gallantly, for he is a warrior's son, and manages to kill two of them with their own weapons. Then the knight strikes him down, and Richard dies, prophesying that the whole land will be stained with his blood.

His murderer is terrified by what he has done and brings the coffined body to King Henry; and Henry is almost as horrified as he.

> *Though I did wish him dead,*
> *I hate the murderer . . .*

Henry banishes the knight from his presence and decides on a voyage to the Holy Land to expiate his guilt. For he has killed a king, the Lord's anointed, and it is a crime that will cast a dark shadow over England for a long time to come.

HENRY THE FOURTH, PART ONE

HENRY IV, PART ONE, tells the story of the opening years of the reign of King Richard's successor. It begins a year after Richard's death and concerns a rebellion in the west of England against King Henry's crown.

But the play does much more than that. It expands into a magnificent panorama of all England, and is not merely a history play but a portrait of the land that Shakespeare knew and loved. It is not a realistic portrait. There was probably never a real man as funny or as outrageous as Falstaff, nor one as lively and charming as Hotspur. But they and the rest of the characters combine into something that is almost better than reality, a quality of Englishness that exists to a certain extent in all Shakespeare's plays but never more than in this one.

Three threads are woven in and out to make up the fabric of the play. The first is the thread of kingship and of the country's welfare, and in this the leading characters are an anxious King Henry and his willful, wayward heir, Prince Hal. The second is the thread of honor and tells of that brilliant and golden young warrior, Hotspur, who lived for military glory and died of it. The third is the thread of Prince Hal's dissolute companions and of that most wonderful fellow, Sir John Falstaff. All the threads combine richly and smoothly, and they make a magnificent play.

The story opens in London in the palace of King Henry. For the past year he has been planning an expedition to the Holy Land, in an attempt to expiate his share in King Richard's death, and now the idea must be postponed again. There have been dangerous rebellions in both Scotland and Wales; and although the Scottish rising has been quelled by young Harry Percy, who is called Hotspur, there is still a threat of trouble in that quarter. Hotspur will not yield up the prisoners he has taken, and Henry intends to demand an explanation. The king has the deepest admiration for Hotspur, who is a gallant and heroic young man, and he cannot help comparing him with his own son Hal. For Prince Hal frequents taverns instead of battlefields, and the king is bitterly ashamed of him.

Then the scene turns to Prince Hal and his favorite companion. This is a fat old knight named Sir John Falstaff, and if Hal misbehaved for no other reason than to have Falstaff's company, that would be reason enough. For Falstaff is one of the world's great comedy creations, and the most famous of Shakespeare's. He is enormously fat, completely outrageous, a drunkard, a coward and a thief, and yet he is so endearing that it is no wonder Prince Hal cannot resist him. No one else can resist Falstaff either. He is so buoyantly charmed by being alive, so delighted with himself and his own disgraceful activities, and such a magnificent realist in a world given to self-deception, that he sweeps through what might have been an orderly play of noble deeds and thoughts and turns everything upside down without even caring. He may be a bad influence on Prince Hal, but he is a wonderful influence on the play.

Falstaff and Hal are on a pleasant basis of good friendship and tease each other endlessly. The prince's barbs are sharp enough to penetrate the average hide, but Falstaff is so resilient that they bounce back upon their author. It is Falstaff's contention that he is a virtuous individual who has been ruined by bad company, and while he is willing to forgive Hal for misleading so good, so fat and so old a man, he does feel that the prince should at least admit his sins. "Thou hast done much harm upon me, Hal, God forgive thee for it! Before I knew thee, Hal, I knew nothing, and now am I, if a man should speak truly, little better than one of the wicked." "One of the wicked" was a Puritan phrase, and Falstaff delivers it in the Puritan singsong, with his old eyes cast up to heaven. Then the prince suggests they commit a small robbery together, and Falstaff lapses into his normal tone of voice. "Zounds! where thou wilt, lad." Hal maintains that there seems to be a little inconsistency here, and Falstaff looks at him in wide-eyed innocence. "Why, Hal, 'tis my vocation, Hal; 'tis no sin for a man to labour in his vocation."

The robbery is to take place early next morning, when the rich merchants pass Gad's Hill on their way to London. The plan has been suggested by a friend named Poins, and when the prince is doubtful about joining it, Poins promises Falstaff he will persuade him. Falstaff removes his fat bulk from the room, still playing his bland portrait of the virtuous Puritan. "God give thee the spirit of persuasion, and him the ears of profiting." As soon as they are alone, Poins tells the prince his real plan, which is to disguise themselves, waylay Falstaff after the robbery and take the stolen money away from him. The prince is delighted with the idea, but as soon as Poins leaves him his thoughts turn to the realities of his position. For he is the son of a king, and he does not intend to spend much more of his time in taverns. He cannot let his own "loose behaviour" last indefinitely, and he is ready at the proper time to throw it off and behave as a prince should.

Back at the palace, King Henry is questioning Hotspur about the Scottish prisoners. Hotspur's father and his uncle had a large share in getting Henry his crown, and the king suspects that the whole family is becoming too proud and independent. Yet Hotspur's explanation is reasonable enough and very characteristic of him. He had been approached by the king's messenger just at the close of the battle when he was leaning, tired and bloody, on his sword. The royal messenger had come mincing along, holding a little perfume box which he sniffed from time to time so that the smell of corpses would not annoy him, and he so maddened Hotspur with his chatter that he could not attend to what he was saying.

> For he made me mad,
> To see him shine so brisk and smell so sweet
> And talk so like a waiting-gentlewoman
> Of guns, and drums, and wounds . . .

King Henry is willing to accept the explanation, but then he and Hotspur get into an argument on the subject of Edmund Mortimer, earl of March. Mortimer was a claimant to the English throne because he was a descendant of Edward the Third, King Henry's grandfather. The Welsh rebel, Owen Glendower, had captured him, and Mortimer married Glendower's daughter. Henry mistrusts him and rebukes Hotspur when he comes to Mortimer's defense. Hotspur is not accustomed to rebuke, even from a king, and when Henry goes from the room he leaves Hotspur in a rage behind him.

> He said he would not ransom Mortimer;
> Forbade my tongue to speak of Mortimer;
> But I will find him when he lies asleep
> And in his ear I'll holla 'Mortimer!'
> Nay,
> I'll have a starling shall be taught to speak
> Nothing but 'Mortimer' and give it him . . .

Hotspur's father and his uncle try to calm him down, but it is a difficult task with anyone so talkative, so high-spirited and so boyishly quick-tempered. Finally Hotspur subsides into a kind of low mutter, and the two older men are able to explain their plan. Instead of fighting the Scotch and the Welsh, they will join forces with them to overthrow the ungrateful king who has already forgotten how they helped him gain the throne. This seems a splendid plan to Hotspur, for military glory means everything to him and nothing seems impossible.

> By heaven, methinks it were an easy leap
> To pluck bright honour from the pale-faced moon,
> Or dive into the bottom of the deep,
> Where fathom-line could never touch the ground,
> And pluck up drownèd honour by the locks . . .

So the conspiracy begins, the conspiracy that Richard prophesied would come if Henry seized the throne.

Early the next morning, in the town nearest to Gad's Hill, the freight carriers on their way to London are packing up to leave the inn. One of them is delivering bacon and ginger and the other a basket of turkeys, and they have some insulting comments to make on the quality of the inn. These range from the multitude of fleas to the worthlessness of the horses' feed, but the inn has a worse aspect yet: it provides information to thieves when rich men are passing by. One of Falstaff's friends hears that a traveler from Kent is carrying gold with him, and he passes the word along to the rest of the gang.

Falstaff gets into difficulties with the project from the start. He loses his horse, and the idea of moving even a few steps on foot is unendurable to so fat a man. He complains bitterly to the unheeding dawn, and only manages to hold his tongue when the rich travelers approach. Then Falstaff finds his voice again and surges to the attack with the vast enthusiasm he puts into everything. "Down with them, cut the villains' throats; ah! whoreson caterpillars! bacon-fed knaves! they hate us youth: down with them . . . What, ye knaves? young men must live." The prince and Poins take no part in this stirring action, but as soon as the gang starts to divide the gold they descend upon them in disguise and take it away with no difficulty at all.

Meanwhile Hotspur, in his castle, is discovering some of the practical disadvantages of organizing a rebellion. He has just received a letter from a friend who refuses to take part in the undertaking because it is dangerous, and Hotspur agrees that it is. " 'Tis dangerous to take a cold, to sleep, to drink; but I tell you, my lord fool, out of this nettle danger, we pluck this flower safety." Hotspur feels he has only himself to blame for trying to persuade such "a dish of skim milk" to take the path of honor. He tells his delightful wife, Lady Percy, he must leave the castle that night, and she makes a final effort to find out what has been occupying his mind; for she is Mortimer's sister and knows how dangerous politics can be. But Hotspur will tell her nothing, although in the end he promises to let her follow him. The two are on excellent terms, high-spirited, charming people who enjoy teasing each other and love each other very much, and their scene together is a delightful one.

Prince Hal, who also enjoys teasing, plays a mild joke on one of the serving boys in the tavern while he and Poins are waiting for Falstaff. That indignant and thwarted warrior arrives to tell his two friends exactly what he thinks of them for not helping with the robbery. It is a question what the world is coming to. "There lives not three good men unhanged in England, and one of them is fat and grows old. . . . A plague of all cowards." Poins indignantly denies that he is a coward, and Falstaff agrees this may be so; "but I would give a thousand pound I could run as fast as thou canst." The prince inquires in deep concern what the matter is, and Falstaff launches into a spirited description of the battle at Gad's Hill. It was a magnificent battle, and it gets more so by the minute. More and more men spring up in the fertile field of Falstaff's imagination, and the prince listens to him gravely. "Pray God you have not murdered some of them." "Nay, that's past praying for," says Falstaff and surges on with his bloody tale. He finally ends up with eleven foes in buckram and three in Kendal-green, and then just as the balloon of his imagination is soaring at its giddiest height the prince unkindly shoots it down by telling exactly what happened at Gad's Hill. Falstaff is trapped by that uncomfortable commodity, the truth, and everyone waits to see how he will get out of the hole he has so enthusiastically dug for himself. But Falstaff is capable of rising above anything so sordid as mere facts, and he remarks beamingly to the prince that of course he recognized him. "Was it for me to kill the heir-apparent? . . . I am as valiant as Hercules, but . . . the lion will not touch the true prince. Instinct is a great matter, I was a coward on instinct. I shall think the better of myself and thee during my life; I for a valiant lion, and thou for a true prince. But, by the Lord, lads, I am glad you have the money."

Mistress Quickly, the owner of the tavern, comes in to report that there is a messenger to see the prince. Falstaff goes out to interview him and comes back with news of the rebellion. "Tell me, Hal, art thou not horribly afeard? thou being heir-apparent, could the world pick thee out three such enemies again as that fiend Douglas, that spirit Percy, and that devil Glendower? Are thou not horribly afraid?" Hal says he is not, and adds unkindly, "I lack some of thy instinct." Falstaff feels that Hal should at least rehearse what he is going to say to his father and kindly offers to play the king. He chooses a stool for his throne and opens with a royal eloquence suitable to the occasion.

For God's sake, lords, convey my tristful queen,
For tears do stop the flood-gates of her eyes.

Mistress Quickly, an admiring audience of one, is overcome by the beauty of his performance, and Falstaff quiets her from his lofty heights. "Peace, good pint-pot, peace, good tickle-brain." Then he turns to his erring offspring, Hal, and informs him in sentences of measured dignity that he has been keeping very bad company. He has only one really virtuous friend—"a goodly portly man, i' faith, and a corpulent; of a cheerful look, a pleasing eye, and a most noble carriage . . . and, now I remember me, his name is Falstaff."

The indignant prince demands that the roles be reversed, so that he can speak for his father, and Falstaff promptly becomes a charming prince, alert and respectful. The playlet is interrupted, however, by the sheriff, who has come to trace the stolen gold and brought a carter along as witness. The carter remembers that one of the attackers was an old man "as fat as butter," and it is fortunate that Falstaff has wisely absented himself from the room. The prince finds him later, asleep behind a wall hanging and snoring like a horse, and in his pockets are the bills that bear witness to his well-balanced habits—a halfpenny-worth of bread to two gallons of strong drink. Having cleaned out his pockets, Hal decides to let his fat friend have a company of foot soldiers, so that he can have some exercise in walking, and then goes off to report to his father the king.

The rebels meet together in Wales, and Hotspur finds it difficult to behave with the patience of a good ally. He is particularly irritated by the great Welsh warrior, Glendower, whose natural self-confidence is heightened by his conviction that he possesses supernatural powers. He informs Hotspur that the day he was born the whole earth trembled at the portent.

> *The frame and huge foundation of the earth*
> *Shaked like a coward.*

Hotspur is not in the least impressed by this information. "Why, so it would have done at the same season, if your mother's cat had but kittened." Glendower tries again: "I can call spirits from the vasty deep," and again Hotspur fails to respond satisfactorily.

> *Why, so can I or so can any man*
> *But will they come when you do call for them?*

Mortimer tries hard to keep the peace between the two men, but Hotspur is not in a sympathetic mood when Glendower brings out a map and plans the future division of England among the rebels. Hotspur claims he is not getting his fair share, and they finally end up arguing whether Glendower has a Welsh accent, which he denies, and whether Hotspur can compose poetry. Hotspur remarks that poetry sets his teeth on edge.

> *I had rather be a kitten and cry mew*
> *Than one of these same metre ballad-mongers.*

Then his ill temper vanishes as suddenly as it came, for Hotspur has a happy, open nature and cannot hold any grudge long. The ladies enter, and Mortimer's Welsh wife sings a little tune. Hotspur listens with reluctance, for he does not like music any better than poetry, and his own wife calls him a "giddy goose" in a voice full of love. It is the last time they ever see each other, for Hotspur rides forth to the battle that destroys him.

Back in London, Prince Hal presents himself at the palace to see his father. It seems to King Henry that Hal is doing everything he can to lose the love of the people of England and that he has become his father's "nearest and dearest enemy." But Hal assures his father earnestly that he will be proud of him in the coming warfare. The news comes that the rebels are gathering their forces in the west at the town of Shrewsbury, and King Henry puts his son in charge of part of the royal army.

Back in the tavern, Falstaff is brooding on the wicked-
ness of the world and composing some especially eloquent
insults on the red nose of a friend of his. He has discovered
that someone has picked his pocket and holds Mistress
Quickly responsible, since it happened in her tavern. There
were many valuable things in his pocket, he claims. "I
have lost a seal-ring of my grandfather's worth forty
mark." Mistress Quickly has her own sense of injury, for
Falstaff owes her a great deal of money, to say nothing of
the twelve shirts she bought for him. Falstaff dismisses
the shirts loftily. "I have given them away to bakers'
wives." When Prince Hal appears they both appeal to
him, with the contents of Falstaff's pocket increasing in
value all the time. Finally the prince informs him that he
was the one who picked his pocket, finding nothing but a
mass of bills and a penny's worth of sugar candy. Falstaff
turns to the highly indignant Mistress Quickly in his
grandest manner. "Hostess, I forgive thee." He is then informed that the prince is going to provide him with a regi-
ment of foot soldiers, and in spite of a fleeting wish that he
could go on horseback, Falstaff has reason to be well
pleased. For he is an experienced army captain and knows
very well how to make money out of his men.

The rebels meet near Shrewsbury, and Hotspur learns
that his father is ill and unable to supply the soldiers he
has promised. The young warrior receives the news well;
the smaller their army, the greater the credit each man in
it will gain. Then he hears that King Henry is marching
toward Shrewsbury with a mighty force and that even
Prince Hal has left playing about in taverns to join it. Still
further bad news arrives, for Owen Glendower has not yet
gathered together his men. But Hotspur's gay spirit is not
shadowed by the possibility of almost certain defeat.
"Doomsday is near; die all, die merrily."

If all King Henry's captains were like Falstaff, the rebels
would be assured of a long life. That wily old campaigner
has drafted cowards who would be sure to buy themselves
off—"toasts-and-butter, with hearts in their bellies no
bigger than pins' heads." They have paid Falstaff more
than three hundred pounds to get them substitutes, and he
has spent a fraction of it in acquiring a hundred and fifty

vagrants, with only a shirt and a half to the lot of them. Prince Hal is startled by the strange crew, and Falstaff points out airily that they will serve well enough in an age of gunpowder. "Tut, tut; good enough to toss; food for powder, food for powder; they'll fill a pit as well as better; tush, man, mortal men, mortal men." He is a deplorable realist, and the golden glories of the field of honor have no interest for him whatsoever.

Meanwhile that most ardent of warriors, Hotspur, is eager to attack that night and is being held back by his uncle and Douglas the Scot. An envoy arrives from the king, asking for a list of their grievances, and Hotspur repeats the story of how his family supported the outlawed Henry and how he turned against them when he got the throne. The next morning, Hotspur's uncle goes to the king and repeats the charge, and Henry offers them all a general pardon if they will lay down their arms. Prince Hal is sure the rebels will not accept the offer, and Falstaff, that reluctant warrior, prepares for battle. "I would it were bedtime, Hal, and all well."

Prince Hal cheers his old friend on—"Why, thou owest God a death"—and leaves Falstaff to meditate on the subject of this particular debt. " 'Tis not due yet; I would be loath to pay Him before His day. What need I be so forward with Him that calls not on me? Well, 'tis no matter; honour pricks me on. Yes, but how if honour prick me off when I come on? How then? Can honour set to a leg? No." It will not set an arm either, or keep a wound from hurting. It is nothing but a word, and who possesses it? "He that died o' Wednesday. Doth he feel it? No." It is no use to the dead and will not remain with the living, for there will always be someone to belittle deeds of valor. And so Falstaff comes to his final conclusion, well suited to a man of his bulk and temperament: "I'll none of it."

Back in the rebels' camp, Hotspur's uncle has decided not to tell him of the king's generous offer, and the excited young hero addresses his soldiers in an eloquent call to arms. The battle is joined and all the threads of the story come together in a bloody conclusion.

The fight sways back and forth, and Falstaff's unhappy ragamuffins die in the thick of it. "There's not three of my hundred and fifty left alive, and they are for the town's end, to beg during life." Falstaff is not anxious to share their fate, especially when he stumbles over the corpse of Sir Walter Blunt. "I like not such grinning honour as Sir Walter hath; give me life." Falstaff is out of place on a field of honor, and he cannot even persuade the prince to stop for a jest in his old fashion.

Prince Hal is fighting so furiously he refuses to leave the battle to have his wounds tended. He is looking for Hotspur, that young and gallant foe, and Hotspur is looking for him. The two men meet at last and cross swords. England cannot hold the two of them and the prince triumphs, with Hotspur falling dead at his feet. Hal knows he has killed a great spirit and gives him a hero's salute. "Fare thee well, great heart!"

Falstaff has decided in the meantime that the only practical way to survive the battle is to sham death, and Hal finds his fat and apparently lifeless bulk stretched out near Hotspur's body. The prince says good-bye to his old friend also—"I could have better spared a better man"—and goes back into the battle. The mock corpse heaves itself up from the ground, and Falstaff has no difficulty in deciding that his action was a valiant one. "The better part of valour is discretion; in the which better part, I have saved my life."

Falstaff eyes the body of Hotspur with some nervousness, wondering if he is safely dead, and then stabs him to make sure. By this time he has decided that he may as well have the reputation for having killed him, and when Prince Hal returns Falstaff triumphantly casts the body of Hotspur at his feet and waits for his reward. "I look to be either earl or duke, I can assure you." The prince protests that he saw Falstaff dead and that he himself killed Hotspur, and Falstaff eyes him with benignant scorn. "Didst thou? Lord, Lord! how this world is given to lying! I grant you that I was down and out of breath, and so was he; but we rose both at an instant, and fought a long hour by Shrewsbury clock." The prince is willing to let him have his way, and the fat knight follows him from the field of battle, resolving to live virtuously "as a nobleman should."

King Henry, merciful in victory, gives Douglas the Scot

his freedom. Then he turns to the next problem that confronts him, the suppression of the rebel forces that are still in existence, led by Mortimer, Glendower and Hotspur's father. And so, with the royal army turning to its next task, the first part of *Henry IV* ends.

HENRY THE FOURTH, PART TWO

HENRY IV, PART TWO, continues the story that was begun in the preceding play, and most of the same characters reappear in it. It closes with the death of King Henry and the crowning of Prince Hal, and again it is Falstaff who dominates the play and the affections of the reader.

The story opens at the castle of the earl of Northumberland, who had failed to send the promised aid to Hotspur his son and so was largely responsible for his defeat and death at the battle of Shrewsbury. The old earl maintained he was ill and could not come, but most people felt his sickness was assumed for the occasion. A rumor that the rebels are victorious reaches the castle, but at last the old earl learns the truth. His son is dead on the field of battle and his gallant game with the "trade of danger" is ended. But the cause Hotspur fought for is not lost, since the archbishop of York has decided to join the rebellion. He is very conscious of the wrongs King Henry has committed and anxious to avenge the murder of King Richard. Many others are ready to do battle for the same reason, and the earl of Northumberland puts his attention to the twin problems of "safety and revenge."

Back in London, that fat old sinner, Sir John Falstaff, is strutting about in his newly-won dignities. His dear friend Prince Hal has given him a little page to attend him, and he has just bought himself twenty-two yards of satin for a new cloak and breeches. He does not have the money to pay for it, but petty considerations of that kind have never bothered Falstaff.

He encounters on the street a grave and reverend chief justice who unwisely attempts to point out to him the error of his ways. Falstaff professes to be amazed that so elderly a man should venture out in the fresh air, and when the

chief justice points out that he is an old man too, Falstaff
cannot imagine what he means. "My lord, I was born about
three of the clock in the afternoon, with a white head, and
something a round belly. For my voice, I have lost it with
hallowing and singing of anthems. . . . The truth is, I am
only old in judgement and understanding." It is a comfort
to the chief justice, struggling to uphold the dignity of the
law against so agile an opponent, that at least Prince Hal
and Falstaff will be separated. For Falstaff has been put
under the command of Hal's younger brother, Prince John,
in a campaign against the archbishop of York and the earl
of Northumberland. Falstaff agrees this is a wise way to use
such an invincible warrior. "There is not a dangerous
action can peep out his head but I am thrust upon it.
Well, I cannot last ever. But it was always yet the trick of
our English nation, if they have a good thing, to make it
too common. . . . I would to God my name was not so
terrible to the enemy as it is." The chief justice gives up,
defeated by so bland a liar, and Falstaff promptly suggests
he might like to lend him a thousand pounds. "Not a
penny," says the chief justice, clear at least about that,
and Falstaff is left to meditate on the eight small coins
in his purse. He is also handicapped by a touch of gout
in his great toe, but it is to be expected that a warrior
should limp a little and the disability might be used to increase the size of a pension.

The archbishop of York holds a consultation with some
of the other rebels, and they agree that their chief problem
is the earl of Northumberland. It is impossible to know if
he can be trusted to give them any assistance. On the other
hand, King Henry has divided his army into three parts,
and Prince John will have a comparatively small force to
lead against them. Moreover, the archbishop is convinced
that the country is growing restive under Henry's rule and
regrets that it ever supported him against King Richard.
"The commonwealth is sick of their own choice."

Back in London, Falstaff's long-suffering landlady, Mistress Quickly, has finally decided to bring suit again him.
He owes her a hundred marks, which is a great deal "for
a poor lone woman to bear; and I have borne, and borne,
and borne, and have been fubbed off, and fubbed off, and

fubbed off, from this day to that day, that it is a shame to be thought on." Two officers try to arrest Falstaff and he creates such a disturbance that the chief justice arrives on the scene. Mistress Quickly wails out Falstaff's sins. "He hath eaten me out of house and home." She also maintains, and this is the root of his offending, that he has ignored his promise to marry her, a promise he made last Whitsuntide, before a coal fire, just before the butcher's wife came in to borrow some vinegar for a dish of prawns. Falstaff denies the whole thing and gravely informs the chief justice that the poor soul is mad, a piece of information the chief justice does not believe. Then the fat knight, superbly undefeated, takes Mistress Quickly aside for a brief chat, and the upshot is that he succeeds in borrowing ten pounds. She does not have it with her, but she will get it by pawning her plate and her wall hangings.

Falstaff is supposed to be on his way to York to join Prince John and the army, but he decides instead to have supper with Mistress Quickly and a warm-hearted, rampageous little tart named Doll Tearsheet. Prince Hal is back in London, and he and his friend Poins decide to dress up as serving boys in the same tavern to see what Falstaff will say about them. Prince Hal's gallant behavior at Shrewsbury has not changed his habits, but he is becoming increasingly aware that he cannot keep up such conduct once he becomes king. "We play the fools with the time, and the spirits of the wise sit in the clouds and mock us."

In the castle of the earl of Northumberland, the old man is torn between his duty to his allies and the persuasions of his wife and his daughter-in-law. Hotspur's widow cannot see why he should give the help to others that he withheld from his own son, and the two women finally persuade the earl to take refuge in Scotland and wait to see what happens to Prince John's forces at York.

Falstaff has his supper with Doll Tearsheet and Mistress Quickly, and all three of them have a fine time. Doll has drunk too much canary, which, as her hostess says, is "a marvellous searching wine," but she recovers from it rapidly except for a slight case of hiccups. The party is interrupted by a friend of Falstaff's named Pistol, who is fond of orating blank verse and has a brisk fight with Doll. Falstaff finally heaves up his fat bulk and chases his friend from the room, and the delighted Doll twines herself around the conqueror's neck. Then she sits on his knee and begins to worry about his future. "Thou whoreson little tidy Bartholomew boar-pig, when wilt thou leave fighting o' days, and foining o' nights, and begin to patch up thine old body for heaven?"

Falstaff does not wish to consider so uncomfortable a subject, and instead he starts discussing that "shallow young fellow," Prince Hal. This is not a wise thing to do, for Hal and Poins have just entered in their serving aprons and are able to hear the uncomplimentary remarks. Falstaff, having drunk too much, then grows maudlin—"I am old, I am old"—while Doll comforts him. "I love thee better than I love e'er a scurvy young boy of them all." Falstaff revives and calls for more drink, and the prince comes forward to serve him. Falstaff does his best to wriggle out of the corner he has worked himself into and is finally saved by the news he must go and join the army. He makes a lofty exit: "Farewell, hostess; farewell, Doll. You see, my good wenches, how men of merit are sought after." Doll is in tears, and Mistress Quickly is equally emotional. "I have known thee these twenty-nine years, come peascod-time, but an honester and truer-hearted man—well, fare thee well." So Falstaff departs, the very picture of a noble soldier and gallant patriot, and then sends a message for Doll Tearsheet to come to him.

In the royal palace at Westminster, King Henry is ill, and sleepless with concern over the state of his kingdom. He cannot forget that the dead King Richard prophesied rebellion and is greatly worried over the gathering of the rebels at York. His lords comfort him as much as they can. The Welsh rising at least is over, for Owen Glendower is dead.

Falstaff, on his way to York, has reached Gloucestershire, where an old school friend has agreed to find him some recruits. The name of the old friend is Shallow, now a justice of the peace, and he and his cousin Silence are waiting for Falstaff to arrive. Justice Shallow is in a reminiscent mood, thinking of the days of his youth when he and Falstaff attended law school at one of the London inns of chancery. "I was once of Clement's Inn, where I think they will talk of mad Shallow yet." He remembers all the wonderful times he had—what a fine fellow Will Squele was and how he himself had a notable fight "with one Sampson Stockfish, a fruiterer, behind Gray's Inn. Jesu, Jesu, the mad days that I have spent! and to see how many of mine old acquaintance are dead!" His memories of the dear dead days are mingled with practical farm talk, for Justice Shallow is a countryman, and his cousin listens to him with the deepest respect.

Falstaff arrives, and the recruits are paraded in front of him. The usual way of checking off a man's name was to put a prick in the paper, and Falstaff holds a roll with the names ready to mark. The recruits as a whole are not eager for battle. As one of their number says, "You could have let me alone; my old dame will be undone now for one to do her husbandry and drudgery: you need not to have pricked me; there are other men fitter to go out than I." Another has a cough and most of them manage to buy their way out of the service. The best of them is a spirited little tailor: "I care not; a man can die but once." Falstaff had called him a "most magnanimous mouse," but he is better than that.

Once his official work is done, Falstaff chats with his old school friend, remembering the nights when they were young and the girls they knew. It seems to Justice Shallow that everything was better in the days of his youth, and when he watches musket practice he remembers how much better muskets were handled when he studied at Clement's Inn. "There was a little quiver fellow, and a' would manage you his piece thus: and a' would about and about, and come you in, and come you in: 'Rah, tah, tah,' would a' say; 'Bounce,' would a' say; and away again would a' go, and again would a' come: I shall never see such a fellow." Everything about the London of his youth is wonderful to Justice Shallow, and a man like Falstaff, who is familiar with London and the court, is a great man in his eyes. As for Falstaff, he still wants the thousand pounds that he failed to borrow from the chief justice, and when he returns from the wars he knows exactly what Justice Shallow ought to do with all his extra money.

In Yorkshire, the rebels are waiting in Gaultree Forest to meet the king's army, and Prince John, as its leader, sends an envoy to talk with them there. They present a list of their grievances which the envoy takes back to the prince, and Prince John promises on his honor that they will be given full redress. As soon as they trustingly dismiss their army, however, he arrests them on a charge of high treason. Falstaff turns up late, having acquired a single prisoner more or less by accident, and Prince John reproves him. "When everything is ended, then you come." Falstaff assures him he wore out nearly two hundred horses in his haste, and the prince, relenting, promises to speak for him at court and let him go back to London through Gloucestershire. But Falstaff does not like Prince John. "This same young sober-blooded boy doth not love me, nor a man cannot make him laugh; but that's no marvel, he drinks no wine." It is Falstaff's theory that the whole royal family is cold by nature, and that Prince Hal has become warm and lively only because he is so intelligent a drinker.

Within his palace at Westminster, the perturbed King Henry is still brooding on the problem of Prince Hal's worthiness to succeed to the crown. His other sons are gathered around him, but Hal is off enjoying himself in a tavern with Poins. The news comes that the rebels have been destroyed and the land is at peace, but the king cannot find happiness even in that. He becomes suddenly ill and is carried to his bedroom. He asks to be left alone, with the crown set beside him on his pillow, and when Prince Hal comes to see him he looks at his father's closed eyes and thinks he is dead. Hal is deeply grieved but he cannot help thinking of the crown, which is his if the king is dead, and he takes it with him into the next room.

The king awakens and immediately assumes that Hal has snatched the crown from him. But his lords report that the prince is in the next room, in tears. King Henry is sure that his eldest son rejoices in the idea of his father's death, but Hal finally manages to convince him how deep his love really is.

King Henry, profoundly comforted, is able to talk to his son and heir about the problems of kingship that have been haunting him.

> *God knows, my son,*
> *By what by-paths and indirect crook'd ways*
> *I met this crown; and I myself know well*
> *How troublesome it sat upon my head . . .*

It is Henry's hope that his son will rule with more assurance than he has been able to do, for the king is still full of remorse for Richard's death. "How I came by the crown, O God forgive!" But Prince Hal has no doubts of the legitimacy of the claim of the Lancastrian line to the throne.

> *My gracious liege,*
> *You won it, wore it, kept it, gave it me;*
> *Then plain and right must my possession be . . .*

King Henry can die in peace, for his wild and wayward son is at last ready to take up the responsibilities of the throne.

King Henry dies and the hearts of most men are heavy, for they believe that the kingdom will be given over to a rule of dice and taverns. Especially worried is the chief justice, for he once had occasion to send Prince Hal to prison and now that the young man is the new King Henry V he has the power to revenge himself for the indignity. The new king enters, and the chief justice heroically tells him he would do the same thing again, since he is sworn to uphold impartially the laws of the land. Hal listens to him with close attention and then asks him to be his chief adviser. For the new King Henry intends to have a reign of dignity, law and "formal majesty," and he is prepared to listen to wise counsels.

Down in Gloucestershire, Falstaff has renewed his acquaintance with Justice Shallow, and they are eating apples in the garden when Pistol arrives from London with the news that the king is dead. Now that his own dear Hal is the ruler of England, Falstaff can see himself as the most powerful man at court with all the laws of England under his fat hand. "We'll ride all night. . . . Let us take any man's horses; the laws of England are at my commandment. Happy are they which have been my friends, and woe unto my lord chief justice."

Some of Falstaff's friends in London have already fallen on evil days. Mistress Quickly and Doll Tearsheet have become involved in a murder case and they are arrested, shouting at the top of their voices as the officers drag them through the streets. Pistol goes off to get Falstaff's help and finds him outside Westminster Abbey, waiting for the king to emerge after his coronation. Falstaff has brought Justice Shallow along to show him how devoted the king is to his old companion; and Shallow has a deep personal interest in the matter since Falstaff, as the climax of a long career of borrowing, has actually succeeded in getting from him the thousand pounds.

King Henry V enters, to the sound of trumpets, and in the procession that accompanies him is the lord chief justice. Falstaff calls out to him, to his darling, his Hal, but the king who answers is a cold stranger.

I know thee not, old man: fall to thy prayers . . .

All the laughter they once knew together is forgotten, and only the sinfulness remains. If Falstaff is willing to reform, the king will see him again; but otherwise they have parted company forever.

The royal retinue continues on its way, leaving Falstaff to face his startled companion, and his first words are those of a true realist. "Master Shallow, I owe you a thousand pound." Then his irrepressible optimism reasserts itself. "I shall be sent for in private to him. Look you, he must seem thus to the world." Surely the king would not betray so old a friendship for a little thing like the laws of the realm.

But he can and he does. Falstaff and his followers are taken away to Fleet prison, and the play closes with Prince John and the lord chief justice talking together. Henry V has just called his parliament together, and there is a rumor that within the year there will be war with France.

HENRY THE FIFTH

HENRY V tells the story of Prince Hal as king of England and deals especially with his military expedition to France. It is a study in patriotism, and Henry is pictured as the most heroic of monarchs, with a nature as simple and as stirring as a trumpet call. Yet the play is in many ways a subtle one, with several points of view represented, and it is not wholly a glorification of war.

It was not easy for Shakespeare to represent, on a small wooden stage, the movements of kings and armies and especially the great battle of Agincourt.

> *Can this cockpit hold*
> *The vasty fields of France, or may we cram*
> *Within this wooden O the very casques*
> *That did affright the air at Agincourt? . . .*

Therefore Shakespeare calls on that mighty force, the collective imagination of the audience, for help. "Piece out our imperfections with your thoughts." Shakespeare knew he could get the members of his audience to follow him anywhere, as long as they took their imaginations with them.

The play opens in London, where the archbishop of Canterbury and the bishop of Ely are discussing a bill which has been presented in parliament. The bill would strip the church of most of its wealth, and both men hope the new king will resist it; for he has shown himself to be a devout monarch and deeply interested in the church's welfare. In return, the churchmen are prepared to give King Henry a huge sum of money for his military preparations if he decides to invade France and to give him full backing in his claim to the French crown.

Henry is not sure he has a right to the French crown

and refuses to start a war unless he is certain of his position. The archbishop gives him a long and learned exposition as to why his claim is legitimate, and also urges the glory of such an expedition. Henry still hesitates, for it is possible that the Scots will invade England while he is gone. The archbishop is convinced the government will continue safely in his absence and gives him an eloquent and reassuring picture of the orderliness of a well-run country like England. It is like a community of bees, with each one doing his special work, from the ones that act as porters bringing in the honey, to "the singing masons building roofs of gold."

The king decides he will invade France and gives audience to an ambassador from the French prince, the dauphin. The dauphin has sent him a highly insulting gift; instead of the valuable jewels that usually pass between princes he has sent him a box of tennis balls, in reference to the king's reputation as a light reveler when he was Prince Hal. The king is furious. In the previous play his father had said of him, "Being incensed, he's flint," and it is a cold and stony anger that takes possession of King Henry as he promises to avenge the mockery of the French prince.

All England is seized by the excitement of the military expedition to France. "Now all the youth of England are on fire." Even the London rapscallions who are friends of Falstaff have caught the infection. One of them has become a corporal and the other a lieutenant, although the corporal is a little doubtful of his sword. "It will toast cheese." The first person he draws it on is Pistol, who is even less valorous than he. Pistol has just married Falstaff's hostess, Mistress Quickly, and the whole crew hears the news that Falstaff is very ill. Mistress Quickly goes to nurse him, convinced that he is dying of sorrow and that he never recovered from King Henry's rejection of him. "The king has killed his heart." The fat old knight will never be able to go on the expedition to France, but his trio of old friends plans to accompany the army and make as much money out of it as they can.

At Southampton, the port of embarkation for France, King Henry has discovered that the three commissioners he sent to France have been bribed by French gold to murder him. He calls them into his presence and with bitter regret accuses them of high treason. Then he sets sail for France, leaving a loyal and united country behind him.

Mistress Quickly says good-bye to her husband in London, since he will not let her go part way with him to Southampton. Pistol and all the rest of Falstaff's friends are in low spirits, for Falstaff is dead. One of them suggests that Falstaff may have gone to hell, but Mistress Quickly knows better. She was with him when he died. She is a fuddled old soul and does not know Arthur from Abraham, but she is kind and she loved Falstaff. She describes his death in a piece of prose that is as remarkable in its way as the greatest of Shakespeare's poetry, and if Falstaff had to die he could never have had a better epitaph.

> *Nay, sure, he's not in hell: he's in Arthur's bosom, if ever man went to Arthur's bosom. A' made a finer end and went away an it had been any christom child; a' parted even just between twelve and one, even at the turning o' the tide: for after I saw him fumble with the sheets and play with flowers and smile upon his fingers' ends, I knew there was but one way; for his nose was as sharp as a pen, and a' babbled of green fields. 'How now, Sir John?' quoth I: 'What, man! Be of good cheer!' So a' cried out, 'God, God, God!' three or four times: now I, to comfort him, bid him a' should not think of God. I hoped there was no need to trouble himself with any such thoughts yet. So a' bade me lay more clothes on his feet: I put my hand into the bed and felt them, and they were as cold as any stone; then I felt to his knees, and so upward and upward, and all was as cold as any stone.*

So Falstaff died, in immortal prose, and after a loving and foolish old woman had pulled the bedclothes up over him, he went on into his own kind of immortality. He could never have remained in the play, for it is dominated by a conception of military glory that would only have made

him laugh, and he and the new king had nothing more to
say to each other. Falstaff belonged to a different world,
and it is this world that mourns him truly. "Would I were
with him."

At the court of France, the dauphin argues that a king
of tennis balls will pose no threat to his country's might,
but the rest of the French aristocracy is not so sure. For
Henry of England is a descendant of that mighty warrior,
Edward III, who defeated the flower of French chivalry at
the battle of Crécy. An ambassador arrives with a warlike
challenge from Henry, coupled with a special warning to
the dauphin, but the French prince is still convinced that
the English monarch is only a man of "youth and vanity."

King Henry sets sail for France, the silken banners
streaming from his ships as they all converge on the French
port of Harfleur. The English king leads his men in an
attack on the walls of the city, and when they are thrown
back it is his shout that rallies them

Once more unto the breach, dear friends, once more;
Or close the wall up with our English dead . . .

Falstaff's friends show little enthusiasm for the fight, and
neither does the boy they have brought with them. "Would
I were in an alehouse in London! I would give all my
fame for a pot of ale and safety." The man who most enjoys the battle, perhaps, is a Welsh captain named Fluellen.
His whole soul is wrapped up in the techniques of warfare, and he likes everything to be done properly and in
the approved manner. He gets into a hot argument with
an Irish captain who is responsible for laying the gunpowder mines, since in Fluellen's opinion the other man
is an ass and does not understand the situation at all.

Whatever their internal disagreements, the English manage to capture Harfleur, and the rest of France can think
of nothing but the invading English army. The daughter of
the king of France goes so far as to take a lesson in the
English language, and the noblemen of France press the
king to let them march against the invaders. The king of
France finally consents and sends his own son and the
flower of the French army against the English, who have

become "sick and famished" in their long winter marches and are in no shape for fighting.

Men like Captain Fluellen try to maintain discipline in the English camp that winter, while men like Pistol try to break it down. King Henry keeps a close watch on everything that goes on, and when one of Pistol's friends robs a French church he is hanged. For the English king is determined to prevent looting by his army, or any cruelty to the peasants. The French herald arrives with a challenge and Henry admits that his army is too "weak and sickly" to meet it. Nevertheless, they will fight. Henry's brother expresses openly what is in the thoughts of all: "I hope they will not come upon us now." But King Henry will not permit that kind of despair. "We are in God's hand, brother, not in theirs."

Through the night the two opposing armies wait for the dawn. On the French side there are sixty thousand fighting men, led by the greatest lords of France, and all night long the excited noblemen talk of their horses and armor and wait impatiently for the day. On the English side there are only twelve thousand men, worn with sickness and as thin as ghosts. They sit by their campfires waiting patiently for the coming battle, and King Henry spends the night going among them. He has borrowed one of his officer's cloaks and the men do not know him.

Captain Fluellen spends the night trying to keep the English up to the high standards of military behavior he has set for them. It seems to him that they are talking much too loudly and that none of the great warriors of the past would have permitted such slackness. "If you would take the pains but to examine the wars of Pompey the Great, you shall find, I warrant you, that there is no tiddle-taddle nor pibble-pabble in Pompey's camp." King Henry, muffled in his cloak, listens to him and then passes on to where three common soldiers are watching the first streaks of the coming dawn. They are afraid of what will happen, since the odds are five to one in favor of the French, and they are sure that the king must be afraid too. "He may show what outward courage he will, but I believe, as cold a night as 'tis, he could wish himself in Thames up to the neck; and so I would he were, and I by him." For it is better to freeze in a London river than to be slaughtered in a foreign land.

King Henry, cloaked and speaking as though he were a common soldier, tries to rouse the three men to a sense of valor. "Methinks I could not die anywhere so contented as in the king's company, his cause being just and his quarrel honourable." But he is talking to men who have been sent out to fight with no knowledge of why they came; and one of their number, a man named Williams, speaks for the long line of common soldiers who have died throughout history for the quarrels of kings.

> *If the cause be not good, the king himself hath a heavy reckoning to make; when all those legs and arms and heads, chopped off in battle, shall join together at the latter day, and cry all, 'We died at such a place'; some swearing, some crying for a surgeon, some upon their wives left poor behind them, some upon the debts they owe, some upon their children rawly left. I am afeard there are few die well that die in a battle; for how can they charitably dispose of any thing when blood is their argument? Now, if these men do not die well, it will be a black matter for the king that led them.*

The king tries to disclaim such a responsibility, but Williams is still mistrustful of royalty, against whom no common man can defend himself. He and the disguised king get into an argument, and they agree to wear each other's gloves in their caps so they can recognize each other by daylight and take up the quarrel again. Another of the soldiers tries unsuccessfully to act as a peacemaker. "Be friends, you English fools, be friends; we have French quarrels enow, if you could tell how to reckon."

The king himself knows well what the reckoning is—five Frenchman against each Englishman—and when he is alone he prays that his men will forget the odds against them.

> *O God of battles! steel my soldiers' hearts;*
> *Possess them not with fear; take from them now*
> *The sense of reckoning . . .*

As for himself he prays that for this single day at least the Lord will not remember the sin his father committed in seizing the crown, since he himself has practiced unremitting repentance and prayed for the soul of murdered King Richard.

Daylight comes, and the French chivalry ride forth in a massed glory of banners and glittering armor to destroy the waiting English. The English know that they face "fearful odds," and one of the earls cannot help wishing they had more men. King Henry hears him and sends out an order that, on the contrary, any soldier who wishes to leave them now and set sail for England may have the money to get him there. For this battle is a privilege that the king would not force on any man, and in a magnificent speech he rallies the fearful hearts of his soldiers.

> *This day is called the feast of Crispian:*
> *He that outlives this day, and comes safe home,*
> *Will stand a tip-toe when this day is named,*
> *And rouse him at the name of Crispian. . . .*
> *Old men forget: yet all shall be forgot,*
> *But he'll remember with advantages*
> *What feats he did that day . . .*

Like the notes of a trumpet, King Henry names the men who will fight on St. Crispin's Day, the handful of Englishmen who will carry their country's banner even when they are so desperately outnumbered.

> *We few, we happy few, we band of brothers;*
> *For he today that sheds his blood with me*
> *Shall be my brother . . .*

Then, with a smile, King Henry turns to the earl who had longed for more men: "Thou dost not wish more help from England?" And the earl says he almost wishes that he and the king could fight the enemy alone. The French herald arrives to suggest that King Henry arrange for ransom since he cannot hope to win the battle, and the English king sends back word that his army may lack gilding and plumes but it does not lack heart.

The battle is joined, the great battle of Agincourt in which the English bowmen routed the French chivalry, and almost from the first the issue is clear. Even an empty braggart like Pistol manages to capture a prisoner, and the only real triumph the French achieve is to slaughter the boys who are guarding the supplies. The excited Captain Fluellen maintains that King Henry is the latter-day image of Alexander the Great, although one was born in Monmouth and the other in Macedon. "If you look in the maps of the 'orld, I warrant you shall find, in the comparisons between Macedon and Monmouth, that the situations, look you, is both alike. There is a river in Macedon, and there is also moreover a river in Monmouth . . . and there is salmons in both." Monmouth is in Wales, and since Fluellen is a Welshman he feels that King Henry could not have chosen a better place to be born.

The battle is over, the victory of the English is complete, and the French herald returns humbly to ask permission to take the dead bodies from the field. Henry grants the request and stands surrounded by his rejoicing army, with Fluellen reminding him that the Welsh also fought at the side of Henry's grandfather in the battle of Crécy. King Henry sees Williams, the soldier who quarreled with him the night before, and recognizes him by the glove in his cap. He gives Fluellen his own glove to wear, and Williams attempts to box the captain's ear. Then King Henry reveals that the blow was intended for him, and Fluellen talks of having the man hanged. But Williams, as a sturdy Englishman, stands up for himself against them all, and the king rewards his courage by filling his glove with gold pieces. Fluellen, equally forgiving, adds twelvepence and some good advice. "I pray you to serve God, and keep you out of prawls and prabbles." Williams, independent to the end, refuses the money, and Fluellen presses it on him most politely. " 'Tis a good shilling."

King Henry returns briefly to England, where he and his men are given a hero's welcome, and peace negotiations are started with the French. Then Henry returns to

France with his men, the indestructible Pistol among them. Most of Pistol's old companions have been hanged, and he himself incurs the wrath of Captain Fluellen for insulting a Welsh leek. In the end Pistol decides to return to England, with a patch on his head where the Welsh captain hit him, to claim it was a wound he received in the wars. His wife is dead and Pistol will turn robber on the English roads, as so many old soldiers were still doing in Shakespeare's day.

The peace negotiations with France proceed successfully, and King Henry arrives at the French court to discuss them. One of the provisions of the treaty is that Henry shall marry the Princess Katharine of France, and they are tactfully left together while he proceeds with his wooing. In spite of her earlier attempts to learn the language, Katharine knows very little English, and the two of them enact a charming scene—the gentle, coy lady who pretends not to understand anything he is saying and the lively, blunt Englishman who cannot woo in silken phrases. "I know no ways to mince it in love, but directly to say, 'I love you' . . . and so clap hands and a bargain." He ruefully admits he has no skill at writing love verses, although he would make a fine lover "if I could win a lady at leap-frog, or by vaulting into my saddle with my armour on my back." He attempts a little French and then retires defeated by the effort to twist his English tongue around a foreign language. But Henry woos well, since he knows how to kiss, and in the end it is decided that he and his Kate will marry.

Peace is declared between England and France, and Henry is made the heir to the French throne. There is hope that the two kingdoms may be united and the long wars between them cease. But Henry dies young, leaving a baby to inherit the crown, and the next reign sees not only the loss of France but the scourge of war descending upon England itself.

HENRY THE SIXTH, PART ONE

THE THREE PARTS of *Henry VI* continue Shakespeare's story of English history and deal chiefly with civil war—the Wars of the Roses. Shakespeare was a comparatively young man when he wrote this trilogy, an inexperienced dramatist writing for an excitable and patriotic audience, and the plays are not to be read as history but rather as a portrait of the way a loyal Englishman in 1590 would look on events that had occurred more than a century earlier.

The first part of the trilogy, *Henry VI, Part One,* has two themes, the growing contention among the English noblemen that finally leads to civil war, and the military conflict in France. England's chief opponent in France is Joan of Arc, and it was quite clear to the members of Shakespeare's audience that she could never have conquered their gallant countrymen except through sorcery. Therefore Joan appears in the play as a peasant girl, half comic and half wicked, who practices open witchcraft and is helped by fiends. This seems a ridiculous characterization today, but it was the one that was believed in England when Shakespeare wrote the play. The real historical Joan had, after all, been executed on a charge of heresy and sorcery, and while the verdict was later reversed, it took the English a long time to admit her innocence.

The play opens with the funeral of Henry V in Westminster Abbey. "This star of England," once the lively Prince Hal and then the heroic victor of Agincourt, is dead, and all England mourns. "Hung be the heavens with black, yield day to night!" He has left behind him a little son to reign as Henry VI, and the boy's uncle, the good Duke Humphrey, has been named Lord Protector.

Another uncle has been named regent of France, to guard the English interests there, and one by one the towns that the English possess in France are being lost. But the gallant English are still fighting. At the moment they are besieging the town of Orleans and holding the suburbs, and the French can do nothing against them. Although the English are as weak as "drowned mice" from lack of food they refuse to give up the siege, and when Joan of Arc arrives with an offer of supernatural services the French gladly accept her aid.

Back in England, a quarrel begins between the good Duke Humphrey and the wicked cardinal of Winchester, and their men riot in the streets, blue-coats against tawny-coats. It is the first sign of trouble in England and a portent of the coming war.

Lord Talbot, England's greatest soldier, arrives at Orleans to give his assistance, and when the leader of the English forces is accidentally killed by a French gunner's boy, Lord Talbot takes command. Yet even he cannot hold the suburbs against Joan, since she is in the devil's service. The French conquer through "baleful sorcery," but when they are carousing after the battle, Talbot attacks in the darkness and rain and captures the town again. A French countess asks him to visit her, hoping to have him murdered; but Talbot is wise enough to bring his soldiers along, and the countess bows to "so great a warrior."

In London, still another English feud is brewing. The earl of Somerset quarrels with young Richard Plantagenet in a garden, and both of them try to win friends to their side. There are roses growing in the garden, white ones and red, and Plantagenet asks anyone who supports him to wear a white rose as a sign. Somerset does the same with the red, and out of this small beginning comes the civil war that was known as the Wars of the Roses, the struggle for the crown between the red rose of Lancaster and the white rose of York.

Richard Plantagenet, of the white rose, is a nephew of old Mortimer, earl of March, who has been in prison ever since the days, long ago, when he and Owen Glendower fought against the power of Henry IV. Mortimer was descended from a third son of the great Edward III, while Henry could only trace his descent from a fourth son. Therefore Mortimer felt he had a better right than the Lancastrian Henry to rule England, and he manages to convince his nephew that their own line of York has been dishonorably treated by the house of Lancaster. What his nephew, Richard Plantagenet, chiefly wants at the moment is to be given his rightful title as duke of York; he does not yet aspire to the thought of becoming king.

The quarrel between Duke Humphrey and the cardinal of Winchester continues in the Parliament House. The youthful King Henry implores them to keep the peace and they finally shake hands, but Duke Humphrey knows that the evil cardinal is still his enemy. During this same meeting of parliament, Richard Plantagenet is made duke of York; and the earl of Somerset, who had quarreled with him in the garden, mutters savagely under his breath. But outwardly everything is peaceful, and King Henry decides to go to Paris. Paris is still held by the English, and Henry wishes to be crowned there as king of France.

Joan of Arc, the "damned sorceress," captures another city from the brave Lord Talbot, this time by a trick, and once again his heroic fighting wins the city back for the English. Since the French cannot win by force of arms, they try guile, and they succeed in winning Talbot's chief ally away from him, largely through the clever pleading of Joan.

Lord Talbot goes to Paris for Henry's coronation, but even here the constant quarreling of the English continues. Henry's subjects are openly wearing red or white roses in their caps, and Henry himself, anxious to keep the peace, puts on a red rose. It belongs to him by right, since he is of the Lancastrian line, but he assures both sides that he will play no favorites. The weak and youthful king wants "peace and love" in his realm, but he has nothing to enforce it with except his good intentions.

Lord Talbot besieges the city of Bordeaux and implores the English to send him aid. But those old enemies, the duke of York and the earl of Somerset, quarrel again over the question of who should send him the soldiers, and as a result Talbot does not get his reinforcements. He and his heroic son die in battle, the young man in his father's arms, in a scene that was the high point of the play in Shakespeare's day and always reduced the audience to tears. Joan of Arc mocks the dead hero, with the malice that might be expected from a sorceress.

King Henry decides to seek peace with France, and although he is young to marry he will ask for a French lady as his bride. But as the battles continue, the tide begins to turn against the French. Joan of Arc is captured, although she calls upon all the fiends to save her, and in the same battle the young earl of Suffolk captures a beautiful Frenchwoman named Margaret of Anjou. He falls in love with her instantly and longs to marry her. But since he is already married, he decides to persuade King Henry to marry her instead.

Joan of Arc is questioned by her English captors and curses them all. They condemn her to be burned at the stake, since she is clearly a "foul accursèd minister of hell," and then the English regent holds a peace conference with the French and ends the war.

The earl of Suffolk returns to London and describes Margaret in such glowing terms that King Henry decides to marry her, even though she is poor and has no dowry. The play ends with the earl of Suffolk congratulating himself on his success. For Henry is weak and will be ruled by his new bride, while the new bride loves Suffolk and will be ruled only by him.

> Margaret shall now be queen, and rule the king;
> But I will rule both her, the king, and realm.

HENRY THE SIXTH, PART TWO

THE SECOND PART of *Henry VI* continues the story of his reign and ends with the opening of the Wars of the Roses. The first half of the play is chiefly concerned with the fall of Duke Humphrey, who is the best and wisest nobleman in the realm, and the second half portrays the rise of the duke of York until he is strong enough to claim the throne.

The play opens at the point where *Henry VI, Part One* ended. The earl of Suffolk, hoping to get full control of the weak young king, has arranged his marriage with Margaret of Anjou; and, to the sound of trumpets, he escorts the new queen into the royal presence. The good Duke Humphrey is the king's uncle and Lord Protector of England, and he is shocked both by the marriage and by the shameful terms of the treaty with France. But his old enemy, the cardinal of Winchester, makes it appear that Duke Humphrey is displeased with the marriage because he is next in line to the throne and does not want Henry to have any children. Equally displeased by Henry's marriage is the duke of York, who has finally convinced himself that he is the true heir to the throne by descent from Edward III. He can do nothing at the moment, but he is sure the time will come when he can raise the white rose of York as his standard and be proclaimed England's king.

Duke Humphrey is handicapped by a stupid and ambitious wife who is sure that her husband should try to win the crown. She has even hired a witch and a conjurer to help her peer into the future and does not know that they are both in the earl of Suffolk's pay. The new queen, Margaret, hates the duchess for her wealth and her pride and finds an excuse to give her a box on the ear. Anxious young King Henry tries to placate them, but he cannot keep the peace even between women; and his aunt tells him what is no less than the truth, that he is letting his wife rule the kingdom.

That night, within Duke Humphrey's garden, his wife watches while the conjurer pretends to raise spirits. They come, in thunder and lightning, to bring prophecies, and then the duchess is arrested on a charge of consulting with witches about the king's death. Her good old husband, who does not know what she has been doing, is out hunting with the king and queen near St. Alban's. Within the town itself a miracle is proclaimed, of a blind man who has suddenly received his sight, but the wise duke exposes him as a fraud. All the noblemen hate him for his intelligence and power, and they rejoice when the news comes that his wife has been arrested.

The duke of York is as anxious as any of the rest to pull Duke Humphrey down from his high place in the realm. For the king's uncle is the "shepherd of the flock," and the kingdom is safe as long as he remains in charge of it. Once Duke Humphrey is disposed of, the unsteady young king will not be able to keep his throne for long. The duke of York, for instance, has already been able to win the powerful earl of Warwick to his side. Warwick is willing to agree that the Yorkist claim to the throne is a good one, but he is sure that the time is not yet ripe to proclaim it.

Duke Humphrey's wife is declared guilty and the duke gives up his position as Lord Protector of the realm. Queen Margaret rejoices, for she is convinced that now she will have complete authority over the king and that she and Suffolk will be able to rule England together.

The quarrels of the great have spread to the common people. An armorer's apprentice named Peter reports that his master claimed the duke of York was the rightful king one evening when they were busy together in the garret cleaning the duke's armor. Peter's master denies the charge, and they fight a duel with sandbags. Peter is sure he will be killed and gives up his small possessions—his hammer and his apron—to his fellow apprentices. But he wins the duel, and the king rewards him, since it was believed in those days that God always intervened on the side of the duelist who was in the right.

Part of the sentence which has been imposed on Duke

Humphrey's proud wife is that she should go barefoot and penitent through the streets clad in a white sheet. Her sorrowing husband watches her go past, and she warns him he will be the next one to be destroyed. Duke Humphrey is sure that he is safe, since the king loves him and he has done no wrong; but at the next meeting of parliament, when he is not there to defend himself, the queen and Suffolk accuse him of taking bribes from France. The latest news from France seems to bear out their accusation, and when Duke Humphrey makes his appearance, Suffolk arrests him on a charge of high treason. King Henry is too weak to stop the arrest, since everyone else has agreed to it, but he weeps bitterly over the fall of his innocent uncle.

As soon as the king has left the room, four people plot Duke Humphrey's death. They are the queen, the earl of Suffolk, the cardinal and the duke of York. They know that the charge of treason can never be proven against him, and so they plan to murder him secretly. News arrives of a rebellion in Ireland and they send the duke of York there to suppress it. York is delighted, for the one thing he has lacked is an army, and now an army will be given him. In his absence he hopes that more trouble will be stirred up in England, and so he gives support to a rebellion led by a peasant named Jack Cade.

The earl of Suffolk hires two murderers who strangle Duke Humphrey in his bed. Then he tries to pretend the death was a natural one but the earl of Warwick accuses him of murder. The House of Commons, enraged by the death of so good a man, decrees that Suffolk must be banished, and he and Queen Margaret bid each other a sad farewell. Then the news comes that his other ally, the cardinal, is dying. The sins on the cardinal's conscience oppress him and he dies shrieking of hell.

The banished earl of Suffolk sets sail for France and is captured by English pirates. He expects to be released when he tells them who he is, but the captain of the band feels that Suffolk is responsible for all of England's troubles, and the earl, shouting defiance to the end, is beheaded by the pirates.

Jack Cade's rebellion gathers strength, for the common people of England have many reasons to hate the nobility.

The rebels plan to make everyone equal by pulling down their rulers, and Jack Cade has decided he is really the heir to the throne instead of a bricklayer's son. He intends to get rid of noblemen and lawyers and also of economics. "There shall be in England seven halfpenny loaves sold for a penny." With such a program he has no difficulty in finding followers, and when they reach London they swarm triumphantly through the streets, with the bloody heads of their enemies brandished on poles in front of them.

Finally a valiant fighter named Lord Clifford calls a parley with the rebels and manages to persuade them to lay down their arms. Jack Cade is forced to flee for his life and wanders about the countryside, starving, for several days. Finally he climbs over a brick wall to steal some greens from a garden in Kent and is killed by its righteous and property-loving owner.

The rebellion is over, but a worse one flares up immediately. For the duke of York comes marching back from Ireland at the head of his troops. He intends to invade the kingdom and claim the crown, but he gives as a pretext the fact that he wants one of the king's friends to be imprisoned. He and King Henry meet, and the duke of York is not sure that he is strong enough to declare his real intentions openly. But Queen Margaret enters in the company of the nobleman who was supposed to be in prison, and York can control himself no longer. In his anger he tells them that he is the true king of England, brushes aside a charge of treason, and calls in his two sons, Edward and the hunchbacked Richard, to stand by their father. Then he summons the rest of his allies, especially the mighty earl of Warwick, and defies the king to keep the throne from him.

So the civil wars begin, the red rose of Lancaster against the white rose of York, and the first battle is fought at St. Alban's. Old Lord Clifford, who had suppressed Jack Cade's rebellion, is killed by the duke of York, and when his son finds the dead body he vows unceasing enmity against everyone in the house of York. The duke's son, the hunchbacked Richard, is an evil man but a magnificent fighter, and he helps turn the tide of battle in his father's favor. The frightened King Henry flees to London,

where he hopes to call his parliament together, and the
victorious forces of the duke of York plan to pursue him
there. So the play closes, with the beginning of civil war
and with the white rose of York in its first moment of
triumph.

HENRY THE SIXTH, PART THREE

THE THIRD PART of *Henry VI* continues the story of the Wars of the Roses, a story that sinks deeper into hatred and treachery and bloodshed until it is climaxed by the murder of King Henry in the Tower of London.

The play opens at the point where *Henry VI, Part Two* ended, with the victorious duke of York arriving in London at the Parliament House. After King Henry had been defeated at St. Alban's, he had hoped to call parliament together and have York declared a traitor; but by the time the king arrives the duke of York is sitting on the throne, and all his supporters, with their swords still bloody from the battle, surround him. Henry's own supporters, and especially the vengeful young Lord Clifford, want to attack, but Henry is still hopefully bent on peace and tries to parley.

Henry is well aware that his own title to the crown is weak, for his grandfather seized it from the rightful king, Richard II, and later Richard was murdered. In the end Henry agrees to accept the duke of York as his heir, and his followers are enraged by what they feel is his cowardice. They enroll under the banner of his warlike wife, Queen Margaret, who is determined to save the throne for her own son instead of letting it go to the rival house of York.

The duke of York's followers are equally displeased, since they feel that their leader should not be obliged to wait until Henry's death before he ascends the throne. The duke of York's two eldest sons, Edward and Richard, are convinced that their father should seize the crown, and the hunchback Richard is especially intent on the idea.

Father, do but think
How sweet a thing it is to wear a crown . . .

The duke of York finally agrees to raise an army, and the news comes that Queen Margaret is marching upon him with twenty thousand men. The outnumbered duke and his sons go out to battle and meet with disaster. A younger son, the duke of Rutland, is too small to bear arms and he is found by the avenging Clifford who has sworn to destroy everyone in the Yorkist line. The child pleads for his life but Clifford slaughters him and then goes to look for his father, the duke of York.

The duke, defeated and alone, stands surrounded by his enemies. Queen Margaret jeers at his helplessness. "Where are your mess of sons, to back you now?" She tells him of the slaughter of his little boy—"your darling Rutland"— and in mockery she puts a paper crown upon his head. Then she and Clifford stab him, and his head is cut from his body to be set up on the gates of the city of York as a warning to all traitors.

Edward and Richard hear of their father's death, and the earl of Warwick brings news of still another defeat. But the three men decide to continue the fight, and the earl of Warwick promises to support Edward in taking up his father's claim to the throne. The two armies meet before the city of York, with a reluctant King Henry pushed along by his warlike queen, and both sides feel a mounting bitterness. Men like Warwick and Richard take a fierce delight in killing, but the gentle and anxious King Henry can only stand and mourn as the toll of the dead rises. He is witness to the final calamity of civil war, for one of his soldiers kills an enemy and discovers it was his father, while another one kills a youth and discovers it was his son.

The tide of battle turns against the king, and even Queen Margaret admits there is no safety except in flight. Clifford is killed, lamenting that King Henry has been so spiritless that all the common people are flocking to the house of York, and Edward plans a triumphal march to London to be crowned there as king. The earl of Warwick decides that Edward must marry the sister of the king of France, to unite the two nations again, and two of Edward's brothers are made dukes. Richard, the hunchback, is made duke of Gloucester and his older brother, George, is made duke of Clarence. As for King Henry, who has been in disguise and hiding in the north of England, he is captured by two keepers in a forest and sent to London and imprisonment.

While the earl of Warwick is in France arranging Edward's marriage, Edward himself meets a beautiful young widow, Elizabeth, Lady Grey. He falls in love with her and in spite of his brothers' protests persuades her to become his queen. Richard, the new duke of Gloucester, watches the courtship sardonically and thinks of all the people who now stand between him and the crown: Edward, Edward's possible children, Clarence, Henry and Henry's son. Yet Richard longs for the crown, turning on it the lustful eye that the thought of his misshapen body prevents him from turning on a woman.

> *Since this earth affords no joy to me . . .*
> *I'll make my heaven to dream upon the crown . . .*

Somehow, somewhere, Richard Crookback will trample them all down and win the throne of England, but in the meanwhile he must pretend to gentleness. "Why, I can smile, and murder whiles I smile."

Over in France, the French king and his sister give audience to Queen Margaret, who has come to implore their aid for her imprisoned husband and her disinherited son. Following her is the earl of Warwick, who brings Edward's offer to take the French princess as his wife. But on Warwick's heels comes the news of Edward's sudden marriage to the beautiful young widow, Elizabeth, and Warwick is furious at the destruction of his plans. In his rage he throws his support to the Lancastrians: he promises Queen Margaret that his elder daughter will marry her son and together they will fight to return her husband to the throne of England.

In London, Edward discovers that most of his followers are displeased with his marriage, although the new queen does her best to be friendly with them all. Especially angered is Edward's second brother, the duke of Clarence, and when he hears that Warwick has changed sides he decides to follow him and marry Warwick's younger daughter. Only Richard remains loyal, and he stays with his brother, not because he loves King Edward but because his own eye is on the crown.

Again the two armies form their battle lines, but this time Warwick and Clarence are on the side of the Lancastrians. King Edward, sleeping in his tent before the battle, is captured by the enemy, and Warwick takes his crown away to place it on Henry's head. Edward's wife Elizabeth takes flight, for she is with child and determined to protect the coming heir to the throne. But Richard Crookback, who has a lion's courage as well as a lion's savagery, manages to free his imprisoned brother, and he sends him across the sea to Flanders and safety.

King Henry, released from the Tower of London, asks his new-found allies, Warwick and Clarence, to rule the kingdom between them, while he retires to live out his days in meditation and prayer. He also asks them to arrange to have his wife, Queen Margaret, and his young son brought back from France.

Edward, meanwhile, has been raising an army across the Channel and he returns to England to be proclaimed king at York. Warwick and Clarence muster their forces, but Henry persists in the pious conviction that since he has been a harmless king his people will not turn against him. He is captured by Edward and Richard, who lock him up in the Tower and go forth to challenge Warwick to battle.

Warwick shuts himself up in the town of Coventry, and Edward besieges him there. The duke of Clarence finds he cannot bring himself to fight against his own brother and leaves Warwick's side to go back to Edward's. In the battle that follows, Warwick is killed, and he dies lamenting the fact that all his glory is now "smeared in dust and blood."

The Lancastrian side has again been defeated, and again the Yorkist Edward is king. No one is left to oppose him except Queen Margaret, but she and her son refuse to give in. They meet him with the remnants of their army near Tewksbury, and the queen and prince are both captured. Now it is the turn of the three sons of the murdered duke of York to avenge their father's death and that of their little brother, the duke of Rutland. When the prince calls them usurpers they stab him, taking turns as he lies twisting on the ground in agony. His mother, Queen Margaret, screams out her rage and defiance of them all, especially of Richard, "that devil's butcher," and she is dragged away still crying for the death they refuse to give her.

Richard has another piece of butchery he must commit if the house of Lancaster is to be wholly destroyed. He goes to the Tower of London, and finds King Henry reading in his cell. Richard describes the murder of the prince his son, and Henry is horrified by Richard's cruelty.

The owl shrieked at thy birth, an evil sign,
The night-crow cried, aboding luckless time,
Dogs howled, and hideous tempest shook down trees . . .

Before he can finish, Richard stabs him, and over the dead king's body he continues the account of his own misshapen birth.

Then, since the heavens have shaped my body so,
Let hell make crook'd my mind to answer it.
I have no brother, I am like no brother;
And this word 'love,' which greybeards call divine,
Be resident in men like one another
And not in me . . .
King Henry and the prince his son are gone:
Clarence, thy turn is next . . .

Clarence and his brother the king are not aware that a tiger is on the prowl in England, and they are sure that from now on there will be peace in the realm. Queen Elizabeth has given birth to a son, named Edward after his father; the widowed Queen Margaret is exiled to France where she can trouble them no more; and the victorious King Edward looks forward to what he mistakenly believes will be a long and happy reign.

RICHARD THE THIRD

RICHARD III continues the account of the Wars of the Roses that was begun in the three parts of *Henry VI*. Richard, the evil hunchback who has been looming larger and larger in the last two plays of the series, now suddenly towers above the action and dominates it. Since there is now a single focus, the result is a much better play; and *Richard III* is a melodrama of glitter and violence, as vigorous and bloody as its chief character.

Shakespeare's portrait of Richard does not have much resemblance to the real King Richard of history, any more than his portrait of a peasant witch has much to do with the real Joan of Arc. But it was the portrait he found in the only history books that were available to him, and he had no reason to question it. Moreover, it gave him the opportunity to show a complete villain in action and he made the most of it.

The story opens at the point where *Henry VI, Part Three* left off, with the house of York settled on the throne of England and peace in the realm.

> *Now is the winter of our discontent*
> *Made glorious summer by this sun of York . . .*

But there is no peace in the heart of the king's brother, Richard, duke of Gloucester. He can find delight in battle but none at all in the "piping time of peace," for with his misshapen body he cannot please fair ladies and he is so ugly that even the dogs bark at him as he limps past. Since he cannot be happy himself, he will make others unhappy and destroy the peace of the realm if he can.

Already Richard has planted in King Edward's mind a suspicion that a third brother, the duke of Clarence, is plotting to seize the crown, and Edward has Clarence arrested and sent to the Tower of London. On his way there he passes Richard, and Richard pretends to be amazed that the king should do such an unreasonable thing. It is clear that the whole thing must be the fault of Edward's wife, Queen Elizabeth, and while she plots against them no one can draw a free breath. "We are not safe, Clarence, we are not safe." Clarence is sure that his hunchbacked brother is his friend, but Richard sees him only as a stumbling block in his own path to the throne. When he hears that King Edward is ill, his chief thought is that his older brother must not die until Clarence has first been disposed of.

> Which done, God take King Edward to His mercy,
> And leave the world for me to bustle in . . .

Richard has another plan also. He intends to marry the beautiful Lady Anne, who is the daughter-in-law of Edward's murdered predecessor, King Henry. The corpse of the martyred king is being borne through the streets of London, with Anne as mourner, when Richard stops the procession. He killed King Henry, and Anne knows it. He also helped kill Anne's young husband, the king's son, at Tewksbury, and Anne knows that too. She hates him as she hates hell; he is a "lump of foul deformity," a butcher, a devil. And yet, with an effrontery that is almost magnificent, Richard openly makes love to her in the London street, and little by little he beats her down. For all Anne's efforts, she cannot make a stand against his vitality, his violence, and his curious, soft, wheedling tongue. He even offers to let her kill him if that will please her and gives up his own sword for that purpose; for he knows by that time he has her helpless and she will wear the ring he gives her. Anne persuades herself that Richard has repented of all his evil actions of the past, but Richard, once he is alone, feels nothing but a fierce contempt for Anne's weakness. He sardonically decides that he must be a very handsome fellow after all, if he can win a fair lady with such ease after murdering her husband.

At the palace, Queen Elizabeth is openly worried about

the future. For King Edward is gravely ill, and their young son is to be put under the protection of Richard Crookback. Richard himself enters, in his favorite role as the blunt, well-meaning man of peace, and accuses the queen of misrepresenting him to the king and plotting against the innocent Clarence. Elizabeth denies all this indignantly, and Richard accuses her of being in sympathy with the Lancastrian cause of murdered King Henry. Behind them, like a vengeful ghost, creeps the dead king's tragic widow, Queen Margaret, exiled to France but now returned to curse the whole pack of them. She hates Richard the most, the "poisonous bunch-backed toad," but she hates all the Yorkists, since they stood by unaiding at Tewksbury while her son "was stabbed with bloody daggers." They remind her that her side did the same to the duke of York and his small son, the innocent Rutland, for evil bred evil in the civil wars and hate was piled on hate. Queen Margaret leaves them with a final curse, and Richard looks after her piously.

> *I cannot blame her: by God's holy mother,*
> *She hath had too much wrong, and I repent*
> *My part thereof that I have done to her.*

As soon as everyone else has left the room, Richard's cloak of holiness drops from him, and again he is the devil who takes such open delight in his own villainy. He hails his visitors, two "hardy, stout, resolved mates" who are on their way to the Tower of London. Their business there is to murder the imprisoned duke of Clarence, and Richard sends them on their bloody way with hearty good will. "I like you, lads."

Clarence, in the Tower, is oppressed by a nightmare he has had. He dreamed of drowning in the English Channel, with the noisy rush of water in his ears and the debris of shipwrecks at the bottom of the sea.

> *Methought I saw a thousand fearful wracks,*
> *A thousand men that fishes gnawed upon,*
> *Wedges of gold, great anchors, heaps of pearl,*
> *Inestimable stones, unvalued jewels,*
> *All scattered in the bottom of the sea . . .*

He dreamed that then he entered "the kingdom of per-
petual night," where he was greeted by the ghosts of the
men he had destroyed: his father-in-law Warwick whose
cause he had deserted, and the prince he stabbed at Tewksbury—"a shadow like an angel, with bright hair." All this
Clarence had done for his brother Edward's sake, and now
Edward has committed him to prison.

The prisoner turns again to sleep, and the two murderers
whom Richard has sent enter the room. They are talkative
men and argue first with each other and then with Clarence.
Then they suddenly grow impatient, stab him when he is
not looking, and drown him in a barrel of wine in the next
room.

The dying King Edward has persuaded his nobles into a
pact of friendship with each other when Richard enters
with the news that Clarence is dead. The appalled king has
to be taken from the room, and Richard implies darkly to
the assembled courtiers that the queen's kindred are responsible for the murder. "God will revenge it." Clarence's
small children are told of the murder but their grandmother
can do nothing to comfort them. For she has just heard the
news that King Edward is dead also, and that means she
has lost two of her sons at once.

Edward's elder son is to be crowned king, but he is only
a boy and the hearts of the people are heavy. "Woe to
that land that's governed by a child!" Queen Elizabeth
waits for the prince to arrive in London, and with her is
her lively younger son, the little duke of York. News comes
that the queen's kindred have been imprisoned by Richard's
order and she is terror-stricken. For it is clear that Richard
is getting command of the realm and will be able to do
what he pleases. "I see, as in a map, the end of all." The
queen goes into hiding, taking the little duke with her, and
the archbishop of York gives her what assistance he can.

The young prince arrives in London to be crowned, and
his uncle Richard suggests he take lodgings in the Tower.
Richard has managed to get his hands on the prince's
brother also, and although he behaves in a very kind and
uncle-like fashion both the boys mistrust him. The little
duke of York says that he will not sleep quietly in the

Tower, and when Richard tenderly asks him what he is afraid of, the child answers:

> *My uncle Clarence' angry ghost:*
> *My grandam told me he was murdered there.*

Both boys know it was their uncle Richard who gave the order for the murder, and when the prince adds, "I fear no uncles dead," he means that he fears one living and has cause to.

Once his two little nephews are safely in the Tower, Richard turns his attention to his own advancement. He orders the queen's kinsmen to be executed, tempts one nobleman to his side, and has another beheaded for high treason. He creates as much havoc as the wild boar on his emblem, but on the surface he maintains his pious attitude and even the mayor of London is deceived by him. Richard sends his agents to rouse the Londoners against the imprisoned prince and to suggest his own virtues as a possible king, and finally a delegation comes to him, composed of the chief citizens of London. They find Richard deep in prayer between two holy bishops, and it is with the greatest difficulty that they prevail upon him to accept the crown.

There are three people who know Richard's true character: his wife, his mother and his sister-in-law. These tragic women have gathered together to visit the children in the Tower when word comes that Richard is to be crowned king. They can now see that old Queen Margaret's curse is coming true and that England will become a "slaughter-house" where no one will escape the murderer's bloody hands. The two older women feel nothing but sorrow for Richard's unhappy wife and she goes her way to be crowned queen with a heavy heart. As for the former queen, Elizabeth, she says a last prayer for the safety of her two little sons in the Tower.

Richard is crowned. But he knows that his "kingdom stands on brittle glass" unless he can make his title secure. He needs a stronger alliance than his marriage with Anne can give him, and so he plans to kill his wife secretly and marry the sister of the little princes instead. As for the

little prisoners in the Tower, Richard is finally able to un-
earth a man named Tyrrel, who is evil enough to do anything, and sends him to murder them. Tyrrel has two men
to help him and among them they manage to do the killing,
although even Tyrrel himself knows that it is a "piece of
ruthless butchery."

Richard finds a kinder way to describe his latest murders.

The sons of Edward sleep in Abraham's bosom,
And Anne my wife hath bid the world good night . . .

He is now free to present himself to the princess as a "jolly
thriving wooer," and even the news that a former ally of
his is raising an army against him does not trouble King
Richard unduly.

Queen Margaret, that gaunt prophetess of doom from
France, meets the mother and grandmother of the murdered boys and they all curse the man whose bloody hands
have destroyed both the house of Lancaster and the house
of York. Even Richard's own mother can find nothing to
say in his favor, and when he enters to the sound of trumpets she curses him to his face. She prays that when Richard faces the final day of battle "the little souls of Edward's
children" will give strength to his enemies, and Edward's
widow says Amen.

Richard turns to Edward's widow, for he has some business to transact with her. He wishes permission to marry
her daughter, the princess Elizabeth, and he ignores the
queen's furious hatred of him. Gentle and unruffled, he
presses his case, and finally he manages to persuade her
that in such a marriage lies the only hope for England's
safety. Again Richard has won, and again he has nothing
but contempt for the weakness of the woman who has
given in to him. "Relenting fool, and shallow, changing
woman!"

News comes that the army which has been raised against
him is drawing supporters from all over England. The
people flock to the rebels' banner and Richard strikes one
of the messengers who bring bad news. "Out on ye, owls!
nothing but songs of death?" He manages to capture the
chief rebel and have him beheaded, but the real heart of

the opposition lies in young Henry Tudor, earl of Richmond, who is the heir to the crown on the Lancastrian side. The noble and virtuous Henry now has an extremely strong claim to the crown, since Richard has slaughtered all the Yorkist contenders, and the king knows that Henry is his chief enemy.

The two armies meet at Bosworth Field and pitch their tents to wait until morning. The two leaders, Richard and Henry, retire to sleep, and in the cold and dark between the tents there rises up a series of avenging ghosts. They are the tragic host of Richard's victims, from the bright-haired boy who was slaughtered at Tewksbury to the little princes smothered in the Tower. There are eleven of them in all, and each turns to Richard with a refrain like the tolling of a bell. "Despair, and die!" Then each in his turn promises victory to Henry, earl of Richmond. "God and good angels fight on Richmond's side."

Richard starts up from his sleep with a cry, sweating in spite of the cold with the fear of his dream. He is tormented by the thought of all the sins that lie on his head, and in his agony he admits for the first time that he feels despair.

> There is no creature loves me,
> And if I die, no soul will pity me . . .

The cock crows, and one of his men comes to help him with his armor. Richard almost breaks down and the man comforts him. "Nay, good my lord, be not afraid of shadows."

On that gray and sunless morning at Bosworth Field, Henry of Richmond calls his soldiers together and strengthens them for battle. King Richard does the same, for he has won his brutal courage back again.

> Let not our babbling dreams affright our souls;
> Conscience is but a word that cowards use . . .
> Our strong arms be our conscience, swords our law. . . .

But Richard's strong arm is not enough. The battle goes against the evil king and his horse is killed under him. Still looking fiercely for his enemy, even "in the throat of death," Richard shouts wildly for another mount.

A horse! a horse! my kingdom for a horse!

Defiant and savagely brave to the end, he goes down fighting, and with his death there is a sudden peace. "The day is ours, the bloody dog is dead."

As soon as Henry of Richmond stands victorious on the field of battle, the long years of civil war are ended. For he is heir to the house of Lancaster and he will marry the princess Elizabeth, heir to the house of York. The new king is the first of the Tudor line to rule England, and as Henry VII he will bring peace and prosperity to the nation again.

A sin against kingship was committed in the first play of the series when Richard II was deposed and murdered. The sin has now been expiated, and England is whole again, with the Tudors about to begin their glorious reign. And so ends the linked cycle of eight history plays in which a young Tudor playwright showed his countrymen the terrors of civil war, the value of strong and wise rulers, and the glory of his beloved England.

HENRY THE EIGHTH

HENRY VIII is the last of the ten history plays, and also the last play Shakespeare wrote. It is almost more of a pageant than a play, and its chief purpose is to describe the events that led up to the birth of King Henry's daughter, the future Queen Elizabeth.

The story opens in 1520, forty-four years before Shakespeare was born. The kings of England and France have recently met at the Field of the Cloth of Gold, and back in London some noblemen are discussing the magnificence of the festivities. The duke of Buckingham dislikes and mistrusts the English minister who was responsible for arranging them and calls him a "butcher's cur." This is Cardinal Wolsey, archbishop of York, and Buckingham hates the cardinal as an upstart commoner who has managed to draw all the power of the kingdom into his hands.

> *The devil speed him! no man's pie is freed*
> *From his ambitious finger. . . .*

Cardinal Wolsey enters with his retinue and the two men look at each other with contempt and fury. Buckingham is convinced that Wolsey is an evil influence on the king and decides to accuse him of high treason for taking bribes. But Buckingham is too late, for Wolsey has reached King Henry before him; and it is Buckingham himself who is accused of treason and imprisoned in the Tower of London.

King Henry's wife, the virtuous Katharine of Spain, tries to offset Wolsey's influence with the king. She persuades Henry to cancel a heavy tax that the cardinal has imposed upon the people, and she also intercedes for the duke of Buckingham. But the duke's own servants testify against him, and Queen Katharine can do nothing to save him from standing trial.

Cardinal Wolsey gives a feast within his palace at Westminster and all the "lords and ladies" are invited to the magnificent entertainment. While some gentlemen of the court are on their way to the cardinal's, they discuss the behavior of the courtiers who have returned from France with a new-found passion for short breeches and tennis and French songs. A lively Englishman named Lord Sands is delighted that a royal proclamation has been made against these French ways, since they are giving him too much competition in his wooing of the ladies.

The gentlemen arrive at the cardinal's feast, and Lord Sands at once settles himself comfortably between two members of the opposite sex. One of them is the queen's beautiful young lady-in-waiting, Anne Boleyn, and in two sentences Sands manages to find an excuse to kiss her. Wolsey enters to bid his guests welcome, and then a sound of trumpets announces the arrival of "a noble troop of strangers." It is King Henry and some of his friends, disguised as shepherds to dance in the revels. Each of them chooses a partner for the dance and the king chooses Anne Boleyn. Then he unmasks and takes his pretty dancing partner in to supper, flirting with her as delightedly as Lord Sands had done.

> *Sweetheart,*
> *I were unmannerly to take you out,*
> *And not to kiss you. . . .*

When the duke of Buckingham stands trial for treason, he defends himself valiantly. But the sentence goes against him, and he is led through the streets of Westminster to execution. The pitying crowds gather to watch him go past, and the fallen duke addresses a speech to them that is worthy of so great a nobleman. He concludes by asking only for their prayers.

> *All good people,*
> *Pray for me! I must now forsake ye; the last hour*
> *Of my long weary life is come upon me.*
> *Farewell . . .*

Among the spectators are two gentlemen who linger after
the duke has been led away to his death. They talk of the
new gossip at court, the "buzzing of a separation between
the king and Katharine." For Wolsey hates the queen and
he has been trying to persuade King Henry that his marriage is illegal.

The noblemen of the court are disturbed by the plot
against the queen but they can do nothing; for Cardinal
Wolsey goes about his plans so "holily" that it is impossible to catch him. He takes the position that he is merely
trying to save the king from the sin of having married a
woman who was once his brother's wife. Wolsey's real
desire is to form an alliance with the French by marrying
Henry to the French king's sister, and he has persuaded
the Pope to send a cardinal to tell Henry that he must
divorce Katharine.

The queen's young lady-in-waiting, Anne Boleyn, is
much troubled by the disaster that threatens her mistress
—"so good a lady" and so innocent of any wrongdoing.
It seems to Anne that it must be a tragic thing to be a
queen and that she herself would not accept such a title
for "all the riches under heaven." The old waiting woman
who is with her is amused by Anne's vehemence.

> 'Tis strange; a threepence bowed would hire me,
> Old as I am, to queen it. But, I pray you,
> What think you of a duchess? . . .

Anne would not be a duchess either. Then the news comes
that King Henry has made her a marchioness, which is
next in rank to a duchess, and the old lady is still amused
but somewhat caustic.

> How tastes it? is it bitter? forty pence, no.
> There was a lady once ('tis an old story)
> That would not be a queen, that would she not,
> For all the mud in Egypt: have you heard it?

Anne does not wish to submit to any more teasing and
says she must return to her mistress the queen. The two
women go out together, the younger one half frightened

and the older one completely fascinated by the turn of events.

King Henry calls a solemn council together to consider the legality of his marriage to Katharine, and after a magnificent procession he seats himself in his chair of state with his lords grouped about him. The lonely and friendless queen disrupts the formality of the proceedings by kneeling at his feet to plead with him. She is a stranger from another land and has been his "true and humble wife" for more than twenty years. Let him at least delay the verdict until she has heard from her friends in Spain.

It is Wolsey who answers her in the king's name, pointing out that the council which has been gathered together consists of the wisest men in the land. Katharine turns on him, for she knows very well who is her enemy, and she accuses him of being her "most malicious foe" and unfit to act as judge. Wolsey takes refuge in his "holiness" and gently defends himself. "Madam, you do me wrong." He admits that she is a good and gracious lady, but he is only trying to serve his king. Katharine knows that she is no match for his cleverness. But she refuses to let Wolsey act as her judge, denies the authority of the court and sweeps from the room.

King Henry looks after his wife with delighted admiration.

> *Go thy ways, Kate:*
> *That man i' the world who shall report he has*
> *A better wife, let him in nought be trusted,*
> *For speaking false in that . . .*

He assures the court that he will not press for a divorce if his marriage is lawful, for Katharine is "the queen of earthly queens." But his conscience has been troubling him ever since the day when the French ambassador questioned the legitimacy of his daughter Mary. Moreover, his wife has given him no sons, and this may be a sign that heaven is displeased with him for marrying his brother's widow.

Katharine has threatened to take her cause to the Pope, and Wolsey and his fellow cardinal visit her apartment in an effort to dissuade her. They find the queen among her maids, with one of them singing a little lute-song, and they attempt to convince Katharine that they are "peace-makers, friends and servants" who want nothing in the world but her good. The queen receives them at first with a pitiful dignity, and then, when she finds what the two men are attempting, assails them in a blaze of anger. But the two cardinals keep their manners gentle and their words soothing, and in the end Katharine is obliged to give way.

But Wolsey has made a miscalculation. He has pinned his hopes on the king's marriage to the French princess after the divorce, while Henry's own thoughts are on Anne Boleyn. An incautious letter which Wolsey wrote the Pope on the subject comes to the king's eye, and so does a paper that lists the vast accumulation of Wolsey's wealth. King Henry thrusts the two papers into his minister's hands and leaves Wolsey staring at the packet that has destroyed him. For Wolsey is a realist and he knows that his power over the king has ended.

The cardinal conducts himself with his usual dignity before the gloating noblemen who have always hated him, and he will not bow his head before them. It is not until he is alone that he cries out in agony over the depth of his fall.

> *Farewell! A long farewell, to all my greatness!*
> *This is the state of man: today he puts forth*
> *The tender leaves of hopes; tomorrow blossoms,*
> *And bears his blushing honours thick upon him;*
> *The third day comes a frost, a killing frost;*
> *And when he thinks, good easy man, full surely*
> *His greatness is a-ripening, nips his root,*
> *And then he falls, as I do. . . .*

Wolsey's secretary, Thomas Cromwell, enters the room in tears and finds his master curiously at peace. Even the news that Henry has openly acknowledged Anne Boleyn as his queen does not stir Wolsey to anger, although she was the one who destroyed him.

> *All my glories*
> *In that one woman I have lost forever. . . .*

His chief thought is that his servant Cromwell must not share his ruin, and he tries to force the weeping man to think of his own safety and forget his master. Out of his own bitterly acquired knowledge, Wolsey has one piece of advice for Cromwell: "Fling away ambition; by that sin fell the angels." As for himself, he will render up to the king the last penny of all his possessions and leave nothing for himself. And then, in spite of all his efforts at self-possession, Wolsey permits himself one last cry of anguish.

> *O Cromwell, Cromwell!*
> *Had I but served my God with half the zeal*
> *I served my king, he would not in mine age*
> *Have left me naked to mine enemies.*

Anne Boleyn is crowned queen of England and moves in splendor from her coronation in Westminster Abbey. Her hair is woven with pearls, a gold crown is upon her head, and a duchess bears up her train. One of the gentlemen in the crowd has seen the actual coronation and he describes the press of people who had thronged the Abbey to watch it. The crown had been put on Anne's head by the holy Thomas Cranmer, archbishop of Canterbury, who had also helped her to gain it. Both the queen and Cranmer belong to the new Protestant religion, which denies the authority of the Pope and follows the teachings of Martin Luther, and Cranmer's greatest enemy at court is Gardiner, bishop of Winchester, who holds to the old way of thinking.

Katharine, the divorced queen, with only a few faithful servants left about her, is so ill that she can no longer reach a chair without help. She hears of the death of her great enemy, Wolsey, fallen like herself, and she can hate him no longer. "Peace be with him!" She herself is at peace too, content to die; but when a messenger arrives and fails to kneel she shows a flash of the old fire. In Katharine's eyes, she is a queen still. Knowing that the time has come to make her will, she leaves her daughter Mary to King

Henry's care and makes sure that the wages of her servants
will be paid. Then she gives the orders for her own burial:

> ... *like*
> *A queen, and daughter to a king, inter me.*
> *I can no more.*

The new queen, Anne, is about to give birth to a child,
and Bishop Gardiner is already plotting against her. He
is plotting too against her friend Cranmer, archbishop of
Canterbury, for Gardiner considers him an "arch-heretic"
who must be rooted out if the kingdom is ever to be safe.
It is midnight and King Henry, anxious about his wife, is
walking through the palace, unable to sleep. He calls Cranmer to him and warns him that he has many enemies; but
the king assures the archbishop that he will remain his
friend and gives him his own ring to affirm it. Then an
old lady of the court brings Henry the news that his wife
has given birth to a little girl, and he hurries off to see his
daughter.

Archbishop Cranmer presents himself before the Privy
Council in answer to charges that have been brought
against him and is kept waiting in the lobby among the
pages and grooms. The archbishop endures the insult with
patience and when he is admitted to the council table defends himself with vigor. He is accused of encouraging
"new opinions, divers and dangerous, which are heresies,"
and Gardiner declares that he will be sent to the Tower of
London as a traitor. Then Cranmer brings out the king's
ring, and the noblemen who have been backing Gardiner
are suddenly afraid.

The king himself enters the room, having watched the
whole thing secretly, and is furious at the treatment that
Cranmer has been given. They have made him "wait like
a lousy footboy," instead of showing him the respect due
the greatest churchman in the land. As for Henry himself,
he has only one request to make of his beloved archbishop,
that he will act as godfather to the little princess who has
just been born.

The day of her christening arrives, and the palace yard
is mobbed with loyal subjects come to watch the proces-

sion. Finally the trumpets sound and the great men of the kingdom enter. Four noblemen carry a canopy under which a duchess bears the little princess, and a herald sends out a proclamation and a prayer: "Heaven, from thy endless goodness, send prosperous life, long and ever happy, to the high and mighty princess of England, Elizabeth!"

Archbishop Cranmer stands looking at the child and is moved to make a prophecy, that the little girl will grow up to be the greatest of England's queens.

> She shall be loved and feared. Her own shall bless her . . .
> In her days every man shall eat in safety,
> Under his own vine, what he plants; and sing
> The merry songs of peace to all his neighbours . . .

This was the Queen Elizabeth in whose reign Shakespeare was born and grew to manhood and under whom he wrote most of his plays. She ruled an England that was free from civil war, united and prosperous, and her reign was very unlike the tragic years he had described in the histories. Equally at peace was the reign of her successor, King James, under whom Shakespeare wrote the rest of his plays, and James is included in the archbishop's prophecy also.

> Peace, plenty, love, truth, terror,
> That were the servants to this chosen infant,
> Shall then be his, and like a vine grow to him:
> Wherever the bright sun of heaven shall shine,
> His honour, and the greatness of his name,
> Shall be, and make new nations. . . .

Queen Elizabeth had her faults, for all her astuteness and her magnificence, and there was much more to criticize in King James. But they both deserved Shakespeare's praise, for they kept the peace and during their prosperous reigns the shadow of civil war did not threaten the land. Moreover, they were both ardent playgoers, and in a land where the theater had many enemies they protected it and helped it to flourish.

Shakespeare had no memory of the early, troubled years

of Queen Elizabeth, and he died before the reign of King
James drew to its confused and saddened close. He lived
and worked in the sunshine days of both monarchs, in a
joyful, self-confident age in which anything seemed possible, and it is fitting that his last play, which was produced
only three years before he himself died, should end with
their praise.

INDEX OF NAMES